THIS BOOK HAS BEEN PLACED

IN THE DWIGHT PUBLIC

LIBRARY IN MEMORY OF

S. Fred Cummings

(A member of

General Society of Mayflower Descendants)

Presented by

Phyllis Cummings Groll

# MAYFLOWER FAMILIES
## Through
## Five Generations

DESCENDANTS OF THE PILGRIMS
WHO LANDED AT
PLYMOUTH, MASS. DECEMBER 1620

## VOLUME ONE

edited by

Lucy Mary Kellogg, F.A.S.G.

**FAMILIES**
**FRANCIS EATON** – *Lee D. van Antwerp, M.D.*
**SAMUEL FULLER** – *Arthur H. & Katharine W. Radasch*
**WILLIAM WHITE** – *Robert M. & Ruth W. Sherman*

Published by
General Society of Mayflower Descendants
1975

Library of Congress Catalog No. 75-30145


4 Winslow St.
Plymouth MA 02360

*First printing, December 1975*
*Second printing, February 1977*
*(with minor non-copyrightable changes)*

Signatures on endpapers were reproduced from the following sources:

*Francis Eaton:* PLYMOUTH COLONY RECS 12:17
*Samuel Fuller:* William Bradford, *History of Plymouth Plantation* (Boston 1912), 2:90
*Peregrine White:* MD 13:1
*Resolved White:* MD 17:1

IN MEMORY OF

L E W I S   E D W I N   N E F F

1892-1966

GOVERNOR GENERAL

1960-1963

His interest and energy
were major factors in
the establishment and perpetuation of
the Five Generations Project

## HISTORY OF THE PROJECT

The idea of tracing both male and female descendants of the Pilgrims down to Revolutionary times was announced in 1899 by George E. Bowman, founder of the Massachusetts Mayflower Society, first Secretary General and fifth Historian General. In fact his goal initially was to trace such descent down to his own time. As editor of the *Mayflower Descendant* (1899-1937) and of *Pilgrim Notes and Queries* he devoted many years to seeking out and publishing authentic data on the Pilgrims and their descendants. The Bowman manuscripts fill several file cabinets at the office of the Massachusetts Society. In 1956 the first three generations of his findings were published under the auspices of the Massachusetts Society: *Families of the Pilgrims*.

Meanwhile, Herbert Folger, first Historian of the California Mayflower Society, was also compiling information on Pilgrim descendants. In 1920 he prepared a pamphlet listing the names of men who married daughters, granddaughters, and great-granddaughters of Mayflower passengers. Later reprinted and revised, this came to be known as the Folger or Four Generations Pamphlet. His manuscripts fill 82 ledgers at the headquarters of the California Society.

During the twenties and thirties Dr. Frank T. Calef of the Rhode Island Society working from published material prepared family sheets showing lines of descent through five or more generations from Mayflower passengers. In his work he corrected many erroneous lineages appearing in print. His 41 volumes of manuscripts at the Rhode Island Historical Society were the starting point for the William White Family in this book.

As proven lineages accumulated at the office of the General Society, it was recognized that a printed compilation of all accepted descendants would help those seeking a Pilgrim ancestor. William A. McAuslan, also of the Rhode Island Society, while Historian General compiled the *Mayflower Index*, an adaptation of Mr. Folger's system. This Index included all names appearing in the lineage papers accepted to 1932, with a numbering system to trace parentage, generation by generation, back to the Mayflower ancestor. In 1959 Lewis E. Neff of the Oklahoma Society, Historian General and later Governor General, corrected, extensively revised and expanded the *Mayflower Index* to include all lineages of members through 1959.

Mr. Neff presented to the General Board of the Mayflower Descendants in September 1959 a resolution to endorse "publication of the tracing out of five generations of all the descendants of all Mayflower passengers from whom descent can be proved." Carroll Alton Means of the Connecticut Society, subsequently Assistant Governor General, in a letter to that Board stated that he and Mr. Neff had discussed in detail "a pet project of ours--a Key." This Key would follow all possible lines of descent, both male and female, as did *Families of the Pilgrims*, but would extend further--to about Revolutionary times. Mr. Means further urged that the Mayflower Society sponsor this project. To Lewis E. Neff belongs the credit for the unique idea of recruiting separate volunteer genealogists to work on each Pilgrim family. Besides securing several such family workers, Mr. Neff also actively solicited funds for research and eventual publication. Thus was born what came later to be called the Five Generations Project.

Mr. Neff remained in charge of the project until his death in 1966. His successor, Mr. Means, expanded the Committee, added family workers, and arranged a meeting of the workers. In 1967 Dr. Lee D. van Antwerp, Surgeon General and later Governor General, became Chairman. Under his leadership volunteer workers were found for the remaining Pilgrim families, additional contributions were actively sought, Committee meetings were scheduled regularly, and an editor was found.

Recognition of the need for an editor led to the recruitment in 1970 of Miss Lucy Mary Kellogg, Historian of the Michigan Society [in 1971 elected a Fellow of the American Society of Genealogists, FASG]. She commenced developing a standard format for the Families, she considered how to deal with the many families which resulted from intermarriages among Pilgrim descendants, and she assisted, encouraged and in many instances visited the workers. She ultimately suggested inclusion of names of the sixth generation. Miss Kellogg insisted that each family should be "authentic, explicit, and easy to use," and as complete as possible.

The death of Miss Kellogg in 1973 left the project for a time rudderless. However, she had outlined a reasonable format and style, and she had submitted five Families to a preliminary editing. Much of the subsequent preparation for publication of this volume was carried forward by Dr. van Antwerp, Prof. Claude W. Barlow, and Mr. and Mrs. Robert M. Sherman. Professor Barlow, FASG, is the Billington and Warren Family worker; the Shermans, both FASGs, are the Samson and White Family workers. Two significant decisions were to publish the three Families most nearly ready, and to sacrifice strict adherence to format and style, in favor of prompt publication.

In 1975 Mr. Sherman, appointed Chairman to succeed Dr. van Antwerp, supervised the preparation of the final versions of the three Families in this volume. The material was reviewed for genealogical content, clarity and reasonable consistency by Professor Barlow and the Shermans. Because of the decision to publish promptly, each Family write-up reflects, perhaps more than was originally contemplated, the authors' choice of detail, extent of citation of evidence, and information regarding the sixth generation.

Each worker donated the time spent on researching his family, and on writing his manuscript. Each of the Chairmen, Editor Kellogg, and others who completed the aforementioned tasks on this volume, also donated their time and expertise. If ever there was a labor of love, this is one!

Robert M. Sherman

## OFFICERS OF THE GENERAL SOCIETY

## 1972-1975

| | |
|---|---|
| GOVERNOR GENERAL | Joseph B. Latimer |
| ASSISTANT GOVERNOR GENERAL | Ward W. Husted |
| SECRETARY GENERAL | Mrs. Robert M. Sherman |
| TREASURER GENERAL | E. Frederick Low |
| HISTORIAN GENERAL | Mrs. Lester A. Hall |
| ELDER GENERAL | Rev. J. Ronald Bogart |
| CAPTAIN GENERAL | Richard Stanton |
| SURGEON GENERAL | Dr. Walter S. Kimball |
| COUNSELLOR GENERAL | Hewitt A. Conway |

### MEMBERS AT LARGE, EXECUTIVE COMMITTEE

Lynmar Brock Jr., Mrs. John R. Orndorff,
Dr. Robert L. Thomas

## FIVE GENERATIONS PROJECT COMMITTEE

## 1975

Mrs. John K. Allen
John D. Austin Jr., F.A.S.G.
Claude W. Barlow, Ph.D., F.A.S.G.
Mrs. W. Carroll Barnes
Mrs. Fenno E. deVries
Mrs. Lester A. Hall
Carroll Alton Means
Miss Lucinda B. Neff
Rev. William Neff Jr.
Mrs. Robert M. Sherman, F.A.S.G.
Col. John Soule
Dr. Lee D. van Antwerp, C.G.
Robert M. Sherman, F.A.S.G., Chairman

## ABOUT THE EDITOR

To find one person possessing all the essential qualifications to serve as editor of the Five Generations Project must have seemed a hopeless task to Dr. van Antwerp. Lucy Mary Kellogg, though, proved right for the position; she had not only the essential qualifications, but others in addition that were of inestimable value.

Lucy Mary possessed a singularly happy disposition which contributed to her remarkable ability to win and retain the friendship of people from all walks of life. She demonstrated never-ending patience in solving difficult problems, and encouraging, instructing, and sharing her vast store of genealogical knowledge with the workers on the various Mayflower families. Although personally a perfectionist, she never lost patience with others less concerned with the accuracy of their work.

Her dedication to the memory of the Mayflower Passengers, and loyalty to the Society of Mayflower Descendants, were beyond question. The devotion of the final three years of her life to the Five Generations Project, without monetary reward, is proof of this. Nevertheless, she never permitted personal sentiment to influence her approach to each problem, even though the result might be invalidation of an accepted line, and cause her grief.

Perhaps alone Lucy Mary realized the immensity of the Project; possibly none were aware of the remarkable progress she made toward completion of volume one. She only once indicated disappointment or regret when she wrote me shortly before her death in 1973, "I wish I had started work on this Project ten years ago!"

Surely Lucy Mary would have been gratified if she could have foreseen that Robert M. Sherman, with whom she had been so closely associated in Mayflower genealogical research, would supervise completion of this volume, and that he would endeavor to complete the plans she had outlined. Her devotion to the Project is an inspiration to the many others who will have had a part in the total Project before it is completed. Lucy Mary would have been most grateful could she have known that her friends, both members and non-members of the Mayflower Society, would show their appreciation for her great contribution by generous donations to the research fund that now bears her name. It is my firm belief that the Pilgrims would have been proud to acclaim Lucy Mary as one of their descendants.

August 1975
Dallas, Texas

Joseph B. Latimer
Governor General

## THE SOCIETY EXPRESSES THANKS


To everyone involved in any way with the preparation of this book for the printer. Some of their names have unfortunately escaped the record, but the contribution of each is appreciated and hereby acknowledged.

Those who played known substantial parts in the preparation of this work include:

RESEARCH ASSISTANCE: For the *Eaton Family* in original records, Lucy Mary Kellogg (Mich. Soc.), Ruth W. Sherman and Robert M. Sherman (both R.I. Soc.). Help was given also on the *Eaton Family* or the *White Family* by Claude W. Barlow (Mass. Soc.), Georgia H. Birkett (of Mass.), Natalie S. Butler (Me. Soc.), Isabelle V. Freeman (Mass. Soc.), Ronald C. Lawson (D.C. and Vt. Socs.), Beatrice Neal (Me. Soc.), Charles F. Putnam (Mass. Soc.), and Edna C. Townsend (Mass. Soc.).

RESEARCH FINANCING: Many State Societies and Colonies, individual members and non-members, whose donations have been recognized in *The Mayflower Quarterly*. Without these contributions this book would not exist.

LIBRARIES and SPECIAL COLLECTIONS: Connecticut State Library (Hartford); Newberry Library (Chicago); New England Historic Genealogical Society (Boston); Rhode Island Historical Society (Providence); Massachusetts Mayflower Society's Bowman files, courtesy of Adele W. Allen; General Society's lineage papers--copies of early generations, courtesy of Corinne D. Hall (Mass. Soc.) and Florence F. deVries (Ill. Soc.).

FINAL EDITING and PROOFREADING: Claude W. Barlow, Ph.D., F.A.S.G., Frank E. Coldwell (of Mass.), Eileen C. Hall (of Conn.), Robert M. Sherman, F.A.S.G., and Ruth W. Sherman, F.A.S.G. The Committee Consultant was Charles W. Farnham, F.A.S.G. (of R.I.).

KEY TO ABBREVIATED TITLES: Ruth L. Douthit (of Ohio), Stuart P. Lloyd (N.J. Soc.), Milton E. Terry (N.J. Soc.), and Elizabeth P. White (Ill. Soc.).

INDEX: Milton E. Terry and his assistant Stuart P. Lloyd.

ARTWORK: Charles F. Mathewson (of Leyden Press).

FINAL TYPING: Jocelyn Rebello (of Mass.).

# TABLE OF CONTENTS

## TO THE READER

Among the immigrants to Massachusetts between 1620 and 1650 were at least eight named Eaton, sixteen Fullers, and twenty-two Whites (MA PIONEERS). These figures permit the reader to estimate the chance that his early Massachusetts Eaton, Fuller, or White ancestor is a member of one of the families in this book.

The authors have assembled families as correctly and as completely as circumstances permitted. Their work is based largely on carefully researched articles in genealogical journals and family histories, together with probate and land records, and town and church vital statistics. Family tradition, in the absence of confirmatory evidence, has not been accepted as proof of a line. This has, regretfully, resulted in the rejection of a few lines which the Society accepted in its early years, but were based on insufficient or erroneous evidence. On the other hand, many new potential lines have been uncovered.

Paucity of records sometimes renders it virtually impossible to follow a family or individual to another town: An entire family disappears, or one or more children are labelled "n.f.r." (no further record found). The authors often offer tentative identifications using the word probably, when evidence is nearly conclusive, and possibly, when evidence is merely suggestive. This is done in the hope that a reader, tracing back his ancestry through such clues, may come upon real proof and so establish the new line.

Spelling was far from consistent even after the Revolution. To a great extent names in this book have been spelled as found in each record. This often provides different spellings of an individual's name at his birth, upon marriage, and in a deed or will. For example, Hayward is found as Heywood and even Howard for the same person; Marcy and Mercy are many times interchangeable. With variant spellings so commonplace, use of "(*sic*)" is restricted to exceptional examples. To assist the reader, most variant spellings of a name are clumped together in the Index, rather than separately alphabetized.

A reader who finds either an error or additional information regarding any family or individual in this volume down to *the birth of sixth generation children*, but not beyond, is urgently requested to send such material to: FIVE GENERATIONS PROJECT, P.O. BOX 297, PLYMOUTH MA 02360.

# F R A N C I S   E A T O N

of the

*M A Y F L O W E R*

Compiled by

LEE DOUGLAS VAN ANTWERP, M.D., C.G.

Lee Douglas van Antwerp is a descendant of Pilgrim William Bradford. He has served as Governor of the Illinois Mayflower Society and as Governor General of the General Society of Mayflower Descendants (1969-1972); he is immediate past Chairman of the Five Generations Project. He holds both A.B. and M.D. degrees from the University of Michigan.

A Certified Genealogist, he is author of the van Antwerp Family (NYGBR 1941 & 1948), and has already submitted for editing a second Mayflower Family--the William Bradford Family.

# FRANCIS EATON

As is the case with most of the *Mayflower* passengers, we know far too little about Francis Eaton. It is likely that he was of the London Contingent, as his name does not appear in any Dutch records yet uncovered.

Governor Bradford lists as *Mayflower* passengers, "Francis Eaton, and Sarah his wife, and Samuell, their sone, a young child." In his "increasings and decreasings" written early in 1651, he remarks that "Francis Eeaton his first wife dyed in the generall sickness; and he maried againe and his 2nd wife dyed and he maried the 3rd and had by her 3 children. One of them is maried and hath a child; the other are living but one of them is an ideote. He [the father] dyed about 16 years agoe. His sone Samuell who came over a sucking child, is allso maried and hath a child."

As indicated above, Francis and Sarah Eaton, with their infant son, cast their lot for the long voyage on the *Mayflower*. At Cape Cod on 11 November 1620 according to the old calendar, Francis was one of the 41 signers of the Mayflower Compact. There can be little doubt that the arrival of the Pilgrims at Plymouth early in the winter made it imperative that shelter be constructed as promptly as possible. Francis Eaton's competence as a carpenter could very well have been a factor in the prevention of even more deaths.

Son and father survived the "general sickeness" of the first winter which carried off half the population, but Sarah succumbed early in 1621. As was the custom of the times, the widower remarried shortly. It is believed that his second wife was John Carver's unnamed maid who came on the *Mayflower* and "Married and died a year or two after, here in this place." There were no children recorded to this marriage. Francis was alloted four shares in the land division of 1623, apparently one for himself, one for son Samuel, and one for each of his deceased wives who had arrived on the *Mayflower*. He married a third time in 1624 or 1625, Christian Penn, a passenger on the ship *Anne* which arrived at Plymouth the summer of 1623. They had three children. The Eaton family was named in the division of cattle and goats 22 May 1627 old style, when Francis, his wife Christian, and children Samuel and Rachel, with nine other inhabitants of Plymouth, obtained "a heyfer of the last years called the white belyd Heyfer & two shee goats."

Eaton, with Bradford and others, was one of the purchasers who assumed Plymouth Colony's debt to the Merchant Adventurers in 1628. Francis Eaton recorded three land sales after this time, all in 1631: four acres to Edward Winslow for a "cow calf"; twenty acres to William Brewster "at the place comonly called Nothingelse"; and twelve more acres to Brewster. The signature of Francis Eaton appears in the record book on the second deed.

The 1633 epidemic swept away Francis Eaton and many other Pilgrims. He died intestate, but his inventory calls him a carpenter and shows, as might be expected, the tools of his trade as well as livestock and household effects.

Christian survived her husband and married another *Mayflower* passenger--Francis Billington, son of John and Ellen. She had nine children by Billington, and she died in Middleboro, Massachusetts about 1684.

*

We have no certain knowledge of Francis Eaton's parentage or even the section of England from which he came, but research in records of England or New England might prove that he came from Bristol or from Sturton-le-Steeple, Nottinghamshire, as the following records show the name existed in those towns:

Although Banks in his *English Ancestry* quotes the record apprenticing one John Morgan to Francis Eaton of Bristol, England, carpenter, and his wife Dorothy, "the Mr. at New England," the document bears the date of 4 December 1626. By that time Pilgrim Eaton was wed to Christian Penn and would have been "of Plymouth." It seems unlikely that the document is pertinent.

Burgess in *The Pastor of the Pilgrims*, says that George and Francis Eaton of Fenton were selling land in that township about 1591. It was the birthplace of Rev. John Robinson, of Bridget White his wife, and of Catherine White, Gov. Carver's wife. Nearby towns of Austerfield, Babworth, Gainsborough and Scrooby had spawned the Separatist movement and many of the other Pilgrim Fathers. It would not be surprising to find Pilgrim Eaton hailing from the same area, but expert research in Nottinghamshire is needed before Eaton descendants should even tentatively claim the shire as their ancestor's home.

References: MD 1:228; 6:146. BRADFORD'S HIST (1952) pp. 443-4, 446-7. BANKS' ENGLISH ANCY p. 52. PASTOR OF PILGRIMS p. 20. PLYMOUTH COLONY RECS 3:102; 12:4, 12, 16-18, 48, 100, 144. Photocopy of apprentice record from Bristol, England.

## FIRST GENERATION

1 FRANCIS[1] EATON, b. England; d. Plymouth, bet. 25 Oct. and 8 Nov. 1633 O.S. He was prob. one of the London contingent.

He m. (1) in England SARAH -----, b. England; d. Plymouth early in 1621; m. (2) Plymouth ----- -----; d. Plymouth ca. 1624; m. (3) Plymouth, in 1624 or 1625, CHRISTIAN PENN, a passenger on the *Anne*; d. Middleboro ca. 1684. His widow m. (2) July 1634 Francis Billington. [See *The John Billington Family*.]

The inventory of Francis Eaton, carpenter, of Plymouth was valued at £64 8s. 7d. He did not have a granddaughter who m. Hugh Calkins, although a typographical error in the Folger pamphlet implies this.

Children (EATON) one by first wife, three by third wife:

2 i SAMUEL[2], b. England 1620
3 ii RACHEL, b. Plymouth 1625
4 iii BENJAMIN, b. Plymouth after 1 June 1627
iv a child, b. Plymouth; living 1651; n.f.r.

References: MD 1:10, 15, 197-200; 2:115-7. STODDARD pp. 128-9. BRADFORD'S HIST (1912) 2:400, 407, 410. FOLGER p. 4.

## SECOND GENERATION

2 SAMUEL[2] EATON (Francis[1]), b. England 1620; d. Middleboro bef. 29 Oct. 1684 O.S.

He m. (1) bef. 10 March 1646 O.S. ELIZABETH -----, d. after 5 Oct. 1652 O.S., but bef. 1661; m. (2) Plymouth 10 Jan. 1660/1 MARTHA BILLINGTON; d. after 9 June 1704, prob. in CT; dau. of Francis and Christian (Penn)(Eaton) Billington. She m. (2) after 7 Dec. 1687 Robert Crossman of Taunton, b. ca. 1621; d. Oct. 1692 ae. 71; son of John Crossman.

Samuel was apprenticed to John Cooke the younger, on 13 Aug. 1636 for a term of seven years. He was of Duxbury 10 March 1646 when he sold land formerly belonging to

---

NOTE: Because *The Eatonian News* and Molyneux's *Eaton Genealogy* each contain many contradictions of primary sources and many assumptions which could not be proved, this account of Francis Eaton's descendants does not include any information found only in one or the other of them.

Christian Billington. In a deed dated 3 January 1663, Francis Billington named his son-in-law Samuel Eaton, "my daughter Martha his wife," and their daughter Sarah. He was still of Duxbury 17 August 1663 when he sold "all my lands, housing, fencing," etc. in Duxbury; both he and Martha acknowledged the deed. Samuel was a freeman in Middleboro 29 May 1670.

On 9 June 1704 Philip Bump (husband of daughter Sarah) transferred to his mother(in-law), Martha Crossman, all his estate both personal and real in Plainfield CT.

The inventory of Samuel Eaton's estate was exhibited 29 October 1684. In considering the settlement of this estate, Bowman wrote "the first wife must have had at least two daughters who had married and had children living when the estate was settled, and that at least one of these daughters was dead. No other construction can be put upon the statement 'and the Children of the first wife to have the sume of twenty shillings a peece & such of them as are Dead the sume to be paid amonge theire Children.'"

Children (EATON) b. prob. Duxbury or Middleboro, two attributed to first wife, four to second wife:*

i a dau.; d. bef. 1684; m. ----- -----
ii a dau.; m. ----- -----
5 iii SARAH[3], b. bef. 3 Jan. 1663
6 iv SAMUEL, b. ca. 1663
v MERCY, b. 1665; d. after 27 Feb. 1704; m. Plymouth 7 Jan. 1685/6 SAMUEL FULLER, b. ca. 1658; d. Plympton 6 Sept. 1728; son of Samuel Fuller. [See *The Samuel Fuller Family*.]
7 vi BETHIAH

References: MD 1:16; 2:117, 172-3, 254; 7:128; 13:204; 17:183. VR PLYMPTON. PLYMOUTH COLONY RECS 1:43; 3:47; 5:279; 12:100, 144. Bristol Co. PR 1:72-3 (Crossman). PLYMOUTH SCRAPBOOK p. 130. DUXBURY REC p. 22. Plainfield CT LR 1:17(Philip Bump). FAM OF PILGRIMS pp. 86-7. BASSETT FAM (1926) p. 216.

3 RACHEL[2] EATON (Francis[1]), b. Plymouth 1625; d. after 3 June 1656 and bef. Oct. 1661.

She m. Plymouth 2 March 1645 JOSEPH RAMSDELL (or Ramsden); d. 25 May 1674. He m. (2) Plymouth 16 Oct. 1661 Mary Savery.

---

*No substantiation has been found for Molyneux's claim that Samuel and his first wife had children Francis, John, Samuel and Elizabeth.

Joseph was in Plymouth by 1641 when he planted a piece of land. Although there is no probate record of Joseph, in 1674 he deeded land to his "eldest son Daniel." No evidence has been found for other children.

Child (RAMSDELL) b. Plymouth:

8 i DANIEL[3], b. 14 Sept. 1649

References: MD 1:153; 8:18-20; 13:86; 16:121; 17:183. PLYMOUTH COLONY RECS 2:132; 3:102, 329. MA PIONEERS p. 378.

4 BENJAMIN[2] EATON (Francis[1]), b. Plymouth after 1 June 1627; d. Plympton 16 Jan. 1711/2.

He m. Plymouth 4 Dec. 1660 SARAH HOSKINS, b. 16 Sept. 1637; living in Plymouth 1692; dau. of William and Sarah (Cushman) Hoskins.

Benjamin was at least 16 in August 1643. In 1685 he, his wife Sarah, and son Benjamin sold land in Dartmouth. No probate record has been found for Benjamin or Sarah Eaton, or for William Hoskins.

Children (EATON):

9 i BENJAMIN[3], b. Plymouth ca. 1664
ii WILLIAM, b. bef. 1669; d. unm. on a Canadian expedition bet. July 1690 and 18 March 1690/1. In July 1690 he made his will because he was "cald forth to go against the French."
10 iii REBECCA, b. ca. 1675
11 iv EBENEZER, b. ca. 1674

References: MD 2:140; 10:113; 12:227; 17:183. VR PLYMPTON. PLYMOUTH COLONY RECS 2:67. Plymouth Col. LR 5:368(Benjamin Eaton). NEHGR 4:255. FAM OF PILGRIMS pp. 86-7. SMALL DESC 2:528-33. GRANBERRY FAM pp. 241, 243.

## THIRD GENERATION

5 SARAH[3] EATON (Samuel[2], Francis[1]), b. prob. Middleboro bef. 3 Jan. 1663; d. after 24 Feb. 1725/6.

She m. ca. 1685 PHILIP BUMPUS (or Bump), b. Plymouth or Duxbury; d. Plainfield CT 20 Jan. 1724/5; son of Edward and Hannah (-----) "Bompasse."

In his first recorded deed, 1681, he is called "of Marshfield." Shortly after their marriage, Philip and

Sarah moved to Bristol (then in MA, now in RI) where he took the oath of fidelity on 17 May 1685. They moved to Middleboro in 1688, but returned to Bristol bef. April 1692. Philip was among the subscribers on 13 November 1699, who purchased land in Quinebaug (now Plainfield CT). He was still in Bristol in April 1702 when he bought about 300 acres of land in Plainfield, where he was living by December 1702.

An agreement of heirs of Philip Bump of Windham (Co.) CT dated 24 Feb. 1725/6 names Sarah Bump, widow; Samuel Bump of Bolton CT; Philip Bump, Josiah Bump, Thomas Herd and wife Lydia, Peleg Ballard and wife Bethia, daughter Sarah Bump, all of Plainfield; and Thomas Smith and wife Jemima of Preston CT.

Children (BUMP or BUMPUS):

i JEMIMA[4], b. Bristol RI ca. 1686; d. after her husband; prob. was the Jemima Smith who was a member of the First Congregational Church of Preston CT 14 March 1744; m. Plainfield CT 9 May 1706 THOMAS SMITH of Preston CT, d. bet. 23 April and 31 July 1739. He bought land in Plainfield in June 1701, then resident of "East------------stable in Mass. Bay" [perhaps "Eastham in the County of Barnstable"]. Thomas left a will dated 23 April and proved 31 July 1739, bequeathing his estate to wife Jemima and to Daniel Thomas "whom I have brought up."

12 ii SAMUEL, b. Bristol RI 20 Feb. 1687

13 iii PHILIP, b. Bristol RI 13 Feb. 1689

14 iv LYDIA, b. Bristol RI 2 April 1692

v MATTHEW, b. Bristol RI 8 June 1695; d. bef. 24 Feb. 1725/6.

vi JOSIAH, b. Bristol RI 9 April 1698; d. Plainfield CT 2 Sept. 1757; m. SARAH HARRIS, b. Plainfield CT 10 Aug. 1702; dau. of Ebenezer and Christoble (Crary) Harris. Ebenezer Harris mentions dau. Sarah Bump in his will dated 1750; Josiah Bump together with wife Sarah and her sisters, all daus. of Ebenezer and Christable Harris, signed an agreement in 1754. The will of Josiah Bump of Plainfield dated 20 Aug. proved 12 Sept. 1757, bequeathed to sisters Sarah Harris and Bathya Ballard; to "kinsman" Thomas Heard. Nephew Josiah Heard and widow Sarah Bump shared most of the estate.

15 vii BETHIA, b. Quinebaug CT ca. 1700

viii SARAH, b. ca. 1702; living 20 Aug. 1757; m. ----- HARRIS, who has not been identified despite considerable searching, but might be

Nathan Harris whose sister Sarah married Josiah Bump (vi above).

References: Plainfield CT VR 1:4, 34. CSL Barbour Index: Plainfield. RI VR Bristol pp. 66-7. CSL Ch Recs: Plainfield 1:219. PRESTON CONG CH p. 153. Plainfield CT PR 2:146(Ebenezer Harris); 3:115-6(Josiah Bump et al); #299 and 3:176(Josiah Bump). Bristol Co. LR 5:160 (Philip Bump). Plainfield CT LR 1:1(Fitch to Smith); 1:13 (Fitch to Bump); 4:24(Ebenezer Harris); 4:504-7(Harris et al). CSL PR #4991(Thomas Smith). Plymouth Col. LR 5:28 (Bumpus). TAG 23:228; 43:150-1. NEHGR 15:53. HARRIS FAM (1909) p. 13.

6 SAMUEL[3] EATON (Samuel[2], Francis[1]), b. prob. Middleboro ca. 1663; d. there 8 March 1723/4 in 61st yr.

He m. Middleboro 24 May 1694 ELIZABETH FULLER, b. ca. 1663; d. bef. husband; daughter of Samuel and Elizabeth (Nichols) (Bowen) Fuller. [See *The Samuel Fuller Family*.]

In Oct. 1695 Samuel Eaton and wife Elizabeth with other "children of Mr. Samuel Fuller" signed an agreement with his widow Elizabeth. Barnabas and Elizabeth Eaton in June 1724 filed an agreement for division of the estate of their father, Samuel Eaton, "Whereby all His Estate falls unto us by Right of Inheritance."

Children (EATON) b. Middleboro:

i MERCY[4], b. 6 Dec. 1695; d. bef. 3 June 1724
ii KEZIAH, b. 16 May 1700; d. 7 Feb. 1709/10 in 10th yr.
16 iii ELIZABETH, b. 26 July 1701
17 iv BARNABAS, b. 12 April 1703

References: MD 2:42, 159; 4:74; 5:69-72; 12:227-9; 26:36-38. MA MARR 2:70. MIDDLEBORO DEATHS. Plymouth Co. PR 1:223, 246(Samuel Fuller). FULLER GEN 2:15.

7 BETHIA[3] EATON (Samuel[2], Francis[1]), d. bef. 12 Jan. 1735/6.

She m. Taunton 5 Nov. 1691 JOSEPH BASSETT, b. Bridgewater ca. 1664; d. there 8 Nov. 1736; son of Joseph and Mary (Lapham) Bassett.

Joseph Bassett of Bridgewater, husbandman, in his will dated 12 Jan. 1735/6 and proved 7 Feb. 1736/7, named oldest daughter Bethia Bassett; 2nd daughter Mehetebell Holloway living at Middleboro; 3rd daughter Lydia Phillips of Norton. The inventory of Joseph Bassett gives his death date.

Children (BASSETT) b. Bridgewater:

i BETHIA[4], b. 25 Dec. 1693; m. bet. 12 Jan. 1735/6 and 19 Sept. 1738 WILLIAM CODDINGTON of Norton; living Norton 24 March 1785. He m. int. (1) Norton 1721 Elizabeth Jones. William was of Norton when he bought land there 19 Sept. 1721 (earliest record of him). He was a carpenter, housewright and millwright. William and wife Bethia on 19 Sept. 1738 sold "the homestead of our father Joseph Bassett late of Bridgewater deceased." In 1742 William and wife Bethia were both admitted to the Norton Church, she from Bridgewater. They both acknowledged the sale of swampland in Bridgewater 21 May 1764. William sold land and dwelling house in Norton and acknowledged the sale the same day--24 March 1785. [Although no evidence was found for any children, might the Abigail Coddington of Norton be their child? She married in Taunton 14 March 1757 James Verrey of Providence.]

ii MEHITABLE, b. 22 June 1697; d. Middleboro bef. 1754; m. there 20 June 1733 NATHANIEL HOLLOWAY, b. Taunton ca. 1702; d. Middleboro bef. 13 Oct. 1757; son of Nathaniel and Deliverance (Bobbit) Holloway. Nathaniel m. (2) Berkley 25 May 1754 Abiah (Crane) Babbitt. No children were found from his first marriage. In 1757 his widow Abiah was appointed administrator on her husband Nathaniel Holloway's estate; in a subsequent division Jedidah and Lois Holloway, two children of his second wife, are called his only surviving heirs.

18 iii LYDIA, b. 29 April 1703

References: MD 15:46. VR BRIDGEWATER, TAUNTON. MA MARR 2:70. Index Berkley Marr Book 1 (Old Col. Hist. Soc., Taunton). BRIDGEWATER BY MITCHELL p. 111. Plymouth Co. PR 7:265, 345(Joseph Bassett). Bristol Co. PR 6:1, 2(Nathaniel Holloway Sr.) Plymouth Co. PR 14:419; 20:448(Nathaniel Holloway). Plymouth Co. LR 37:155; 52:152 (William Coddington). Bristol Co. LR 39:437(Holloway agreement); 41:28(Blake to Coddington); 63:396(William Coddington). Bristol Co. Ct. Gen. Sess. 1746-77 p. 250 (m. Abigail Coddington). NORTON HIST pp. 167-8. BASSETT FAM (1926) p. 14.

8 DANIEL RAMSDELL[3] (Rachel[2] Eaton, Francis[1]), b. Plymouth 14 Sept. 1649, name recorded Ramsden; d. bef. 12 March 1721/2.

He m. HANNAH CASWELL, b. Taunton 14 July 1661; d. after 10 July 1722; dau. of Thomas Caswell. The earliest reference to Hannah as wife of Daniel occurs in her father's will dated 28 Sept. 1691. The latest record of Hannah is her acknowledgement of a deed 10 July 1722, wherein "Hannah, widow, relict of Daniel Ramsdell, now living in Taunton" signed with her siblings a quitclaim deed to the estate of "our honoured father Thos Caswell of sd Taunton deceased," dated 12 March 1721/2. In the original vital records of Plymouth, four children are ascribed to Daniel Ramsden and his wife "Sarah" [apparently an error for Hannah].

Children (RAMSDELL or RAMSDEN), last four born Plymouth:

19 i THOMAS[4], b. ca. 1680*
20 ii SAMUEL, b. 5 June 1690
21 iii JOSEPH, b. 15 Aug. 1693
iv BENJAMIN, b. 1 June 1699; n.f.r.
v HANNAH, b. 28 Sept. 1700; n.f.r.

References: MD 3:14. HANOVER BY DWELLEY p. 323. VR TAUNTON. Bristol Co. LR 14:316, 317(Caswell et al). Bristol Co. PR 1:196-197(Thomas Caswell). Plymouth VR 1:46(last four children to Daniel and Sarah). KING PHILIP'S WAR p. 429. Proprietors' Records of Greenwich, typescript, Swift River Valley Hist. Soc. pp. 2, 27. MIDDLEBORO BY WESTON p. 550.

9 BENJAMIN[3] EATON (Benjamin[2], Francis[1]), b. Plymouth ca. 1664; d. Kingston bet. 23 April and 7 Dec. 1745.

He m. (1) Plymouth 18 Dec. 1689 MARY COOMBS, b. Boston 28 Nov. 1666; d. Plympton 2 July 1728 in 63rd yr.; dau. of John and Elizabeth (-----) (Barlow) Coombs; m. (2) Hingham 11 March 1728/9 SUSANNA (LEWIS) BEAL, b. 1669 poss. Barnstable; d. Kingston 13 April 1739 "aged 70 the same month she died"; dau. of James and Sarah (Lane) Lewis and widow of Lazarus Beal of Hingham; m. int. (3) Kingston 4 Oct. 1740 Mrs. MARCY VAUGHAN; she received "mourning for the widow" from Benjamin's executor.

Benjamin Eaton, housewright, drew his will 23 April probated 7 Dec. 1745. He gave to oldest son William, lands from his home estate, and "whereas I look upon my son William Eaton non compos mentis" these lands were to revert

---

*The Mayflower Society presently accepts lines through this Thomas. No proof was found to support DWELLEY'S statement that this Thomas belongs in this family. Also, who is Thomas Ramsdell of Middleboro who between 1734 and 1738 claimed land in Narragansett Number Four (subsequently Greenwich MA) in the right of his father, Daniel Ramsdell, for the latter's service in King Philip's War?

to his brothers Benjamin and David "if they take care of (William) and provide for him...during his Natural life." To his sons John, Benjamin and David, he devised lands, his pew in the meeting house and his carpenter and joiner tools; to sons Francis and Elisha, cash bequests or equivalent; and to "the children of my daughter Sarah Cushman," to daughter Mary Soule, to daughter Elizabeth Stertevant, and to the children of daughter Hannah Bryant, deceased, amounts with what had been given previously to make the "Full share." The son Benjamin was executor.

On 15 June 1748 a distribution was made of "that part of the Real Estate that was not Particularly bequeathed & Given away by Benjamin Eaton, late of Kingston, dec'd" 1/9 part each to sons David, Elisha, Benjamin and John, and 1/2 of 1/9 part to Michel Bryant and Marcy Leach the wife of Nathaniel Leach, children of Hannah Bryant, deceased; "whereas Capt. John Loreing of Plympton hath bought the several rights in said land that did belong to Mary Soul the wife of Zechariah Soule; the right of son Francis Eaton deceased; the ninth part in the right of his daughter Elizabeth Sturtevant the wife of Cornelius Sturtevant; the right of the heirs of his daughter Sarah Cushman dec'd who was late the wife of Benjamin Cushman and also one half of that Ninth Part which did belong to the heirs of his daughter Hannah Bryant deceased who was the wife of Benja Bryant deceased, wherefore." Capt. John Loring got 4/9ths and 1/2 of 1/9th part.

Children (EATON), all to Benjamin and Mary:

i WILLIAM[4], b. Plymouth 1 June 1691; d. after April 1745 but bef. 15 June 1748; unm.*

22 ii HANNAH, b. Plymouth 10 Feb. 1692

iii JABEZ, b. Plymouth 8 Feb. 1693; d. Plympton 19 May 1722 ae 28 years

iv SARAH, b. Plymouth 20 Oct. 1695; d. Plympton 13 Sept. 1737 in 42nd yr.; m. there 8 Jan. 1712 BENJAMIN CUSHMAN, bp. Plymouth 1 March 1691; d. Plympton 17 Oct. 1770 in 78th yr.; son of Thomas and Abigail (Fuller) Cushman. [See *The Isaac Allerton Family* for an account of their children.]

v JOHN, b. Plymouth 6 Oct. 1697; d. Halifax 30 March 1766 in 70th yr. He m. Middleboro 31 July 1729 ELIZABETH FULLER "of Middleborough," b. ca. 1697; prob. d. bef. 1750; daughter of John and Mercy (Nelson) Fuller. [See *The Samuel Fuller Family*.]

He sold in 1749 "all that piece of land...set off to me as my part of 33 1/2 acres not

*No substantiation has been found for Molyneux's claim that William had sons William, Joseph and David.

particularly given away in my father Benj. Eaton's last will."

In June 1750 Benjamin Cushman Jr. was made guardian of John Eaton, adjudged non-compos mentis. On 23 Dec. 1751 John Eaton of Kingston was "warned" from Halifax, having come into Halifax "27 September last and at the desire of his guardian was there received by Ebenezer Fuller Jr. of sd Halifax." In 1754 money was received from David Eaton for John's care and payments were made to Mary Soule and Robert Waterman. In 1755 payment was made to Ebenezer Fuller Jr. as guardian and for keeping John "now of Halifax."

It is presumed that Elizabeth died before John and that they had no children.*

23 vi BENJAMIN, b. 1698

vii MARY, b. ca. 1699; d. Middleboro 14 May 1773; m. Plympton 9 June 1720 ZACHARIAH SOULE, b. Plymouth 21 March 1694; d. Plympton 3 May 1751 in 58th yr.; son of Benjamin and Sarah (Standish) Soule. [See *The George Soule Family* for an account of their children.]

24 viii FRANCIS, b. Kingston ca. 1700

25 ix ELISHA, b. ca. 1701

26 x ELIZABETH

27 xi DAVID, b. ca. 1708

References: MD 2:78; 3:91; 4:113; 8:250; 10:113; 12:243; 13:205. VR KINGSTON, PLYMPTON. TAG 46:131. Plymouth Co. PR 10:70-74; 11:10-11, 160-3(Benjamin Eaton); 11:451; 12:457; 13:368, 406, 454(John Eaton, gdn.). Plymouth Co. LR 40:54; 41:89(John Eaton). Minutes Court of General Sessions of the Peace 23 Dec. 1751 [original records at Pilgrim Hall Plymouth MA]. HINGHAM HIST 2:57, 209, 441. SMALL DESC 2:555-6.

10 REBECCA$^3$ EATON (Benjamin$^2$, Francis$^1$), b. ca. 1675; d. Plympton 13 Nov. 1770 in 95th yr.

She m. Plymouth 21 Nov. 1699 JOSIAH RICKARD, b. ca. 1672; d. Plympton 22 Jan. 1765 in 93rd year; son of Giles and Hannah (Dunham) Rickard.

Josiah Rickard made his will on 17 Dec. 1750 probated 4 Feb. 1765 naming wife Rebecca; sons Giles, Benjamin, David and Josiah; daughter Desire Frazier; daughter "Deborah" Allen (mis-copied for Rebecca); and granddaughter Elizabeth Doggett. On 14 June 1765 "Rebeckah" Allen with all her siblings acknowledged receipt from the estate.

---

*No substantiation has been found for Molyneux's claim that John had children Susanna, Benjamin, Mary, Elijah and John.

Children (RICKARD):

28 i GILES[4], b. Plymouth 14 Oct. 1700
29 ii BENJAMIN, b. Plymouth 20 or 28 Feb. 1702
iii JOSIAH, b. Plymouth 21 Oct. 1703; d. Plympton 2 Jan. 1769 in 66th year. No probate rec. found.
30 iv DESIRE, b. Plympton 18 Feb. 1706
31 v REBECCA, b. Plympton 24 Aug. 1708
vi DAVID, b. Plympton 24 Dec. 1711; living in 1765 when brother Benjamin agreed to care for him. Did he m. Plympton 20 Oct. 1740 MARY MORSE of Middleboro? No probate rec. found.

References: MD 3:13-14, 163; 11:115, 116; 13:207. VR PLYMPTON. (PLYMOUTH) ANC LANDMARKS p. 214. Plymouth Co. PR 19:160(Josiah Rickard). Plym. Co. LR 50:44(Giles Rickard).

11 EBENEZER[3] EATON (Benjamin[2], Francis[1]), b. ca. 1674; d. North Yarmouth ME 25 July 1736; m. Plymouth 2 Nov. 1701 HANNAH RICKARD, d. North Yarmouth 26 April 1765; daughter of Giles and Hannah (Dunham) Rickard. In the division of the estate of Giles Rickard of Plymouth after his wife's decease, daughter Hannah Eaton received a portion 25 June 1709.

Ebenezer was a housewright. He arrived in North Yarmouth ME by 1730 from Kingston. In an agreement dated 27 Dec. 1736 and recorded 19 April 1737, the widow Hannah was to be supported by eldest son Ebenezer in consideration of "his having more than any of the rest of the children." The two daughters, Marcy Lake wife of Benjamin, and Joanna Eaton, and the three sons, Ebenezer, Elisha and Gideon, divided the estate. In 1748 Ebenezer Bishop and wife Mercy, and Elisha French and wife Joanna, all of North Yarmouth, sold their rights to brother Gideon.

Children (EATON), b. Plymouth:

i EBENEZER[4], b. 17 Sept. 1702; d. North Yarmouth "being killed by Indians" 20 June 1748. His brother Gideon was appointed administrator of his estate 5 Oct. 1748; sisters Mercy Bishop, wife of Ebenezer, and Joanna French, wife of Elisha, had quitclaimed their interest to Gideon on 1 Sept. 1748.
ii BENJAMIN, b. 23 Nov. 1704; d.y.
32 iii MERCY, b. 15 March 1705/06
iv ELISHA, b. 11 Oct. 1708; d. Plympton bet. 23 Nov. 1737 and 3 July 1738 when his widow resigned as executor. In his will dated 23 Nov. 1737, Elisha Eaton of Plympton, yeoman, left his entire estate to wife Elizabeth. On 11 April

1740, Elizabeth Eaton received £16, "set off to me out of my husband's estate." Elizabeth has not been identified and no further record has been found. On 7 Aug. 1744 administrator Nathaniel Fuller sold "all the right in Land & Meadows & Islands which the sd Elisha Eaton died seized of ... in North Yarmouth ... reference being had to an agreement of the said Eaton & his Brothers & Sisters for the Settlement of their Hon$^{d}$ Fathers Eben$^{r}$ Eaton Estate."

v GIDEON, b. 5 Feb. 1711/12; d. North Yarmouth ME 18 Oct. 1787 ae 75; m. there 10 May 1749 MARY or HANNAH BAILEY (called "Mary" in the marriage record; "Hannah" in North Yarmouth int. 18 March 1749, and death record); she d. prob. North Yarmouth 1 May 1752.

vi HANNAH, b. March 1715; d.y.

33 vii JOANNA, b. 29 April 1716

References: MD 2:165; 13:207. (PLYMOUTH) ANC LANDMARKS pp. 99-100. OLD TIMES 7:653, 655, 658, 1025, 1106-08, 1182. Plymouth Co. PR #7043 3:44(Giles Rickard); 8:10, 68, 69, 88, 128; 9:409-10(Elisha Eaton). York Co. ME LR 24:254(estate Elisha Eaton); 28:40(Gideon Eaton). York Co. ME PR 4983, 4984(Ebenezer Eaton). NORTH YARMOUTH BY ROWE p. 100.

## FOURTH & FIFTH GENERATIONS

12 SAMUEL BUMP or BUMPUS$^{4}$ (Sarah$^{3}$ Eaton, Samuel$^{2}$, Francis$^{1}$), b. Bristol RI 20 Feb. 1687; d. Bolton CT 1747.

He m. (1) Bolton CT 4 April 1723 ABIGAIL ROUSE, b. Rochester 28 March 1693; d. Bolton CT 1 Dec. 1725; daughter of Edward and Rebecca (-----) Rouse; m. (2) Bolton CT 18 May 1727 MARY RAY of Haddam CT; d. Bolton CT 8 Feb 1727/8; daughter of James Ray Sr.

James Ray Sr. of Haddam CT in his will dated 14 Jan. 1730/1 probated 28 June 1731 instructed his son James Ray to pay "my grandson Samuel Bump of Bolton £30" when he becomes 21.

"Sam$^{l}$ Bump of Bolton" made his will 15 April 1730, inventory 20 March 1747, dividing his property between his two sons and asking that Edward Rose of Bolton be guardian to eldest son Mathew, and Lieut. Able Shaylor [not "Gaylord" as reported in TAG], be guardian to son Samuel. In 1747/8, Samuel "of East Haddam" and Matthew of Bolton sold their inheritances.

Children (BUMP), b. Bolton CT, two by Abigail and one by Mary:

i PATIENCE[5], b. 23 Jan. 1723/4; d. Bolton CT 1 May 1725

ii MATTHEW, b. 27 Nov. 1725; living 1747/8; possibly removed to Frederickstown (now Carmel), Putnam Co. NY with his Ballard cousins [See #15]. A Matthew Bump was living in 1790 in Fredericks-town with one female.

iii SAMUEL, b. 5 Feb. 1727/8; living 1747/8; n.f.r.

References: TAG 43:151. BOLTON CT VR pp. 13, 21, 24, 63. VR ROCHESTER. Hartford CT PR #894(Samuel Bump). Bolton CT LR 2:523, 525, 619(Matthew & Samuel Bump). MANWARING 3:99(James Ray); 3:514-5(Samuel Bump). 1790 CENSUS NY:83.

13 PHILIP BUMP or BUMPUS[4] (Sarah[3] Eaton, Samuel[2], Francis[1]), b. Bristol RI 13 Feb. 1689; living Sharon CT 3 March 1762.

He m. (1) Litchfield CT 4 Feb. 1722/3 MARY HORSFORD, b. Windsor CT 15 Feb. 1690/1; d. Sharon CT 1 Dec. 1751; daughter of Samuel and Mary (Palmer) Horsford; m. (2) Sharon CT 3 Dec. 1754 ESTHER (-----) WARNER.

Philip lived in Plainfield CT from May 1725 to 1733; he was in Hebron CT from Oct. 1733 to 1736 according to deeds; in Bolton CT from Dec. 1736 to 1749 when he and wife Mary sold 117 acres in Bolton; and in Sharon CT by June 1749 when he bought land, which he "of Sharon" sold 3 March 1762.

Child (BUMP), b. Plainfield CT:

i WILLIAM[5], b. 26 Oct. 1723; d. Sharon CT 2 Aug. 1750

References: VR SHARON CT. CSL Barbour Index:Litchfield, Plainfield, Sharon. TAG 23:228. HORSFORD FAMS. Bolton CT LR 1:553, 555, 564; 2:24, 489; 3:16 (Philip Bump). Hebron CT LR 3:52, 64(Philip Bump). Plainfield CT LR 3:75, 103, 147, 153, 154, 160(Philip Bump). Sharon CT LR 2:458/9; 5:183(Philip Bump). Voluntown CT LR A1:227, 229(Philip Bump); 2:266(Owen to Bump).

14 LYDIA BUMP or BUMPUS[4] (Sarah[3] Eaton, Samuel[2], Francis[1]), b. Bristol RI 2 April 1692; d. Plainfield CT 14 May 1740.

She m. THOMAS HERD (or Heard or Hurd) who d. Plainfield CT 24 April 1751.

Thomas' will dated 19 Dec. 1750 probated 14 May 1751, names sons Thomas, Josiah, Jacob and John; daughters Mary, Bathyah, Sarah and Ame; brother-in-law Josiah Bump executor.

Children (HERD) b. Plainfield CT:

i BETHIA[5], b. 18 June 1720; living Preston CT 18 April 1765; m. bef. 1745 EBENEZER YERRINGTON; prob. the one bp. Preston 29 July 1710 to Peter Yerrington; d. Preston bef. 3 Jan. 1757 (estate inventory). On 18 May 1751, "Bethiah Yearinton" and six siblings signed a receipt as heirs to their father, Thomas Heard, deceased.

The names of Bethia's husband and children are confirmed by the following records: On 18 April 1765 Bethia Yerrington of Preston posted bond at Norwich CT as guardian of Ebenezer Yerrington, minor son of Ebenezer of Preston deceased. In 1758 Reuben Yerrington, son of Ebenezer of Preston deceased, chose Thomas Heard as guardian, and in 1766 Abraham Yerrington, son of Ebenezer deceased, chose Samuel Tyler guardian.

Six (YERRINGTON) ch. bp. No. Preston CT (now Griswold): Abraham, Mary, Reuben, Sarah, Ebenezer and Lydia.

ii SARAH, b. 23 March 1722; living 1751 when she signed a receipt with sister Bethia.

iii THOMAS, b. 10 Oct. 1724 (twin); m. Plainfield 27 Oct. 1752 KEZIAH RICHARDSON, b. Plainfield 10 June 1731; daughter of Richard and Hannah (Park) Richardson. A year after their marriage, Thomas and Keziah sold "land wch fell to us by our hond. father Richard Richardson of Plainfield decd."

Two (HERD) ch. b. Plainfield: Anne and Zadock.

iv JOHN, b. 10 Oct. 1724 (twin); m. Plainfield 12 May 1757 JEMIMA HUNTER of Norwich CT. He received his father's buildings, land and tools in 1751; he sold the land in 1756; and in 1765 John Heard and his family were warned out of Plainfield.

One (HURD) ch. b. Plainfield: John.

V JOSIAH, b. 23 Sept. 1726; m. bef. 1759 PHEBE -----. In 1757 Josiah inherited land and moveables from his uncle Josiah Bump. Two years later he traded all his land in Plainfield for £100 and 150 acres with dwelling house and barn in Voluntown CT.

Seven (HEARD) ch. b. Voluntown CT: William, Phebe, Hannah, Rhoda, Joseph, Rachel and Martha.

vi JACOB, b. 7 Feb. 1729; m. Plainfield 8 Aug. 1750 AMY WELCH, b. Voluntown CT 25 July 1735; daughter of Samuel and Amy (Williams) Welch, and a descendant of Pilgrim John Billington.

Five (HERD) ch. first b. Plainfield, rest b. Voluntown: Lydia, Sarah, Josiah, Robert and Jacob.

vii MARY, b. 20 Jan. 1731; m. Preston CT 27 March 1755 OBED BENJAMIN; bp. No. Preston (now Griswold) 9 May 1729; son of Obed Benjamin. Obed and wife Mary owned the covenant of the First Ch. in No. Preston 23 April 1758. On 24 March 1759 Obed of Preston bought from two of his siblings their rights to their deceased father's estate. This is almost certainly the Obed Benjamin living in Horton, Nova Scotia in 1770 with one woman, five boys and one girl.

Two (BENJAMIN) ch. b. Preston: Stephen and Caleb.

viii AMY, b. 3 Oct. 1735; living 1751 when she signed a receipt with sister Bethia; n.f.r.

References: CSL Barbour Index:Plainfield, Preston, Voluntown. CSL Ch Recs:Plainfield 1:215; 1:295; Griswold 1:77, 79, 82, 86. Plainfield CT copy book p. 66. PRESTON CONG CH p. 140. CT MARR 4:39. Preston CT LR 7:225, 265(Obed Benjamin grantee). Plainfield CT PR 1:89(Amy Hurd); 2:153(Thomas Hurd); 4:131(Reuben Yerrington). CSL New London PR #493(Obed Benjamin); Norwich PR #11854(Abraham Yerrington); #11858-9(Ebenezer Yerrington). Plainfield CT LR 4:264-5(Thomas Heard); 4:374-5; 5:219(John Heard); 4:504-7; 5:481, 508-9(Josiah Heard). Preston CT PR #1120(Thomas Herd). Plainfield CT TR (in MSS at CT Hist. Soc., Hartford, "Notes by L. B. Barbour"). NOVA SCOTIA CENSUSES p. 39. Voluntown CT LR 2:179(Welch).

15 BETHIA BUMP or BUMPUS[4] (Sarah[3] Eaton, Samuel[2], Francis[1]), b. Quinebaug CT ca. 1700; d. bef. 1790.

She m. Plainfield CT 23 Aug. 1721 PELEG BALLARD, b. Andover 20 Sept. 1694; d. Frederickstown (now Kent) Putnam Co., NY prob. bef. 1762; son of William and Hannah (Hooper) Ballard.

Peleg sold lands and tenement in Plainfield in 1739. He probably moved to NY about this time. In 1790 there were living in Frederickstown NY: John, Peleg, Peleg Jr, William, Tracy and Caleb Ballard.

Children (BALLARD) b. Plainfield CT:

i WILLIAM[5], b. 29 Nov. 1722; d. bef. 1774; m. Frederickstown NY, MARY CREED, b. ca. 1724; d. 18 April 1811 ae. 87; daughter of William Creed of Jamaica L.I. whose will of 1774 called his daughter Mary Ballard a widow.

Two (BALLARD) ch: William and Rebecca.

ii HANNAH, b. 20 Aug. 1726; n.f.r.

iii PELEG, b. 6 Dec. 1728; n.f.r.

iv JOHN, b. 24 Feb. 1730/1; n.f.r.

References: CSL Barbour Index:Plainfield. Plainfield CT LR 3:261, 303(Peleg Ballard). TAG 43:151. BALLARD FAM pp. 13-7, 29, 43-4. BALLARD GEN pp. 71-2, 81-2. 1790 CENSUS NY:82-4.

16 ELIZABETH$^{4}$ EATON (Samuel$^{3-2}$, Francis$^{1}$), b. Middleboro 27 July 1701; d. there 5 May 1780.

She m. Middleboro 21 June 1727 WILLIAM CANEDY, b. Plymouth 8 March 1689; d. Taunton 23 or 24 June 1774; son of Alexander and Elizabeth (-----) Canedy.

William Canedy's will dated 26 Jan. 1773 names wife Elizabeth; sons William and Barnabas, executors; and daughters Hannah Pierce, Thankful Macomber, Fear Perkins and Mercy Williams.

Children (CANEDY):

i WILLIAM$^{5}$, bp. Middleboro 16 Oct. 1729; d. there 26 March 1804; m. Middleboro 6 Dec. 1753 CHARITY LEONARD, b. there 27 Feb. 1731/2; d. Middleboro 13 Oct. 1805; daughter of Elkanah and Elizabeth (-----) Leonard. Charity, wife of William Canedy, was among the children of Elkanah Leonard of Middleboro in an agreement of 1765. William's will dated 17 March 1804, proved 11 April 1804, names wife Charity; sons William and Noble, daughters Charity Stiner, Bathsheba Howland; and grandsons William and Alexander Canedy.

Four (CANEDY) ch. b. Middleboro: Charity, Bathsheba, William and Noble.

ii NATHAN, bp. Middleboro 15 Aug. 1731; d. bef. 1773

iii HANNAH, b. Middleboro 1737; d. there 10 June 1783; m. Taunton 3 Nov. 1757 ABIEL PIERCE, b. Middleboro 10 Sept. 1733; d. there 26 Dec. 1811 in 78th yr.; son of Ebenezer and Mary (Hoskins) Pierce. Abiel m. (2) 1783 Theodora (Godfrey) Robinson. He served as a Capt. of MA troops in the Revolutionary War. The will of Abiel "Peirce" of Middleboro, gentleman, dated 1 May 1795 probated 7 Jan. 1812, names wife "Theadona"; sons William, Nathan and Abiel; daughters Selah wife of Elisha Clarke, Charity wife of Silas Williams, Hannah wife of Godfrey Robinson, Betsey wife of Silvanus Thomas Jr., Thankful, Mercy Dardania, Abigail and Polly. On 23 Dec. 1812 Abial Pierce, executor of Abial Pierce, distributed furniture and wearing apparel to the daughters of the deceased, including Thankful Richmond, Mercy King and Dardana Godfrey.

Eleven (PIERCE) ch. to Abiel and Hannah: William, Nathan, Selah, Charity, Hannah, Abiel, Betsey, Thankful, Mercy, Dardana and Abigail.

iv THANKFUL, b. ca. 1738; d. Middleboro 13 Jan. 1794 in 56th yr; m. Taunton 16 March 1762 JOSEPH MACOMBER, b. there 28 March 1732; d. Middleboro 25 Jan. 1800 in 68th yr; son of John and Elizabeth (Williams) Macomber, and a descendant of Pilgrim Thomas Rogers.

Eleven (MACOMBER) ch. b. Middleboro or Taunton: Joseph, Thankful, Betsey, twins Nancy and Nathan, Frederick, Elijah, Judith, Olive, Luraney and Hannah.

v FEAR, d. bef. 1 Oct. 1801; m. Taunton 18 April 1765 DAVID PERKINS, b. 3 March 1739; d. after 2 Oct. 1801. He served as a private of MA troops in the Revolutionary War. On 2 Oct. 1801 David Perkins of Taunton, blacksmith, sold to his three sons, David, Barnabas and William, and to his daughter Hannah, land which had been conveyed by William Canedy deceased to Fear Perkins "my deceased wife." The same month David Perkins Jr. of Rochester, Barney Perkins of New Bedford and Thomas Cain of Taunton and wife Hannah, "children of Fear Perkins deceased," divided the land.

Four (PERKINS) ch: David, Barnabas, William and Hannah.

vi MERCY, d. bet. 13 March 1775 and 23 Jan. 1783; m. bef. 10 Feb. 1763 JOSEPH WILLIAMS, son of James Williams. On 10 Feb. 1763 William Canedy of Taunton gave land in Taunton to his daughter "Marcy" Williams. On 24 May 1765, Joseph Williams of Taunton sold to James Williams Jr. land of "my father James Williams," wife Mercy releasing dower on the property. Other deeds show that Joseph lived in Taunton from 1763 to 1783. On 29 May 1786 Joseph Williams Jr. [of Savoy] sold all rights, etc. to land in Taunton that William Canedy deceased gave to "my late mother Marcy Williams decd." The last deed involving Mercy was dated 13 March 1775, unless the release of "Mary" in a deed of 15 Feb. 1781 was a mistake for Marcy. Marcy was certainly dead by 23 Jan. 1783 when Joseph Williams sold land in Taunton which was conveyed by William Canedy deceased to "my late wife."

One (WILLIAMS) ch. pos. others: Joseph.

vii BARNABAS, d. Taunton 22 Jan. 1776; m. (1) Freetown 17 Nov. 1757 BETSEY HATHAWAY of Freetown, prob. the one b. 1737 to John and Miribah (Simmons) Hathaway; Betsey d. 6 Nov. 1758. Barnabas m.

(2) Freetown 9 Feb. 1763 ELIZABETH BARNABY, b. Freetown 9 Feb. 1737/8; drowned Berkley 8 Oct. 1785 ae. 48; daughter of Ambrose and Elizabeth (Gardiner) Barnaby, and a descendant of Richard Warren. Elizabeth m. (2) 1777 Elijah Burt of Berkley. John Hathaway's will in 1783 does not mention dau. Betsey or Canedy grandch. The will of Ambrose Barnaby of Freetown dated 18 Feb. 1774, proved 24 April 1775, names wife Elizabeth and dau. Elizabeth "Cannady if she be living." Barnabas Cannedy of Taunton, gentleman, in a will dated 31 March 1775, probated 30 July 1776, named wife Elizabeth, his brother, his sisters and a nephew. Apparently no children.

References: MD 1:209; 5:39; 12:130; 18:157; 24:40; 25:107; 107; 30:9; 32:3, 10. MIDDLEBORO DEATHS. VR TAUNTON. Freetown VR. Middleboro VR 4:148, 151, 162 and card index. Berkley Intentions, book 2 and Town Burial Lot (MSS. Old Colony Hist. Soc., Taunton). Bristol Co. PR 23:455(Ambrose Barnaby); 24:220(Barnabas Cannedy); 31:211 (John Hathaway); 23:268 and original papers(William Canedy). Plymouth Co. PR 40:43-4(William Canedy); 44:124-5, 437(Abiel Peirce). Bristol Co. LR 48:558; 59:92; 61:333; 62:541; 67:132(Joseph Williams); 55:61; 56:182, 185 (William Canedy); 71:451(Barnabas Canedy); 80:336; 117:23 (David Perkins). Plymouth Co. LR 64:24(Elkanah Leonard). Thatcher Papers (MSS at Middleboro Pub. Lib.). HATHAWAY GEN (1970) p. 55. PEIRCE FAM(1870) pp. 98, 108-9, 114. PEIRCE'S CONTRIB p. 9. DAR PATRIOT INDEX p. 527.

17 BARNABAS$^{4}$ EATON (Samuel$^{3-2}$, Francis$^{1}$), b. Middleboro 12 April 1703; d. there Nov. 1790 ae. 87y 7m.

He m. (1) MEHITABEL ALDEN, b. Bridgewater 18 Oct. 1707; d. Middleboro 11 April 1739 in her 32nd yr.; daughter of Joseph and Hannah (Dunham) Alden. [See *The John Alden Family*.] He m. (2) Middleboro 21 Feb. 1743 ELIZABETH CLEMENS, d. there 6 Dec. 1796 in her 80th yr.

In a series of deeds from 1773 to 1790, Barnabas Eaton of Middleboro gave land to sons Samuel, Seth, Nathan, Ziba (all of Middleboro), and Lot of Stoughton, and to "my six daughters Hannah, Mary, Elizabeth, Welthy, Keziah and Merebah," (no last names given for the daughters).

Children (EATON) b. Middleboro, five by Mehitable, eight by Elizabeth:

i HANNAH$^{5}$, b. 29 Oct. 1730; living Yarmouth, Nova Scotia, 13 Aug. 1791; m. bef. 1750 JOHN CLEMMONS (or Clements), b. 1715; living Yarmouth N.S. 13 Aug. 1791; pos. son of John and Mary (Hinderson)

Clemens. John and Hannah arrived in Yarmouth in 1769. On 13 Aug. 1791 Hannah Clemmons of Yarmouth, Co. of Shelburn (N.S.) wife of John Clemmons, sold to David Weston Jr. her one-sixth part of land "our father Barnabas Eaton gave to his six daughters."

Eight (CLEMENTS) ch., last b. Yarmouth: John, Mehitable, William, Silas, Elkanah, Hannah, Elizabeth and Wealthy.

ii SAMUEL, b. 16 May 1732; d. Middleboro 18 Jan. 1820 ae. 87y 7m 22d; m. Middleboro 8 Nov. 1753 PATIENCE TINKHAM, b. there 9 April 1732; d. there 19 Jan. 1812 ae. 79y 9m; daughter of Peter and Eunice (Thomas) Tinkham. A division of real estate of Peter "Tincom" was made 12 March 1756 to his widow "Eunis," daughter Patience Eaton, and others. Samuel Eaton's will dated 1 May 1815, probated 21 Feb. 1820, names sons Israel, Enos, Daniel and Darius; ch. of son Samuel; ch. of daughter Mehitable Wood; daughter Eunice Edy; and grandson Zenas Eaton.

Eight (EATON) ch. b. Middleboro: Israel, Enos, Daniel, Darius, Samuel, Mehitable, Eunice and Barnabas.

iii MARY, b. 14 May 1735; living 21 Oct. 1790 when she received land from her father; n.f.r.

iv SARAH, b. 16 June 1737; n.f.r.*

v SETH, b. 6 April 1739; d. Middleboro 20 Feb. 1823 in his 84th yr; m. int. (1) Dartmouth 3 March 1764 SARAH DELANO, prob. b. there 30 June 1734; n.f.r.; m. int. (2) Dartmouth 12 March 1768 BETHIA DELANO, b. there 17 March 1730; d. Middleboro 16 Dec. 1803 in 74th yr; daughter of Jethro and Elizabeth (Pope) Delano. No proof was found that he actually married Sarah, who was prob. Bethia's sister. In Seth's first marriage intention he was of Middleboro, in the second of Dartmouth. He continued to reside at Dartmouth until at least 10 Oct. 1774 when he bought land in Middleboro; presumably he moved to Middleboro shortly after this. He was a private in MA troops in the Revolutionary War. The death record in Middleboro of his son Seth is the only evidence of children.

One (EATON) ch. pos. others: Seth.

vi LOT, b. 9 Nov. 1744; m. Middleboro 22 May 1766 MARTHA COBB, b. 9 June 1748; daughter of John

*No proof was found of Molyneux's claim that Sarah married George Middleton and that her sister Mehitable married John Shoemaker. An unnamed child of Barnabas Eaton died 19 Dec. 1751, perhaps Sarah or Mehitable (Isaac Backus Record, Middleboro). They did not receive land from their father in 1790.

and Priscilla (-----) Cobb. Lot was living in Stoughton in 1781 when his father gave him land; n.f.r.

vii MEHITABEL, b. 30 April 1747; n.f.r.*

viii ELIZABETH, b. 22 Feb. 1748/9; d. 13 Jan. 1808; m. Middleboro 10 Jan. 1771 PEREZ LEONARD, b. 1747; d. Middleboro 6 Jan. 1801 ae. 52. Widow Elizabeth was appointed administratrix of his estate 23 Jan. 1801. No evidence was found that they had ch.

ix ZIBA, b. 14 Sept. 1750; m. Middleboro 31 Aug. 1773 RUTH LEONARD, b. Middleboro 28 Aug. 1754; daughter of Joseph and Ruth (White) Leonard. Ziba served as a private during the Revolution. Ziba and Ruth were living in Middleboro in 1781 when they sold land. In deeds he is called joiner and housewright. Might he have been the Ziba Eaton in Bakerstown Plantation ME in 1790?

Four (EATON) ch. b. Middleboro: Solomon, Betty, Clemons and Ruth.

x NATHAN, b. 11 Aug. 1753; m. Bridgewater 18 Aug. 1774 MARGARET CHERRY. They were living in Middleboro in 1796 when daughter Elizabeth was born.

Nine (EATON) ch. b. Middleboro: Hannah, Martha, Barnabas, Ziba, Sarah, Mehitable, Nancy, Luther and Elizabeth.

xi WEALTHY, b. 19 June 1755; d. Minot ME 23 July 1831; m. Middleboro 24 Jan. 1776 ELIJAH HACKET, b. Middleboro 26 April 1753; d. Minot 25 May 1823; son of Elijah and Prudence (-----) Hacket. He served in the Revolutionary War. "Elisha" Hacket of Middleboro, cordwainer, and wife "Welthy" sold to David Weston Jr. on 21 Oct. 1790 (the same day they received it), one-sixth part of land which "our father Barnabas Eaton" gave to his six daughters. This deed was signed and acknowledged by Elijah Hacket. Elijah and Wealthy shortly afterward moved to Poland ME where a son was born 16 Oct. 1791.

Seven (HACKET) ch. first four b. Middleboro, all recorded Poland ME: Salmon, Elijah, James, Wealthy, Barnabas, Nathan and Elizabeth.

xii KEZIAH, b. 8 Oct. 1757; d. Middleboro 16 June 1816 in 59th yr.; m. Middleboro 6 Jan. 1779 DAVID WESTON JR., b. Plympton 1 Feb. 1754; d. Middleboro 4 Feb. 1836 in 83rd yr.; son of David and

---

*No proof was found of Molyneux's claim that Sarah married George Middleton and that her sister Mehitable married John Shoemaker. An unnamed child of Barnabas Eaton died 19 Dec. 1751, perhaps Sarah or Mehitable (Isaac Backus Record, Middleboro). They did not receive land from their father in 1790.

Susanna (Churchill) Weston. The will of David Weston of Middleboro dated 8 April 1835, proved 5 April 1836, names eldest daughter Susanna Lincoln, 2nd daughter Polly Weston singlewoman, youngest daughter Keziah Lincoln widow woman, youngest son Enoch Weston; "their eldest brother, my son Andrew Weston" to receive land of their mother Kezia which she received from her father Barnabas Eaton.

Five (WESTON) ch. b. Middleboro: Susannah, Polly, Keziah, Andrew and Enoch.

xiii MERIBAH, b. 10 Feb. 1760; d. Middleboro 1 March 1838 ae. 78; m. (1) Middleboro 12 March 1782 ANDREW MURDOCK, b. Plympton 31 Oct. 1758; d. bef. 3 Dec. 1789; son of James and Hannah (Tillson) Murdock. She m. (2) Middleboro 3 Dec. 1789 GIDEON PERKINS, b. Plympton 25 Feb. 1750/1; d. Middleboro 8 Oct. 1828 ae. 78; son of Joshua and Hannah (Samson) Perkins. Gideon had m. (1) Plympton 1771 Desire Dunham. In 1791 Gideon Perkins and "Marabah" Perkins of Carver sold to David Weston Jr., one-sixth part of land in Middleboro from her father Barnabas Eaton. Gideon Perkins "of Middleboro" sold his farm in Carver in 1806.

Two (MURDOCK) ch. b. Carver: Edmund and Andrew.

Five (PERKINS) ch. b. Carver: Betty, Seabury, Sylvia, John Clammans and Josiah.

References: MD 12:131; 14:244-5; 15:24, 220; 16:134-5; 18:125-6, 156; 19:46; 25:87-8; 31:135-6. VR BRIDGEWATER, CARVER, DARTMOUTH, PLYMPTON. Middleboro VR 4:10; 17:173; and card index. MIDDLEBORO DEATHS. MA MARR 2:79, 80, 84, 86, 95, 98. NEHGR 88:65. Plymouth Co. PR 16:141(Peter Tincom); 34:260(Perez Leonard); 78:125(David Weston). Plymouth Co. LR 58:208(Alden to Eaton); 62:64 (Barnabas Eaton); 62:141; 64:10(Ziba Eaton); 72:191(Hannah Clemmons, Elisha Hacket, Gideon Perkins); 108:116(Gideon Perkins); 64:229; 70:175, 191; 83:18(Barnabas Eaton). YARMOUTH N.S. HIST p. 112. YARMOUTH N.S. GEN 15 Feb. 1898 #49. COBB FAM p. 125. MURDOCK GEN. Tinkham MSS (at NEHG Soc. Boston) p. 44. WESTON GEN p. 22. Minot ME Town Clerk.

18 LYDIA BASSETT[4] (Bethia[3] Eaton, Samuel[2], Francis[1]), b. Bridgewater 29 April 1703; living at Norton 17 May 1764.

She m. 17 Nov. 1726 SAMUEL PHILLIPS, pos. b. Taunton 10 Feb. 1697 to James Phillips; living Norton 23 April 1771.

In 1738 Samuel and Lydia sold land "by the meadow that was our father Joseph Bassett's." They were living in Norton when they acknowledged a deed in 1747. In 1763 William Coddington and wife Bethia, and Samuel Phillips and wife Lydia, all of Norton, sold their rights to a swamp in Bridgewater; the Phillips acknowledged this deed 17 May 1764. Samuel Phillips of Norton sold his dwelling house and barn in Norton to son Daniel Phillips of Norton on 23 April 1771; the land was bounded by "land of my son Joseph Phillips."

Children (PHILLIPS) b. prob. Norton:

i JOSEPH[5], b. bef. 1734; m. Norton 12 Sept. 1754 the widow MERCY (-----) TITUS; n.f.r.

ii DANIEL, b. bef. 1736; d. Norton bet. 4 Dec. 1799 and 5 Jan. 1802; m. (1) Norton 16 Sept. 1756 ELIZABETH FISHER, b. Norton 21 Dec. 1728; daughter of Eleazer and Elizabeth (-----) Fisher; m. (2) Taunton 25 Nov. 1782 RACHEL LINCOLN. Daniel Phillips of Norton was named among heirs of Eleazer Fisher, late of Norton deceased, father of Daniel's deceased wife Elizabeth, in 1791. In 1788 Daniel Phillips of Norton gave to his son Daniel, land in Norton bounded by land lately belonging to "my brother Joseph Phillips."

In his will dated 4 Dec. 1799, probated 5 Jan. 1802, Daniel Phillips of Norton, yeoman, bequeathed to his wife Rachel; eldest son Daniel Phillips; children (heirs at law) of his second son Samuel; daughters Betty, wife of Isaac Taylor, Lurena Phillips, Sarah Phillips, Julia Phillips, and Ruth Phillips; and two youngest sons, Minor Phillips and Arba Phillips.

Ten (PHILLIPS) ch. b. Norton, seven to first wife, last three to second wife: Elizabeth, Lurana, Daniel, Samuel, Nathan, "Salle," Ruth, Miner, Julia and Arba.

and possibly:

iii LYDIA, d. Norton 16 May 1826 ae. 91; m. Norton 25 July 1765 GEORGE WETHERELL, b. Norton 1 Jan. 1735; son of William and Mary (-----) Wetherell. They had seven children in Norton.

References: VR NORTON, TAUNTON. Bristol Co. PR 7:485 (James Phillips); 23:522(Eleazer Fisher); 38:456(Daniel Phillips). Bristol Co. LR 54:100(Samuel Phillips); 66:476; 69:438(Daniel Phillips). Plymouth Co. LR 37:154; 38:250(Samuel Phillips); 52:122(Coddington and Phillips).

19 THOMAS RAMSDELL[4] (Daniel Ramsdell[3], Rachel[2] Eaton, Francis[1]), b. Plymouth c1680; d. Hanover 16 Sept. 1727.

He m. Scituate 23 March 1702/3 SARAH ALVERSON (or Alberson), b. ca. 1682; d. Hanover 4 Aug. 1773 ae. 91 yrs; prob. daughter of Nicholas Alverson.

Thomas was living in Duxbury in 1702, later in Pembroke and Scituate, and moved to Hanover before 1725.

Children (RAMSDELL)*:

i MARY[5], b. Pembroke 9 May 1706; d. Hanson 14 March 1798 ae. 93 yrs.; m. Scituate 16 Feb. 1726/7 WILLIAM COX (or Cokes or Cocks), b. ca. 1700; d. Hanson 10 Aug. 1784 in 84th yr. William Cocks of Pembroke left a will dated 6 April 1771, probated 26 Aug. 1784, naming wife Sarah, sons William and Seth, daughters Mary, Sarah, Rachel and Ruth, and children of daughter Lydia deceased.

Eight (COX) ch. b. Scituate, Pembroke and Hanover: Mary, Sarah, Rachel, Ruth, Lydia, William, Seth and Isaac.

ii JOSEPH, b. Pembroke 29 May 1708; d. Hanover 24 Aug. 1788 in 81st yr.; m. (1) Hanover 23 April 1730 MARY HOMER (or Hosmer), b. Boston ca. 1708; d. Hanover 2 June 1754 ae. 46 yrs. Joseph m. (2) Hanover 25 Nov. 1755 MERCY (DELANO) PRIOR b. ca. 1715; d. Hanover 1 Jan. 1800 in 82nd yr.; daughter of Nathaniel and Mercy (Bonney) Delano, widow of John Prior, and a descendant of Pilgrim Henry Samson. [See *The Henry Samson Family* for her daughters Marcy and Lydia Prior.] Joseph's will dated 18 Aug. 1788 and probated 27 Sept. 1788, names wife Mercy; son Joseph; daughters Mary Whitten, Priscilla Prouty wife of Isaac, Avis Dwelle, Sarah Pool wife of Oliver, Mercy Estes wife of Richard, and Lydia Ramsdell; and granddaughter Hannah Ramsdell, daughter of son Thomas.

Eleven (RAMSDELL) ch. b. Hanover, last two by second wife: Mary, Avis, Priscilla, Thomas, Joseph, Avis, Joseph, Japhet, Sarah, Marcy and Lydia.

iii JEMIMA, b. Pembroke 28 July 1710; living 19 Nov. 1781 when her dower was set off; m. Hanover 20 Feb. 1728/9 RICHARD HILL, d. Pembroke bef. 5 March 1779. They lived in Hanover and Pembroke. On 5 March 1779 Thomas Hill of Pembroke was appointed administrator on the estate of Richard Hill late of Pembroke deceased. On the back of his bond is written "Thomas Hill's bond admr. on his father's estate." This is the only evidence for son Thomas. The only evidence of daughter

---

*No evidence was found to support the claim that Thomas had a daughter Elizabeth.

Jemima is a deed of 1787 in which Jemima Hill of Pembroke sold "all my right in...land...my father Richard Hill died siezed of."

Seven (HILL) ch., first five b. or bp. Hanover, last bp. Pembroke: Richard, Leonard, Lettice, Samuel, Joseph, Thomas and Jemima "daughter widow Hill."

iv GIDEON, b. Scituate 13 Sept. 1712; d. Abington 28 Feb. 1795; m. (1) Hanover or Bridgewater, 24 June 1736 SARAH FARRINGTON; he m. (2) Marshfield 3 Sept. 1755 ABIGAIL EAMES, daughter of Nathaniel and Abigail (Oldham) Eames, and a descendant of Pilgrim Samson. [See *The Henry Samson Family*.] Gideon m. (3) Abington 11 Sept. 1766 RUTH PALMER, d. there Feb. 1812 ae. 83 yrs. Gideon was a "settwork cooper." The last record of his wife Abigail was Gideon's accusation that in 1763 she was carried off by Nathaniel Eames (her father) and "detained from him ever since." After the death of his third wife, Ruth, the balance of Gideon's estate was divided among sons John, Gideon, Micah, Noah, David and Thomas Ramsdell; the heirs of Job Ramsdell; and daughters Content Cudworth, Deborah Gurney and Abigail Thomson. The will of Nathaniel Eames in 1767 names grandchildren Thomas and Abigail Ramsdell.

Eleven (RAMSDELL) ch. seven to first wife in Abington or Hanover, two to second wife, two in Abington to third wife: Sarah, John, Content, Gideon, David, Job, Micah, Thomas, Abigail, Deborah and Noah.

v SARAH, b. Scituate 12 July 1715; bp. 14 Aug. 1715; n.f.r.

vi MERCY, b. Scituate 5 Nov. 1717; d. Abington 28 Nov. 1797 ae. 81 yrs.; m. Hanover 9 March 1737/8 PELEG STETSON, b. Pembroke 30 April 1715; d. Abington 16 May 1806 ae. 93 yrs.; son of Isaac and Elizabeth (Pray) Stetson. In 1806 there was an order to divide the estate of Peleg Stetson among: the heirs of Isaac Stetson dec., the heirs of Mercy Townsend dec., the heirs of Peleg Stetson dec., Ephraim Stetson, Laban Stetson, Betty Studly, Hannah Stetson, Levi Stetson and Oliver Stetson.

Eleven (STETSON) ch. first seven bp. Hanover, last two b. Abington: Isaac, Ephraim, Ephraim, Mercy, Levi, Betty, Peleg, Laban, Betty, Hannah and Oliver.

vii LYDIA, b. Scituate 5 Sept. 1719; n.f.r.

viii DAVID, b. Abington 24 Oct. 1721; d. Hanover bef. 2 Sept. 1754, when brother Joseph was appointed his administrator.

ix GRACE, b. Hanover 5 June 1725; d. bef. 1761; m. Hanover 19 Jan. 1743/4 ADAM PROUTY, b. Scituate 14 Dec. 1721; d. Spencer bef. 23 April 1793; son of Isaac and Elizabeth (Merrit) Prouty. Adam m. (2) in 1761 DOROTHY HOWE. Adam was a housewright in Hanover when he sold his house and barn in 1757, and wife Grace released her dower. He was in Spencer when he remarried. Adam's widow Dorothy was appointed administratrix of his estate on 23 April 1793. An account after Dorothy's death mentions the eleven children of said deceased.

Five (PROUTY) ch. to Adam and Grace, bp. Hanover: Grace, Sarah, Desire, Adam and Isaac.

References: MD 16:100. VR ABINGTON, BRIDGEWATER, DUXBURY, EAST BRIDGEWATER, HANSON, PEMBROKE, SCITUATE, SPENCER. HANOVER VR pp. 6, 9, 111, 116, 128, 192, 194, 205, 251. MARSHFIELD VR p. 147. HANOVER FIRST CH pp. 72, 89, 90, 112, 113, 115, 118, 122, 123, 124-134, 181. NEHGR 58:171-2; 126:258-63; 127:105. HANOVER BY DWELLY pp. 323-35. DAR PATRIOT INDEX p. 555. Plymouth Co. PR #4630, 24:77(William Cox); 36:354-5(Mary Cox); 21:264(Nathaniel Eames); #10095, 27:7, 28:234(Richard Hill); 13:340(David Ramsdell); 34:26, 35:485, 36:289, 44:510, #16339(Gideon Ramsdell); 30:430(Joseph Ramsdell); 40:550(Peleg Stetson). Worcester Co. PR #48073(Adam Prouty). Plymouth Co. LR 77:123(Jemima Hill); 43:204, 44:177, 55:41(Adam Proute); 78:197(Gideon Ramsdell); 18:99(Thomas Ramsdell). Plymouth Co. Ct. Recs., C.C. Pleas 12:516(Nathaniel Eames). STETSON DESC 2:104-5. PROUTY GEN pp. 26-7, 45-7.

20 SAMUEL RAMSDELL[4] (Daniel Ramsdell[3], Rachel[2] Eaton, Francis[1]), b. Plymouth 5 June 1690; d. Pembroke bet. 21 Aug. and 3 Dec. 1759.

He m. (1) Scituate 24 Dec. 1712 MARTHA BOWKER, b. there 8 July 1684; d. bef. Aug. 1750; daughter of James Bowker. He m. (2) Pembroke 20 Aug. 1750 ANNAH NORRIS, d. after 21 Aug. 1759.

The will of Samuel Ramsden of Pembroke dated 21 Aug. 1759, probated 3 Dec. 1759, names wife Anna, son Samuel Ramsden, granddaughter Mercy Hersey, grandson Samuel Ramsden, granddaughter Betty Crooker, and "my two daughters" Mary Crooker and Susanna Hersey. Daniel Crooker was executor.

Children (RAMSDELL or RAMSDEN), all by first wife:

i SAMUEL[5], b. Pembroke 4 June 1714, bp. Scituate 2 Sept. 1716; d. Pembroke 28 March 1801 ae. 86 yrs.; m. Pembroke 26 Jan. 1743/4 DOROTHY BISHOP, b. Pembroke 28 Jan. 1715/6; d. there 31 March 1801 ae. 85 yrs.; daughter of John and Elizabeth

(-----) Bishop. The will of John Bishop dated 19 Feb. 1756 names daughter "Dorotha Ramsden."

Eight (RAMSDELL) ch. b. Pembroke: Content, Samuel, Elizabeth, Gershom, Martha, Content, Abigail and John.

ii MARY, bp. Scituate 2 Sept. 1716; d. Pembroke 19 Jan. 1776; m. Pembroke 28 April 1736 DANIEL CROOKER, b. there 20 April 1717; d. there 6 Nov. 1773. The will of Daniel Crooker of Pembroke, cordwainer, dated 8 Oct., probated 6 Dec. 1773, names wife Mary, son Daniel, daughter Betty Bates, sons Tilden, Elijah and Nathan, and daughters Bethia and Deborah.

Eleven (CROOKER) ch. first five b. Hanover, next five bp. Pembroke: Lemuel, Betty, Daniel, Ensign, Lazarus, Nathan, Mary, Tilden, Bethia, Deborah and Elijah.

iii CONTENT, bp. Scituate 3 April 1720; d. bef. 21 Aug. 1759 (not in father's will).

iv SUSANNA, d. Yarmouth N.S. 1 July 1791; m. Pembroke 20 May 1743 DAVID HERSEY JR., b. there 24 Jan. 1721; son of David and Elizabeth (Joyce) Hersey. David sold his house in Pembroke and with his family moved to Nova Scotia in 1763.

Seven (HERSEY) ch., first bp. Pembroke, second in grandfather's will, others from Yarmouth N.S. Herald: Elizabeth, Mercy, Daniel, Samuel, Martha, Levi and Deborah.

References: MD 9:87. VR PEMBROKE, SCITUATE. MARSHFIELD VR p. 143. HANOVER VR pp. 8-9, 116, 117, 205. Plymouth Co. PR 14:38(John Bishop); 15:450(Samuel Ramsden); 21:430(Daniel Crooker). Plymouth Co. LR 56:85(David Hearsey). YARMOUTH N.S. HERALD GEN, 6 May 1902 (p. 235 of scrapbook in NEHG Society, Boston). YARMOUTH N.S. HIST. p. 113.

21 JOSEPH RAMSDELL$^4$ (Daniel Ramsdell$^3$, Rachel$^2$ Eaton, Francis$^1$), b. Plymouth 15 Aug. 1693; d. bef. Nov. 1770.

He m. Scituate 10 Dec. 1718 MARY BOWKER, b. Scituate 20 Feb. 1688; living in Hanover Jan. 1771; daughter of James Bowker.

Children (RAMSDELL) b. Pembroke:

i JOSEPH$^5$, b. 22 Sept. 1719; d. Hanover 27 Oct. 1778; m. (1) Pembroke 30 Dec. 1741 MARY DAWS of Bridgewater, b. 3 April 1726; d. Hanover 20 July 1766; daughter of Samuel and Sarah (Howland) "Dooars." Joseph m. (2) Hanover 1 Jan. 1767 MERCY BATES, b ca. 1727; d. Hanover 19 June 1805 ae. 78; pos.

daughter of Edward and Margaret (White) Morse and widow of Amos Bates Jr.

Ten (RAMSDELL) ch. by first wife, first eight b. Pembroke, last two Hanover: John, Hannah, Lydia, Lot, Lois, Simeon, Olive, Ruth, Mary and Joseph Dose.

ii BENJAMIN, b. 1 Oct. 1721; d. Hanover 5 Oct. 1804 ae. 80; m. Pembroke 8 Dec. 1743 LUSANNA BISHOP, bp. Scituate 17 Nov. 1717; d. Hanover Jan. 1807; daughter of Hudson and Abigail (-----) Bishop. The will of Hudson Bishop of Pembroke dated 1 June, probated 7 Aug. 1758, names daughter Lusanna "Rambsden."

Six (RAMSDELL) ch. b. Pembroke: Benjamin, Lusanna, Deborah, Content, Edmond and Charles.

iii DANIEL, b. 28 Sept. 1723; m. Pembroke 18 May 1749 MARY DILLINGHAM "of Pembroke"; n.f.r.

iv SIMEON, b. 24 Dec. 1726; d. Pembroke 13 Oct. 1799 in 73rd yr.; m. (1) Pembroke 9 June 1757 MARY TURNER, bp. Scituate 12 Nov. 1732; d. East Bridgewater 22 March 1781; daughter of Joshua and Elizabeth (-----) Turner. He m. (2) Pembroke 18 July 1790 SARAH TURNER, b. there 27 Jan. 1733/4; d. there 29 April 1796; daughter of Joshua and Sarah (Winslow) Turner. On 20 Oct. 1779 the constable was requested to warn the following people to depart from Hanover: Simeon Ramsdell, Mary Ramsdell, John Stockbridge Ramsdell, Mercy Munro Ramsdell and Anne Stockbridge Ramsdell.

Four (RAMSDELL) ch. by first wife, first three bp. Pembroke: John Stockbridge, Mercy Munro, Abner Turner and Anne Stockbridge.

v NATHANIEL, b. 30 March 1730; d. Bridgewater bef. 6 Dec. 1762; m. East Bridgewater 10 Jan. 1753 MARY PRATT; daughter of Joshua and Experience (Nash) Pratt; pos. the Mary Ramsdell who d. Bridgewater 18 April 1821 ae. 90. The will of Joshua Pratt of Bridgewater dated 11 July, proved 2 Nov. 1772, names wife Experience, daughter Mary Ramsdell and her daughter Margaret Ramsdell. Nathaniel's estate was inventoried 13 Dec. 1762.

Five (RAMSDELL) ch. first four b. Bridgewater: Daniel, Mathew, James, Joseph and Margaret.

and very probably:

vi NEHEMIAH, b. Hanover 13 Nov. 1734; d. Harvard 30 Sept. 1800; m. Pembroke 29 Dec. 1757 REBECCA CHAMBERLAIN, b. there 28 Feb. 1736; d. Harvard 15 Sept. 1818 ae. 82 yrs.; daughter of Freedom

and Mary (Soule) Chamberlain. [See *The George Soule Family*.] Nehemiah was called a housewright when he bought land in Pembroke in 1770.
Nine (RAMSDELL) ch. first eight bp. Pembroke, last bp. Harvard: Freedom, Nehemiah, Nathaniel, Seth, Bartlett, Rebecca, Ezekiel, Betty and Nabby.

References: MD 10:75. VR BRIDGEWATER, EAST BRIDGEWATER, HARVARD, PEMBROKE, SCITUATE. HANOVER VR pp. 6, 7, 124, 128, 134, 197, 199, 207, 253. NEHGR 126:258-63; 127:105. Plymouth Co. PR 25:170, 276, 334(Joseph Ramsdell); 16:438, 17:91, 19:276(Nathaniel Ramsdell); 15:76 (Hudson Bishop); 21:202(Joshua Pratt). Plymouth Co. LR 57:34(Chamberlain to Ramsdell). Plymouth Co. Ct. Recs., Recs. C. Sessions 3:523(Simeon Ramsdell). BRIDGEWATER BY MITCHELL p. 291. HANOVER BY DWELLEY p. 323.

22 HANNAH$^{4}$ EATON (Benjamin$^{3-2}$, Francis$^{1}$), b. Plymouth 10 Feb. 1692; d. Plympton 4 March 1723/4.

She m. Plympton 31 July 1712 BENJAMIN BRYANT, b. Plymouth 16 Dec. 1688; d. "on Plymouth shore" 4 May 1724; son of John and Abigail (Bryant) Bryant.

The children of Benjamin Bryant signed receipts for their portions of his estate on the following dates: David Sears and wife Phebe in 1733; David Curtis and wife Hannah in 1735; Nehemiah Leach and wife Marcy in 1736; Micha Bryant in 1742; Jesse Bryant in 1744; and Solomon Leach in 1746 for his wife Jerusha deceased.

Children (BRYANT) b. Plympton:

i PHEBE$^{5}$, b. 18 Sept. 1713; d. Middleboro 9 Oct. 1779 in 67th yr.; m. Plympton 29 Nov. 1733 DAVID SEARS, b. Yarmouth 2 Oct. 1710; d. Middleboro 20 Aug. 1788 ae. 78; son of Josiah and Marcy (Howes) Sears. David m. (2) Hannah (Tinkham) (Vaughn) Werton. David was a millwright.
Four (SEARS) ch. b. Middleboro to David and Phebe: Zebedee, Huldah, Abner and David.

ii MERCY, b. 3 Jan. 1714/5; d. Bridgewater 27 Jan. 1775 in 60th yr.; m. Plympton 11 Nov. 1735 NEHEMIAH LEACH, b. Bridgewater 18 Dec. 1709; d. there 17 May 1769 in 60th yr.; son of John and Alice (-----) Leach. Nehemiah m. (1) Mary Staples by whom he had two ch.
Nine (LEACH) ch. to Nehemiah and Mercy, first five b. Bridgewater: James, Ruth, Robert, Huldah, Mehitable, Lydia, Nehemiah, Caleb and Susanna.

iii HANNAH, b. 24 March 1716/7; living 8 Nov. 1774; m. bef. 2 Aug. 1735 DAVID CURTIS; d. Bridgewater 27 Feb. 1756 in 48th yr. They were living in Halifax in 1735 and still there in 1747 when they sold land that was formerly Benjamin Eaton's. In 1756 widow Hannah Curtis of Bridgewater was appointed administratrix of David Curtis' estate. In 1774 Silvanus Curtis sold land in Middleboro; Hannah Curtis, widow of David, and David Curtis, Jonathan Curtis, Luke Curtis, and Hannah Curtis, on behalf of her son Ezekiel Curtis, quitclaimed their rights to the land. Hannah acknowledged her signature on 8 Nov. 1774.

Eight (CURTIS) ch. b. or bp. Halifax: Japhet, Jesse, Ezekiel, David, Jonathan, Hannah, Silvanus and Luke.

iv MICAH, b. 2 April 1719; d. Middleboro 28 Jan. 1776 in 57th yr.; m. int. Kingston 19 April 1740 ELIZABETH NORCUT ("Worcut" in VR), b. Marshfield 19 Feb. 1715; d. Middleboro 23 Jan. 1776 in 60th yr.; daughter of Ephraim and Elizabeth (Bonney) Norcut, and a descendant of Henry Samson. [See *The Henry Samson Family*.] In 1786 Micah Bryant of Middleboro rendered his account on the estate of his father Micah Bryant. In 1787 Benjamin and Amasa Bryant, Hannah Bryant 3rd, Cornelius Ellis and wife Jerusha sold to Micah Bryant land set off to Ephraim Bryant deceased from the estate of "our father Micah Bryant deceased."

Seven (BRYANT) ch. first two b. Middleboro: Benjamin, Micah, Abner, Amasa, Hannah, Jerusha and Ephraim.

v JERUSHA, b. 7 Feb. 1721/2; d. Bridgewater 25 April 1743; m. there 19 April 1739 SOLOMON LEACH, b. Bridgewater 19 Feb. 1712; son of John and Alice (-----) Leach. Solomon m. (1) 1736 Tabitha Washburn; m. (3) 1743 Hannah Leach. On 18 April 1746 Solomon Leach of Bridgewater, husbandman, received the share of "wife Jerusha Leach, otherwise Bryant, deceased" of the estate of her father Benjamin Bryant.

Three (LEACH) ch. b. Bridgewater to Solomon and Jerusha: Abisha, and two daughters who d.y.

vi JESSE, b. ca. 1723; d. Middleboro 3 Dec. 1758; m. there 10 April 1744 SUSANNA (CONANT) WINSLOW, b. Middleboro 7 Aug. 1711; d. there 17 April 1801 in 92nd yr.; daughter of Josiah and Elizabeth (Washburn) Conant and widow of James Winslow. In 1759 Micah Bryant of Middleboro, housewright, was appointed administrator on the estate of Jesse Bryant late of Middleboro, housewright deceased.

Five (BRYANT) ch. bp. Middleboro: Jesse, Betty, Solomon, James and Susanna.

References: MD 1:210; 2:141, 236; 3:93; 4:68; 9:253; 13:6, 248; 14:131; 15:2, 220; 16:14; 27:118-9. VR BRIDGEWATER, KINGSTON, PLYMPTON. MARSHFIELD VR p. 40. MIDDLEBORO DEATHS. BRIDGEWATER BY MITCHELL. Card index, Middleboro town hall for d. David Curtis, d. Abner[6] Bryant, and bp. of children of Jesse[5] Bryant. Middleboro VR 1:243. Plymouth Co. PR #12459(Mercy Leach); 5:179-180; 6:80; 8:31; 12:417-9(Benjamin Bryant); 14:66; 15:585(David Curtis); 15:184, 516(Jesse Bryant); 23:87; 30:77(Micah Bryant). Plymouth Co. LR 38:267(David Curtis); 58:142(Sylvanus Curtis et al); 38:266(Jesse Bryant); 77:166 (Benjamin Bryant et al). CONANT FAM p. 172. LEACH GEN 1:29-30. SEARS DESC pp. 108, 191.

23 BENJAMIN[4] EATON (Benjamin[3-2], Francis[1]), b. pos. Plymouth ca. 1698; d. Kingston 3 March (or May) 1751 in 53rd yr.

He m. (1) Plympton 7 July 1726 MARCY STURTEVANT, b. Plympton 24 May 1706; d. Kingston 2 Aug. 1741 in 35th yr.; daughter of Nehemiah and Ruth (Sampson) Sturtevant. He m. (2) Kingston 27 Jan. 1742/3 MARY TILSON, b. Plympton 13 Dec. 1708; daughter of John and Lydia (Rickard) Tilson. He m. (3) Plymouth 28 Oct. 1746 MARY TINKHAM, b. there 14 Sept. 1724; daughter of Helkiah and Elizabeth (Heister) Tinkham. Widow Mary Eaton m. (2) Kingston in 1760, as his second wife, Andrew Barce of Halifax. [See *The Peter Brown Family*.]

Proof of the identity of Benjamin's first wife is found in the will of Nehemiah Sturtevant of Plympton, who bequeathed on 28 July 1744 "to my two Grandsons Noah Eaton & Seth Eaton, the sons of my daughter Mary Eaton deceased." [The original will is not on file; it is assumed that "Mary" in the record book is a miscopy of "Marcy".]

Benjamin's third wife "Mary, wife of Benjamin Eaton of Kingston" was to receive payment from her brother Isaac Tinkom in 1748 as her share of the estate of their father, Helkiah Tinkom.

A division of Benjamin's estate was recorded on 2 May 1757, allowing the widow Mary Eaton her dower; eldest son Noah Eaton received 2/6 parts plus 1/5 part of the share of Thadeus, deceased; Seth, James and Benjamin each received 1/6 part plus 1/5 part of Thadeus' share.

Children (EATON) five by Marcy, one by Mary (Tilson), and three by Mary (Tinkham):

i RUTH[5], b. Kingston 21 March 1726/7; d. there 14 or 21 May 1727; bur. Plympton

ii JABESH, b. Kingston 7 Aug. 1728; d. there 26 Sept. 1728

iii NOAH, b. Kingston 29 May 1734; d. Plympton 30 Nov. 1798 in 66th yr.; no m. rec.; in 1790 he was head of a household in Plympton with three boys under 16 and two females. [He may have been the Noah Eaton who enlisted in the MA line in 1778, and was placed on the Continental List of Pensions in 1782.] In 1795, at the request of the Selectmen of Plympton, he was placed under guardianship, so that the town would not have the expense of supporting him or his family. A DAR lineage names Noah's wife as Elizabeth Freeman, with one son Ebenezer.

Children (EATON): prob. Seth (d. 1769 "son of Noah and Hannah"); pos. Ebenezer, son of Noah and Elizabeth (Freeman).

iv MARY, b. Kingston 6 March 1734/5; d. there 5 May 1735

v SETH, b. Kingston 1 Jan. 1738/9. In March 1760 Seth Eaton of Kingston, cooper, acknowledged the sale of land in Plympton bounded by land of "Mary Eaton alias Bearse"; n.f.r.

vi JAMES, bp. Kingston 15 April 1744 "son of Benjamin & Mary." Jonathan Tilson of Plympton on 8 April 1754, was appointed guardian of James Eaton, minor son of Benjamin late of Kingston deceased. The last record found is his receipt for his father's estate on 2 May 1757.

vii HANNAH, bp. Halifax 22 Nov. 1747; d. bef. 2 May 1757

viii BENJAMIN, bp. Halifax 19 March 1748/9; d. bef. 1790; m. Plymouth 3 Jan. 1771 HANNAH HOLMES, d. Plympton 29 Oct. 1824 ae. 78; bur. in Kingston. In 1790 Hannah was head of a household, in Kingston, with three females. In May 1804 Hannah Eaton, widow of Benjamin late of Kingston deceased, sold land "descended to me from my deceased children who was heirs to my late husband Benjamin. My husband's right came to him from his grandfather Benjamin Eaton."

Children (EATON): prob. Benjamin who d. Kingston 2 March 1787 age 6 son of widow Eaton, and Polly who d. Kingston 19 Jan. 1791 ae 17.

ix THADDEUS, bp. Halifax 19 May 1751 "after his father's death"; d. bef. 1757

References: MD 5:99, 181; 7:85; 17:5; 27:180. VR KINGSTON, PLYMPTON. MA MARR 2:24. MIDDLEBORO DEATHS. 1790 CENSUS MA:171, 178. Plymouth Co. PR 9:393-4 (Nehemiah Sturtevant); 11:441(Ebenezer Tinkham); 12:260 (Benjamin Eaton); 11:100(Helkiah Tinkcom); 13:229(James Eaton); 26:504; 35:227(Noah Eaton). Plymouth Co. LR 58:155(Seth Eaton); 58:156(Benjamin Eaton); 99:202(Hannah Eaton). PLYMOUTH CH RECS. FAM OF PILGRIMS p. 57. Tinkham MSS. TILSON GEN pp. 39-40, 388. DAR LINEAGE 59:101.

24 FRANCIS[4] EATON (Benjamin[3-2], Francis[1]), b. Kingston ca. 1700; d. Middleboro bef. 11 July 1749.

He m. (1) Middleboro 14 Dec. 1727 THANKFUL ALDEN, b. there 30 May 1700; d. Middleboro 29 Oct. 1732 in 27th yr.; daughter of John and Hannah (White) Alden; m. (2) Middleboro 12 June 1733 LYDIA FULLER, bp. Middleboro 9 Nov. 1718; d. prob. Middleboro 24 Oct. 1780; daughter of John and Mercy (Nelson) Fuller. [See *The John Alden Family* and *The Samuel Fuller Family*.] The will of John Alden in 1730 names wife Hannah and daughter Thankful Eaton.

Lydia Eaton of Middleboro was appointed administrator of the estate of Francis Eaton on 11 July 1749; the final accounting was allowed on 10 Nov. 1755. On 3 Nov. 1755 Azariah Thresher was appointed guardian of the five younger children of Francis Eaton: John, Mary, Elijah, Benjamin and Susanna.

Children (EATON) first b. Kingston, rest b. Middleboro; two by first wife, seven by second:*

i JOSEPH[5], b. 26 Nov. 1728; living Middleboro in May 1766; m. Middleboro 22 Nov. 1750 HANNAH CROSSMAN, b. 6 Feb. 1730/1; living in May 1766; daughter of Barnabas and Hannah (-----) Crossman. Hannah, wife of Joseph Eaton, was among the heirs in a division of Barnabas Crossman's estate in 1754. Joseph and Hannah each acknowledged sale of rights in a swamp formerly of Barnabas Crossman deceased, on 6 May 1766.

Four (EATON) ch. b. Middleboro: Joel, Abigail, Francis and Mary.

ii JABEZ, b. 29 Jan. 1730/1; d. Pike, Wyoming Co. NY about 1815-8; m. Middleboro 4 Jan. 1759 ELIZABETH WILLIAMS of Taunton, b. there ca. 1740; d. Easton 26 Nov. 1783; daughter of John and Elizabeth (Caswell) Williams. The will of John Williams of Taunton, dated 31 Oct. 1765 and probated 1780, names wife Elizabeth and daughter Elizabeth, wife of Jabez Eaton. He was prob. the Jabez Eaton who was in Easton in 1790, for in 1777 Jabez Eaton of Middleboro bought land in Easton. Jabez was back in Middleboro in 1791 when he sold the last of his Easton land.

Eleven (EATON) ch. b. Titicut and Middleboro: Lucy, Elizabeth, Simeon, Jabez, Luraney, Oliver, Olive, Solomon, Cyrus, Timothy and Selah.

iii SYLVANUS, b. 8 May 1734; prob. d. New Salem bet. 1 Dec. 1791 and 2 Jan. 1792; m. (1) Middleboro 11 March 1756 DEBORAH CASWELL, bp. there 1 June 1735; d. after 1778 but bef. Sept. 1791; daughter of Daniel and Mary (-----) Caswell. He prob.

---

*No evidence was found for sons David and Francis claimed by Molyneux, nor for the marriage of daughter Thankful to Josiah Cogswell.

m. (2) Bridgewater 25 Sept. 1791 ANNA LEACH. She m. (2) New Salem 1793 John Chamberlain. On the 10th of A-- 1778 Silvanus Eaton of Middleboro sold his homestead with barn and dwelling in Middleboro and wife Deborah gave up her dower. If he was the Sylvanus Eaton who appeared later in New Salem, he moved there with his family sometime between 1778 and 6 Aug. 1780. The will of Salvenus Eaton of New Salem, dated 1 Dec. 1791 proved 2 Jan. 1792, names wife Anna, sons Nathan and Abner, daughters Hulda Twitchell deceased, Annis Forster, Thankfull Mourton deceased, Deborah Mourton, Tryphosa, and son Salvenus.

Nine (EATON) ch. prob. b. Middleboro, prob. to Sylvanus and Deborah: Sarah (d. there 1770), Sylvanus, Nathan, Annis, Hulda, Tryphosa, Abner, Deborah and Thankful.

iv THANKFUL, b. 21 Dec. 1735; prob. d. 29 Sept. 1754

v JOHN, b. 12 Aug. 1737; living in Greenwich in 1788; m. (1) Middleboro 23 or 29 Sept. 1764 PATIENCE SHELLEY of Raynham, b. 23 Jan. 1745; d. 10 April 1777. He m. (2) Bridgewater 15 May 1780 SARAH (PRYOR) FOBES, bp. East Bridgewater 21 Jan. 1738/9; d. Bridgewater 29 Sept. 1839 in 103rd yr.; daughter of Joseph Pryor and widow of Josiah Fobes Jr. She m. (3) 1798 Lt. Joseph Bassett. John Eaton served as a private in MA troops during the Revolutionary War. In 1760 John Eaton of Middleboro sold his share of the farm of his father Francis Eaton deceased. On 11 Jan. 1787, still living in Middleboro, John sold land which he had purchased of Sylvanus Eaton; his wife Sarah gave up her dower. John was living in Greenwich, Hampshire Co. on 1 March 1788 when he sold part of the home place in Middleboro where he had formerly lived.

Eight (EATON) ch. seven by first wife: Lois, Hannah, John, Jairus, Eliphaz, Lydia, Patience and Anna.

vi MARY, b. 16 Feb. 1738/9. On 26 April 1760 Mary Eaton of Middleboro acknowledged the sale of her share of the farm of her father Francis Eaton deceased; n.f.r.

vii ELIJAH, b. 7 Nov. 1740; d. Titicut 20 Jan. 1831 ae. 90; m. Middleboro 1 Nov. 1763 SARAH SHAW; d. Middleboro 4 July 1819 ae. 76. Elijah of Middleboro in 1761 sold his share of his father Francis Eaton's farm. The will of Elijah Eaton, dated 31 Oct. 1825 and proved 11 April 1831, names sons Barzillai and Zabina, daughters Lucretia Perkins, Mersena Eaton, Bethana Leonard and Salona Fobes; and four grandch. including two "children of David Eaton who married my daughter."

Six (EATON) ch.: Barzillai, Zabina, Lucretia, Mersena, Bethana and Salona.

viii BENJAMIN, b. 26 March 1742. He was living in Middleboro in 1763 when he sold his share of the farm of his father Francis. In 1782 Benjamin Eaton of Bennington VT, housewright, sold his rights in his mother Lydia Eaton's thirds of the real estate of his father Francis Eaton. Possibly Benjamin was the one in Pownal VT, in 1790, listed with eight males and five females.

ix SUSANNA, b. 13 Sept. 1743; living in Middleboro 8 Feb. 1765 when she acknowledged the sale of her share of her father Francis' farm; n.f.r.

References: MD 2:201; 5:39; 6:111; 12:131; 13:5, 250; 16:14, 15, 19; 18:83; 19:48, 175; 23:111-117, 133; 24:55; 25:107; 26:30. VR BRIDGEWATER, EAST BRIDGEWATER, KINGSTON, NEW SALEM, PELHAM. Raynham VR. Middleboro VR 1:58, 137; 2:31, 96, 108; 4:10; bp. pp. 6, 31; Isaac Backus Recs. MIDDLEBORO DEATHS. NEHGR 11:189; 57:76. MASS MARR 2:70, 77, 81, 86. (PLYMOUTH) ANC LANDMARKS p. 100. Plymouth Co. PR 11:250; 15:18, 19; 14:2 (Francis Eaton); 13:482(Barnabas Crossman); 70:116 & #7042 (Elijah Eaton). Plymouth Co. LR 50:83-4(Mary, Elijah, Benjamin, and Susanna Eaton); 58:147(Elijah Eaton); 66:255; 68:63(John Eaton); 61:33(Benjamin Eaton); 59:204 Silvanus Eaton). Bristol Co. PR 26:272(John Williams). Bristol Co. LR 50:430(Elias Crossman et al). Hampshire Co. PR Box 52-43(Salvenus Eaton). New Bedford Mercury Obits p. 124. WAITFIELD VT BY JONES pp. 300-301.

25 ELISHA$^{4}$ EATON (Benjamin$^{3-2}$, Francis$^{1}$), b. ca. 1701; d. Harpswell ME 19 April 1764.

He m. Braintree 5 Dec. 1734 CATHERINE (BELCHER) CLOUGH, b. Braintree 24 Dec. 1706; d. Harpswell ME 12 April 1767; daughter of Gregory and Elizabeth (Ruggles) Belcher and widow of William Clough of Boston.

Elisha graduated from Harvard College in 1729 and was the first Congregational minister in Randolph, 1731-1750, and in Harpswell ME from 1753-1764.

Children (EATON) b. Braintree (now Randolph):

i ELISHA$^{5}$, b. 12 Sept. 1735; d. Boston 21 July 1774 ae. 38 yrs.; bur. in the Granary Burying Ground, Boston. He was a housewright in Boston in 1771. His estate was settled by Samuel Eaton of Harpswell ME; no indication of wife or children.

ii SAMUEL, b. 22 March 1736/7; d. Harpswell ME 5 or 6 Nov. 1822 unm. He graduated from Harvard

College in 1763 and became the second minister of the Congregational Church in Harpswell, succeeding his father, from 1764 until 1822. He lived with two maiden sisters until they died. He brought up a nephew who lived with him.

iii MARY, b. 1 Dec. 1738; d. 9 Oct. 1793 ae. 54 yrs. unm. A son Joseph was born 4 April 1781 to Mary Eaton of Harpswell; this is presumably the nephew brought up by her brother Samuel.
Child (EATON) b. Harpswell: Joseph.

iv ELIZABETH, b. 9 May 1740. One of the following records may apply to her: an Elizabeth who died 13 Jan. 1806 ae. 65; or an Elizabeth who died 20 July 1818 unm.; or an Elizabeth Eaton of Harpswell who filed int. of m. 31 Aug. 1767 with Josiah Harden of Georgetown ME.

v HANNAH, b. 30 or 31 May 1742; d. 19 Jan. 1806 unm.

vi THADDEUS, b. 1 April 1744; d. "infant"

vii RUTH, b. 21 Feb. 1746; n.f.r.

viii THADDEUS, b. 26 Feb. 1747/8; n.f.r.

References: BRAINTREE RECS pp. 686, 750, 772, 776, 779, 782, 785, 788, 794. VR GEORGETOWN ME. RANDOLPH FIRST CH pp. 14-9, 146. NEHGR 60:135. York Co. ME LR 30:380(Elisha Eaton). BOSTON NEWS OBITS 2:338; 3:100 (Elisha Eaton). HARVARD GRADS 8:569-72; 15:382-6. Account book of Elisha Eaton (MSS. at ME Hist. Soc., Portland). (BOSTON) GRANARY BUR GD p. 88. Suffolk Co. PR 74:95(Elisha Eaton). Suffolk Co. LR 120:36; 123:222; 127:46(Elisha Eaton). Records of Harpswell ME compiled into families by Putnam (MSS. at ME State Lib., Augusta). BRUNSWICK-TOPSHAM-HARPSWELL HIST p. 833. BOWDOIN COLLEGE CAT p. 10. BOWDOIN COLLEGE HIST pp. 73-4.

26 ELIZABETH[4] EATON (Benjamin[3-2], Francis[1]), b. prob. Plymouth; living 27 April 1764.

She m. int. at Kingston 25 Jan. 1728/9 CORNELIUS STURTEVANT, b. Plympton 10 Nov. 1704; d. there 17 Dec. 1762 ae. 58y 23d; son of Nehemiah and Ruth (Sampson) Sturtevant.

The estate of Cornelius Stertevant of Plympton, deceased, was divided between eldest son Silas and Cornelius in 1763; on 27 April 1764 the division was confirmed, reserving the widow's dower.

Children (STURTEVANT) b. Plympton:

i SILAS[5], b. 27 June 1730; d. 1814 ae. 84; m. Middleboro 18 Nov. 1756 ELIZABETH SAMSON, b. Plympton 29 March 1732; d. Brockton 29 Jan. 1802 in her 70th yr.; daughter of Ephraim and Abigail

(Horrel) Samson and a descendant of Pilgrim Myles Standish. Not a Mayflower Samson line. Silas was living in Bridgewater in 1790.
Eight (STURTEVANT) ch. b. Plympton: twins Abigail and Elisebeth, Levy [Lucy], Isaac, Ephraim, Mary, Silos and Elisebeth.

ii CORNELIUS, b. 7 Nov. 1734; d. Keene NH 8 March 1826 ae. 91 yrs.; m. Plympton 16 Dec. 1766 SARAH BOSWORTH, b. Halifax 5 Dec. 1737; d. Keene NH 25 April 1826 ae. 88 yrs.; daughter of Nehemiah and Sarah (Tomson) Bosworth, and a descendant of John Howland. [See *The John Howland Family*.] Cornelius moved to Keene NH after 1777 (birth of last child), but before 1790.
Seven (STURTEVANT) ch. b. Plympton: Luke, Elias, Cornelos, Luther, Luther, and twins Isaac and Sarah.

References: VR BROCKTON, HALIFAX, KINGSTON, PLYMPTON. KEENE NH VR p. 231. Plymouth Co. PR 19:21-3 (Cornelius Stertevant). BRIDGEWATER BY MITCHELL p. 326. (PLYMOUTH) ANC LANDMARKS p. 254. 1790 CENSUS NH:Keene. BOSWORTH GEN 4:581.

27 DAVID[4] EATON (Benjamin[3-2], Francis[1]), b. ca. 1708; d. Kingston 8 July 1759 in his 51st yr.

He m. int. Kingston 24 Dec. 1743 DEBORAH FULLER, b. Plympton 23 Nov. 1727; d. Kingston 25 July or 1 Aug. 1809 ae. 81 yr.; daughter of Jabez and Priscilla (Sampson) Fuller, and a descendant of Pilgrim John Alden. [See *The Samuel Fuller Family*.] Deborah m. (2) 1768 Ebenezer Fuller Jr. of Halifax.

David was a cordwainer. Administration on the estate of David Eaton was granted to Deborah Eaton of Kingston on 8 Sept. 1759. A division of property took place on 13 April 1771, in which the widow Deborah Eaton received her thirds. The remainder was divided into seven parts, with two shares to Lot Eaton the eldest son, and single shares to Jabez, Job, Consider, Joshua and Unis. On 7 May 1810 the widow's thirds were divided among: Lot Eaton oldest son, Jabez Eaton, Job Eaton, heirs of Consider Eaton deceased, heirs of Joshua Eaton deceased, and heirs of Eunice Cook late wife of Amos Cook.

Children (EATON) rec. Kingston:

i LOT[5], b. 18 May 1744; d. Kingston 1822 ae. 78; m. there 23 July 1772 ELIZABETH (RICKARD) EVERSON, b. Plympton 2 March 1732/3; d. Kingston 26 Dec. 1803 in her 72nd yr.; daughter of Samuel and Rachel (Whiton) Rickard, and widow of John Everson, by whom she had three children. A share of

Samuel Rickard's estate was paid to Elizabeth Everson in 1771. On 7 March 1774 Lot Eaton and wife Elizabeth swore to her account as administratrix of John Everson, late of Kingston deceased. Lot and Elizabeth apparently had no children.

ii JABEZ, b. 2 Aug. 1746; living Kingston in March 1818 when he acknowledged a deed in which he, together with Lot Eaton and Amos Cook, had sold rights to a swamp which David Eaton had purchased. He seems not to have married or left any descendants.

iii JOB, b. 26 Oct. 1749; d. Kingston May 1811 ae. 53 unmar. On 7 April 1812 three equal parts of Job's estate went to Lot Eaton "late of Kingston," Jabez Eaton, and the heirs of Eunice Cook.

iv CONSIDER, b. 1 March 1752; d. Kingston 25 Dec. 1776 ae. 24y 8m 25d

v JOSHUA, b. 12 July 1755; d. in Canada 23 Dec. 1777 in his 23rd yr.

vi EUNICE, b. 12 April 1759: d. Kingston 1799 ae. 40; m. Kingston 11 Jan. 1787 AMOS COOKE, b. 12 March 1756; son of Caleb and Sarah (Adams) Cooke. Amos m. (1) 1780 Lydia Stetson; (3) 1801 Sally Bradford. On 30 Dec. 1816 the heirs of Eunice Cook were Lydia Bradford wife of Thomas, Deborah Cook, Eunice Cook, and David Eaton Cook.

Six (COOK) ch. to Amos and Eunice, first five b. Kingston: Bartlett, Prissilla, Lydia, Deborah, Eunice and David Eaton Cook.

References: MD 7:85, 87. VR KINGSTON, PLYMPTON. Plymouth Co. PR 15:304, 313, 402; 16:121; 21:443-4; 43:229(David Eaton); 48:321-2(Job Eaton); 20:184; 21:433-4, 436(David Eaton ch.); 20:525(Samuel Rickard); 21:336(Lot Eaton). Plymouth Co. LR 45:149; 53:192(David Eaton); 57:166(John Ford et al); 137:124(Lot and Jabez Eaton). HINGHAM HIST 3:129, 290. (PLYMOUTH) ANC LANDMARKS p. 99. FULLER GEN 2:132.

28 GILES RICKARD[4] (Rebecca[3] Eaton, Benjamin[2], Francis[1]), b. Plymouth 14 Oct. 1700; d. Kingston bef. 15 Jan. 1770.

He m. Plympton 18 Nov. 1724 MARY EDDY, b. there 24 Jan. 1701/2; daughter of Jabez and Mary (Rickard) Eddy. The will of John Rickard Sr. of Plympton, dated 27 Sept. and proved 7 Nov. 1726, names daughter Mary Eddy and granddaughter Mary Rickard, wife of Giles Rickard.

In 1751 Giles Rickard of Kingston, schoolmaster, sold all rights "to my dwelling which joins the westerly end of my father Josiah's dwelling," which he acknowledged in 1765. In 1763 Jabez Eddy of Middleboro sold to Giles Rickard and wife Mary of Kingston, schoolmaster, all his personal estate after his decease.

Children (RICKARD) b. Kingston:

i NATHANIEL[5], b. 18 Oct. 1725; d. 3 June 1729
ii HANNAH, b. 30 Nov. 1727; d. 2 Dec. 1727
iii SUSANNA, b. 18 March 1729/30; d. 12 April 1730
iv SOLOMON, b. 13 July 173*; d. same day
v SOLOMON, b. 15 Aug. 173*; d. 31 Aug. 173*
vi MARY, b. 4 Aug. 173*; d. Carver 26 May 1778 in her 44th yr.; m. Kingston 8 March 1753 JOSEPH LUCAS, b. Plymouth 12 June 1729; d. Carver bef. 12 Oct. 1807; son of William and Mehitable (Doty) Lucas. [See *The Edward Doty Family* and *The Richard Warren Family*.] Joseph m. (2) at Carver 1790 Sarah Doten. The widow Sarah was appointed administrator of the estate of Joseph Lucas late of Carver on 12 Oct. 1807.
Seven (LUCAS) ch. b. Plymouth: Benjamin, Phebe, Lovisa, Elnathan, Ansell, Molle and Lazarus.
vii SUSANNAH, b. 21 Sept. 173*; d. 3 Nov. 173*
viii LUCY, b. 3 May 173*; d. 30 June 173*
ix CORNELIUS, b. 27 May 173*; d. 30 June 173*
x REBECCA, b. 14 June 17*; did she die at Kingston 16 Jan. 1825, or did she m. at Plympton 18 Dec. 1764 Robert Barrows?
xi JOHN, b. 29 or 24 Oct. 17*; bp. 9 Nov. 1746; d. bet. 1775 and 1790; m. Plymouth 23 Feb. 1769 LYDIA KING, b. Plymouth 8 Nov. 1747; d. Kingston 29 March 1839 ae. 90 yrs.; daughter of Jonathan and Deborah (-----) King. Jonathan King's will dated 1782 names wife Deborah and daughter Lydia Rickard. John Rickard was a blacksmith. When he bought land in Plympton in 1770, he was called a son of Giles Rickard late of Kingston deceased; at this time he was living in Plymouth. In 1774 he was living in Plympton when he sold land, with wife Lydia releasing dower, in a deed which he acknowledged 13 Feb. 1775. In 1790 a Lydia Richard (sic) was living in Carver with another female. In June 1829 widow Lydia Rickard of Kingston sold rights to the Doten swamp in Carver. John and Lydia apparently had no children.
xii NATHANIEL, b. 14 July 17*; bp. 15 July 1750; d. 7 July 17*

References: MD 2:139; 13:168-9; 21:164. VR CARVER, KINGSTON, PLYMPTON. Plymouth VR 2:264. Plymouth Co. PR 5:251 & #16909(John Rickard); 30:321(Jonathan King); 39:140(Joseph Lucas). Plymouth Co. LR 48:236(Jabez Eddy); 50:45(Giles Rickard); 55:107(Benjamin Rickard, John Rickard); 58:177(John Rickard) 166:86(Lydia Rickard).

---

*Record worn.

(PLYMOUTH) ANC LANDMARKS pp. 178, 213. DAR PATRIOT INDEX p. 428. EDDY GEN pp. 29, 63. DOTY GEN p. 160. 1790 CENSUS MA:Carver.

29. BENJAMIN RICKARD[4] (Rebecca[3] Eaton, Benjamin[2], Francis[1]), b. Plymouth 20 or 28 Feb. 1702; d. Plympton 28 March 1788 ae. 86y 1m.

He m. Plympton 12 Feb. 1729/30 THANKFUL PINCHEON, b. Scituate 22 Dec. 1702; d. Plympton 10 Feb. 1794 in her 92nd yr.; daughter of Ebenezer and Deborah (-----) Pincheon.

Benjamin Rickard's will drawn 2 April 1785, probated 2 June 1788, mentions his wife Thankful; heirs of kinsman John Rickard late of Plympton; Seth Fuller son of Benjamin Fuller late of Plympton deceased; Rebecca Rickard daughter of Theophilus Rickard, late of Plympton deceased and her heirs; and the balance of the estate to daughter Deborah Stranger and her heirs.

Children (RICKARD) b. Plympton:

i BENJAMIN[5] (twin), b. 12 April 1732; d. Plympton 10 July 1747 in his 13th yr.

ii THANKFULL (twin), b. 12 April 1732; possibly the Mrs. Thankful Rickard who d. Plympton 9 Dec. 1781 in her 50th yr.

iii ELIJAH, b. 21 Sept. 1734; d. Plympton 11 July 1747 in his 16th yr. [sic]

iv NATHANIEL, b. 10 Oct. 1736 n.f.r.

v DEBORAH, b. 19 Oct. 1738; d. Plympton 19 April 1794 in her 56th yr.; m. there 15 Dec. 1775 EDWARD STRANGER, d. Plympton bef. 29 Feb. 1796. In 1786 land in Pembroke occupied by Edward Stranger was taken in a judgement against him. In 1790 he was living in Plympton with three females. Edward and Deborah sold the farm where they lived in April 1794, together with all the estate given her by Benjamin Rickard; on 11 July 1794 Edward sold the homestead farm and dwelling left by Benjamin Rickard to his daughter Deborah in his will. Edward was named in various deeds as a trader, a weaver, a laborer and a yeoman. On 29 Feb. 1796 administration was granted on the estate of Edward Stranger, late of Plympton trader; the administrator's account of 7 Oct. 1797 listed "corn for use of family." No children.

References: MD 5:210; 11:115-6. VR PLYMPTON, SCITUATE. Plymouth Co. PR 11:450; 30:410-1(Benjamin Richard); 34:67; 35:411-3(Edward Stranger). Plymouth Co.

LR 65:168; 73:215; 75:125, 210(Edward Stranger). 1790 CENSUS MA:Plympton.

30. DESIRE RICKARD[4] (Rebecca[3] Eaton, Benjamin[2], Francis[1]), b. Plympton 18 Feb. 1706; d. Plymouth 10 Jan. 1783.

She m. int. (1) 11 Aug. 1733 "both of Plymouth," EBENEZER DOGGET, b. Marshfield 22 Aug. 1693; d. Boston in Dec. 1746; son of Samuel and Bathsheba (Holmes) Dogget. Ebenezer m. (1) Plymouth 1720 Elizabeth Rickard. Desire was appointed administratrix of Ebenezer's estate on 9 Dec. 1746; she rendered an account 21 April 1748 as Desire Frazier.

She m. (2) Boston 30 July 1747 JOHN FRAZIER; he very likely died in the summer of 1749, since "Desire Frazier with her daughter were warned from Plimton 26 Jan. 1750; she came sometime last August from Boston."

Josiah Rickard (#10) in his will named his daughter Desire Frazier and granddaughter Elizabeth Doggett. Desire Frazier in 1765 acknowledged a settlement made with her siblings of the estate of their father, Josiah Rickard.

Child (DOGGETT):

i ELIZABETH[5], b. Marshfield 14 May 1738 "Bethy"; d. Plymouth 6 Dec. 1798; m. Plympton 24 Nov. 1764 BENJAMIN DREW of Plymouth, d. Plymouth 22 Dec. 1820 ae. 82; son of Seth and Margaret (James) Drew. In 1811 Benjamin Drew, cordwainer of Plymouth, sold a pew to daughters Elizabeth Sherman widow and Margaret Richard.
Nine (DREW) ch. b. Plymouth: Elizabeth, Benjamin, Bathsheba, Ebenezer, Margaret, Ebenezer, Mallechi, Desire and Simeon.

References: MD 6:20; 9:185; 14:39; 18:119; 22:105. VR PLYMPTON. MARSHFIELD VR pp. 25, 47. BOSTON VR 28:346. PLYMOUTH CH RECS p. 412. (PLYMOUTH) BURIAL HILL pp. 81, 137. Suffolk Co. PR 39:276; 41:99(Ebenezer Doggett). Plymouth Co. LR 50:44(Giles Rickard); 117:104; 142:90(Benjamin Drew). Plymouth Co. Ct. Recs., Gen. Sess. of the Peace 1:285(at Pilgrim Hall, Plymouth). DOGGETT FAM pp. 363, 388-91.

31. REBECCA RICKARD[4] (Rebecca[3] Eaton, Benjamin[2], Francis[1]), b. Plympton 24 Aug. 1708; d. East Bridgewater 29 March 1791 ae. 82.

She m. (1) Bridgewater 19 Nov. 1735 SETH ALLEN, b. Bridgewater 5 Aug. 1710; d. there 1 Jan. 1760; son of Samuel and Mary (-----) Allen; m. (2) Bridgewater 29 Jan. 1767 THOMAS WHITMAN, b. there 24 Oct. 1702; d. East

Bridgewater 15 Dec. 1788 ae. 86; son of Nicholas and Sarah (Vining) Whitman. Thomas m. (1) 1727 Jemima Alden.

In 1749 brothers Matthew and Seth Allen sold a piece of land; since the deed was lost, on 8 Nov. 1762 Matthew Allen Jr. of Bridgewater and Nathan Whitman with wife Betty, surviving heirs of Seth Allen deceased, released their rights to this land.

For some inexplicable reason, no action was taken on Seth Allen's estate for 24 years; then on 7 June 1784 Benjamin Whitman and Seth Allen Whitman, both of Bridgewater, were simultaneously appointed administrators on the estate of Seth Allen, and on the estate of Nathan Whitman, late of Bridgewater deceased (son-in-law of Seth). Inventories were ordered on both on 17 Aug. 1784. (Benjamin Whitman was Nathan's brother, and Seth Allen Whitman was Nathan's son.)

The will of Thomas Whitman of Bridgewater, dated 29 June 1785 and probated 2 Feb. 1789, named wife Rebeccah, and several children including son Benjamin Whitman, and ch. of his son Nathan Whitman: Seth Allen Whitman, Nathan Whitman, and the latter's sisters Rebecca and Sela Whitman.

Children (ALLEN) b. Bridgewater:

i child[5], stillborn 20 Nov. 1736

ii BETTY, b. 23 Oct. 1739; d. East Bridgewater 29 March 1784 ae. 45; m. Bridgewater 19 March 1761 NATHAN WHITMAN, b. there in Feb. 1736; d. East Bridgewater 13 May 1784 ae. 48; son of Thomas and Jemima (Alden) Whitman. [See *The John Alden Family*.] On 2 May 1785 the estate of Nathan Whitman was divided among Seth Allen Whitman, eldest son; Nathan Whitman, Rebecca Whitman, and Celia Whitman.

Seven (WHITMAN) ch. first three b. Bridgewater, all bp. E. Bridgewater: Seth Allen, Rebeka, Nathan, Celia, Eliab, Asa and Betty.

iii MARY (twin), b. 25 April 1743; d. Bridgewater 16 June 1747

iv REBECCA (twin), b. 25 April 1743; d. Bridgewater 20 June 1747

References: MD 16:100. VR BRIDGEWATER, EAST BRIDGEWATER, PLYMPTON. NEHGR 10:226. Plymouth Co. PR 27:160; 29:191(Seth Allen); 30:512(Thomas Whitman); 27:159; 29:274(Nathan Whitman). Plymouth Co. LR 49:155; 133:77-8 (Seth Allen). BRIDGEWATER BY MITCHELL p. 353. WHITMAN DESC pp. 51, 164.

32 MERCY[4] EATON (Ebenezer[3], Benjamin[2], Francis[1]), b. Plymouth 15 March 1705/6. No. Yarmouth ME First Church Records state "Mrs. Mercy (Lake) Bishop removed by death, n.d."

She m. (1) North Yarmouth ME 27 June 1731 BENJAMIN LAKE, b. there ca. 1706; d. "before 1747." She m. (2) North Yarmouth ME 5 Nov. 1747 EBENEZER BISHOP, d. there either in 1752 or more likely 4 Feb. 1778.

Children (LAKE) b. North Yarmouth ME:

i BENJAMIN[5], b. 22 Dec. 1732; d. bef. 1790; m. No. Yarmouth ME 22 Jan. 1759 LYDIA HUTTON d. bef. 1800 ae. 75. She was prob. the Lydia Lake in Freeport ME in 1790. She was bp. No. Yarmouth 19 June 1774 with five children.
Six (LAKE) ch. bp. No. Yarmouth: Joshua, Benjamin, John, Eleazer, Molly and Mercy (bp. 1776).

ii EBENEZER, b. 17 Sept. 1734. Did he marry No. Yarmouth 18 Oct. 1759 Sarah Merrill, b. Salisbury 5 Jan. 1736/7; daughter of Samuel and Anna (Evans) Merrill?
One (LAKE) ch. bp. No. Yarmouth: Joanna "daughter of Ebenezer."

iii HANNAH, b. 17 Sept. 1738; d. after 1804; m. int. No. Yarmouth ME 21 July 1753 EDWARD BREWER, b. Middletown CT 24 Aug. 1728; son of Daniel and Eleanor (Goodale) Brewer.
Six, pos. eight (BREWER) ch. b. or bp. No. Yarmouth: Daniel, Joseph, Hannah, Eleanor, Reuben, Miriam; and pos. Ebenezer and Joanna.

iv MERCY, b. 24 Feb. 1740; m. No. Yarmouth ME 23 Nov. 1758 DAVID PETTINGILL, b. there 5 Sept. 1734; d. Saratoga NY 6 Jan. 1778; son of Abraham and Anna (French) Pettingill. They lived in New Gloucester ME.
Eight (PETTINGILL) ch. first two bp. No. Yarmouth: Mary, Benjamin, Rachel, David, Ephraim, Edward, Mercy and Emily.

v ELISHA, b. 30 July 1742; living Lewiston ME in 1790; m. int. New Gloucester ME 19 Oct. 1776 SUSANNA HILDRICKS (or Hildreth), b. Dracut 5 Dec. 1748; living Lewiston ME in 1790; daughter of Robert and Sarah (-----) Hildreth. No others were enumerated in their household in 1790, and no ch. have been found.

Child (BISHOP) b. North Yarmouth ME:

vi JOANNA, b. 26 Aug. 1750; n.f.r.

References: VR DRACUT, SALISBURY. OLD TIMES pp. 653, 660, 667, 714, 909, 968, 1025, 1107, 1162. North Yarmouth ME First Church Recs. North Yarmouth ME T.R. PETTINGILL GEN pp. 89-90, 154-6. HILDRETH ANCY p. 16. MERRILL MEM p. 263. 1790 CENSUS ME:16, 40. DAR PATRIOT INDEX p. 529.

33 JOHANNA[4] EATON (Ebenezer[3], Benjamin[2], Francis[1]), b. Plymouth 29 April 1716; d. North Yarmouth ME 28 Dec. 1774.
She m. North Yarmouth ME 29 Dec. 1736 ELISHA FRENCH.

Children (FRENCH) b. North Yarmouth ME:

i MARY[5], b. 6 Oct. 1737; m. 9 Nov. 1755 BURRILL TUTTLE. [Did he m. (2) 13 March 1775 Mrs. Susannah Eaton?]
Five (TUTTLE) ch. to Burrill and Mary, bp. No. Yarmouth: Libbeus, Lorania, Thadeas, Archilaus and Trueworthy.

ii JOANNA (or Hannah), b. 28 July 1740; d. 1 or 3 April 1743

iii JOSEPH, b. 6 June 1747; d. 22 April 1750

References: OLD TIMES pp. 472, 658, 660, 794, 991, 1037, 1182.

# S A M U E L   F U L L E R

of the

*M A Y F L O W E R*

Compiled by

KATHARINE WARNER RADASCH

and

ARTHUR HITCHCOCK RADASCH

Katharine Warner Radasch is a descendant of Pilgrims John Alden, Isaac Allerton, William Bradford, Francis Cooke, Stephen Hopkins and John Howland. She is a member of the New Jersey Mayflower Society.

Arthur Hitchcock Radasch, who died without seeing this work in print, held an S.B. degree from M.I.T. (1920).

Mr. and Mrs. Radasch are known for their articles and books on families of Barnstable and Plymouth (Mass.) counties, the most recent of which is the *Thomas Clark Family*, (1972).

# SAMUEL FULLER

## FIRST GENERATION

1 SAMUEL[1] FULLER, born in England, was baptized in the parish of Redenhall in Harleston, County of Norfolk, 20 January 1580. He and his brothers Edward and Thomas were sons of Robert Fuller, a butcher in Redenhall, and were mentioned in Robert Fuller's will of 19 May 1614. The will was proved 31 May 1614, and is recorded at the Norfolk Archdeaconry Court, Norwich Register, 1614, folio 259.

Samuel Fuller married first ALICE GLASCOCK, who died before 1613. He was betrothed in Leyden, Holland as the widower of Alice Glascock, 16 March 1613, to Agnes Carpenter from Wrington, England, one of the daughters of Alexander Carpenter. She was baptized in Wrington 16 December 1593. At his betrothal Samuel was accompanied by Alexander Carpenter and William Hoyt*, Samuel's brother-in-law, and by Roger Wilson and Edward Southworth, acquaintances. Agnes was accompanied by her sister Alice, and by Agnes White. Samuel Fuller and AGNES CARPENTER were married 24 April 1613. She died in Leyden in 1615. Samuel married third in Leyden 27 May 1617 BRIDGET LEE, daughter of Josephine (from Dutch "Joos") Lee and sister of Samuel Lee, who were witnesses to the marriage.

Samuel Fuller was one of the band of Pilgrims that fled from England to Leyden, Holland, in 1609. On 7 October 1611 he witnessed the betrothal of Degory Priest, and on 27 January 1612, the betrothal of a William White to Ann Fuller. Ann was possibly a kinswoman of Samuel.

Later, Samuel lived in Pieterskerkhof; after marrying Bridget Lee, he took up residence near Marepoort. On 10 June 1620, he joined with Isaac Allerton, William Bradford, and Edward Winslow in a letter to their associates, John Carver and Robert Cushman, then in England, concerning the affairs of the Pilgrims.

---

*Hoyt in the Dutch record in Leyden; translated as "Hoyt" by Edward Arber (*The Story of the Pilgrim Fathers*) and as "White" by Morton Dexter (*Mayflower Descendant* 8:129-30).

According to Bradford's *History of Plimoth Plantation,* Samuel Fuller brought with him on the *Mayflower* a servant by the name of William Butten, who died at sea. Samuel left his wife and a child behind; after they came over, "he had tow children by her, which are living and growne up to years, but he dyed some 15 years agoe."

Samuel Fuller was a deacon of the church in Leyden and later in Plymouth. He was one of the forty-one signers of the Mayflower Compact. In the land division of 1623, Samuel was allotted two shares. The family was named in the division of cattle and goats 22 May 1627 old style, when "Samuell Fuller, his wife Bridgett, and Samuell Fuller Jr." with ten other inhabitants received a "red Heyfer" and "two shee goats." He was a physician and surgeon, and his services were in demand in the Massachusetts Bay Colony as well as in Plymouth. In 1629 he was sent to Salem where many of the newly arrived colonists were ill. On May 11 Mr. Endicott wrote to Bradford in Plymouth expressing appreciation for Dr. Fuller's services. Debts for these services in 1629 and others rendered by the doctor may have gone unpaid, as Samuel Fuller in his will four years later wrote, "Whereas Capt. John Endecott oweth me two pownds of Beaver I give it to his sonne... Whatsoever mr. Roger Williams is indebted to me upon my booke for Phisick I freely give him... Whatsoever is due me from Capt. Standish I give unto his Children..."

In 1632 Samuel Fuller was a member of the Governor's Council, called Assistants. In 1633 Plymouth suffered an epidemic, believed to have been smallpox. Bradford wrote, "It pleased the Lord to Visite them this year with an infectious fevoure, of which many fell very sicke, and upwards of 20 persons dyed...and in y^e^ end (after he had much helped others) Samuell Fuller, who was their surgeon and phisition, and had been a great help and comforte unto them; as in his facultie, so otherwise, being a deacon of y^e^ church, a man godly, and forward to doe good, being much missed after his death..."

Samuel Fuller died in Plymouth between 9 August and 26 September 1633. He made his will 30 July 1633, and it was proved 28 October 1633. The will and the inventory of his estate have been published in full. In his will he mentioned three youths entrusted to his care and education: Sarah Converse, who was to be brought up by his wife or by Thomas Prence; Elizabeth Cowles, who was to be returned to her parents in Charlestown; and George Foster, who was to be returned to his mother in Saugus. He bequeathed "the education of my children to my brother Will Wright & his wife (Priscilla, a sister of Agnes

Carpenter) onely that my daughter Mercy be & remaine wth goodwife Wallen so long as she shall keepe her at a reasonable charge." Others mentioned were: his neighbor Thomas Prence, his servants Thomas Symons and Robert Cowles, his sister (in-law) Alice Bradford, John Jenny, Joh. Winslow, Mrs. Heeks (Hicks), "old mr. Willm Brewster," Rebecca Prence, and his "Cozen" (i.e., nephew) Sam. Fuller, who had been left in Dr. Samuel Fuller's care upon the death of Edward[1] Fuller and the latter's wife during the winter of 1620-21. Samuel named his executor and overseers as follows: "I institute my son Samuell my Executor and because he is young and tender I enjoyne him to be wholly ordered by Edw. Wynslow m[r] Wil Bradford & m[r] Tho. Prence whom I make his Overseers & the Overseers of this my last will & Testm[t]."

Samuel's third wife, Bridget (Lee) Fuller, came to Plymouth in 1623 on the *Anne*, bringing one child with her. Shortly after her husband's death she opened a small private school. In 1633 the town of Rehoboth voted to invite Mrs. Bridget Fuller to "come and dwell amongst us, to attend on the office of midwife, to answer the town's necessity, which at present is great." The date and place of Bridget's death are not recorded, but she died after 1 March 1664 O.S.

Children (FULLER)*:

i a child[2], bur. Leyden, Holland 29 June 1615
ii a child, b. Holland; d.y. in Plymouth
2 iii SAMUEL, b. about 1624
iv MERCY, b. after 22 May 1627; d. after 1650

References: MD 1:24-8, 152; 2:8, 117; 8:129-30; 13:85; 25:55. BRADFORD'S HIST (1898) p. 374. DEXTER p. 615. ARBER p. 163. STODDARD p. 88, 131-2. FAM OF PILGRIMS p. 94-96. NEHGR 55:193, 410-16; 110:182-83; 113:236. PLYMOUTH COLONY RECS 2:23; 12:4, 11, 164.

## SECOND GENERATION

2 SAMUEL[2] FULLER (Samuel[1]), b. Plymouth ca. 1624; d. Middleboro 17 Aug. 1695 in 71st yr.

He had a first wife whose name is not known. He m. (2) ca. 1665 ELIZABETH (NICHOLS) BOWEN, b. ca. 1637; d. Plympton 11 Nov. 1713; daughter of John Nichols (son of

*No proof was found for the claim (FAM OF PILGRIMS) that Bridget Fuller who m. 30 Sept. 1641 Henry Sirkman was daughter of Samuel Fuller.

Francis) of Fairfield CT and widow of Thomas Bowen of New London CT and Rehoboth. (The death of "Widow Elisabeth Fuller, the aged relict of Rev. Samuel Fuller" is also recorded as 4 Nov. 1713 in *Middleboro Deaths*.)

On 16 March 1648/9 Samuel Fuller, with the consent of his mother Bridget Fuller, sold to Lt. Matthew Fuller two acres of land in Plymouth.

Samuel Fuller was a physician and minister. In 1663 the Town of Rehoboth voted to ask him to become their physician, but he never settled there. His mother was also asked to go there as a midwife. However, as there was no resident doctor in Rehoboth at the time, Dr. Fuller may have gone there temporarily to attend Thomas Bowen and in that way may have become acquainted with Elizabeth Bowen whom he afterwards married.

In 1676 the Indians burned his home in Middleboro, and he returned to Plymouth until the war with the Indians was over. On 19 Dec. 1678 he was called to preach in Middleboro and became their first minister. He was ordained 26 Dec. 1694, a few months before his death. His gravestone is pictured opposite page 193 volume 18 of the *Mayflower Descendant*.

Samuel's widow Elizabeth was appointed administratrix of his estate 25 Sept. 1695. An agreement of the heirs, including the widow and "all of the children of Mr. Samuel Fuller," was signed 1 Oct. 1695 and acknowledged 27 July 1696 with John Nelson signing as guardian for Isaac Fuller.

It is believed that all of Samuel Fuller's children named below, with the exception of his son Samuel, were by his second wife. Mr. Richard LeBaron Bowen stated however in 1942, that Samuel "had four motherless children ranging from nine down to two years of age" when he married for the second time.

Children (FULLER), the eldest by first wife, six by second wife; prob. b. Middleboro:

3 i SAMUEL[3], called eldest son, b. about 1658

ii ELIZABETH, b. about 1666; m. Middleboro 24 May 1694 SAMUEL EATON, b. probably Middleboro about 1663; d. there 8 March 1723/4 in 61st year; son of Samuel and Martha (Billington) Eaton. [See *The Francis Eaton Family*.]

4 iii JOHN, b. about 1667

5 iv EXPERIENCE, b. about 1669

6 v HANNAH, b. about 1671

vi MERCY, b. in 1672 or 1673; d. Eastham 25 Sept. 1735 in 63rd year; m. before 1 Oct. 1695 DANIEL COLE, b. in 1666 or 1667; d. Eastham 15 June 1736 in 70th year; son of Daniel and Ruth Cole. Daniel made his will 20 Nov. 1735, two months after the death of his wife, and it was probated 7 July 1736. He left no issue; no sons, daus., or grandchildren were mentioned. The legatees have been identified as his brothers or sisters or their heirs.

7 vii ISAAC, b. about 1674, possibly later; under 21 in Sept. 1695

References: MD 3:180; 5:65-72; 12:27; 23:76; 26:38. VR PLYMPTON. TAG 34:81-84. MIDDLEBORO DEATHS. REHOBOTH BY BLISS p. 53. NEHGR 96:252, 253. MIDDLEBORO BY WESTON p. 443. Plymouth Co. PR 1:223, 224, 246, 247 (Fuller). Barnstable Co. PR 5:296(Cole).

## THIRD GENERATION

3 SAMUEL[3] FULLER (Samuel[2-1]), b. Plymouth about 1658; d. Plympton 6 Sept. 1728 in his 70th year.

He m. Plymouth 7 Jan. 1685/6 MERCY EATON, b. about 1665; d. after 27 Feb. 1704, the date her last child was born; daughter of Samuel and Martha (Billington) Eaton. [See *The Francis Eaton Family*.]

Samuel Fuller probably lived in that part of Plymouth that later became Plympton. In July and August 1728, he made deeds of gift of his lands in Plympton and Kingston to his sons Nathaniel, Seth, Ebenezer, Benjamin, John, Jabez and James. On 15 Aug. 1728, he made a deed of gift "to my two daughters, viz., Elizabeth Rayment and Mercy Rayment of all my household stuff...the remainder of my personal estate...to be equally divided among all my children, sons and daughters...."

Children (FULLER), rec. Plymouth:

8 i NATHANIEL[4], b. 14 Nov. 1687

ii SAMUEL, b. 30 Aug. 1689; d. Plympton 18 April 1728. His estate was administered by his brother, Nathaniel Fuller of Plympton, 1 Dec. 1728

iii WILLIAM, b. 14 Feb. 1691; d. 26 Aug. 1692

9 iv SETH, b. 30 Aug. 1692

10 v EBENEZER, b. 24 March 1695

11 vi BENJAMIN, b. 7 March 1696

12 vii ELIZABETH, b. 30 March 1697

13 viii JOHN, b. 19 Dec. 1698

14 ix JABEZ, b. "sometime in the beginning of June" 1701

15 x MERCY, b. 3 Oct. 1702

16 xi JAMES, b. 27 Feb. 1704

References: MD 3:14; 13:204. VR PLYMPTON. Plymouth Co. LR 23:111, 119; 24:55, 116, 131, 178; 27:138; 28:122(Samuel Fuller). Plymouth Co. PR 5:407(Fuller).

4 JOHN[3] FULLER (Samuel[2-1]), b. about 1667, very prob. in what is now Middleboro; d. there bef. 10 March 1709/10, age 42 years.

He m. about 1688 MERCY NELSON, daughter of William and Ruth (Foxel) Nelson. "Marcy" Fuller was named by William Nelson Jr., as one of his daughters in his will, dated 20 March 1717 and probated 12 April 1718.

John Fuller took the oath of fidelity in Middleboro in 1688. Mercy Fuller, widow of John Fuller late of Middleboro, was appointed administratrix of his estate 10 March 1709/10. Mentioned in the settlement, which was ordered 19 Sept. 1712, were: Ebenezer Fuller and John Fuller, who were to have all the housing, and pay the shares due each of the other children, respectively, when they became of age or married, viz., Samuel, Jabez, Elizabeth, Joanna, Mary, Marcy and Lydia.

Mercy Fuller, John's widow, m. (2) Middleboro 2 Dec. 1720 Capt. Joseph Vaughan; d. 2 March 1733/4 in his 81st year.* Capt. Vaughan's first wife, Joanna, had d. 11 April 1718, ae. 61.

Children (FULLER), b. prob. Middleboro:

17 i EBENEZER[4], b. in 1689
18 ii JOHN, b. 20 March 1691/2
iii ELIZABETH, b. about 1697; m. Middleboro 31 July 1729 JOHN[4] EATON, b. Plymouth 6 Oct. 1697. [See *The Francis Eaton Family*.]
19 iv JABEZ, b. about 1698
20 v JOANNA, b. about 1701
21 vi SAMUEL, b. about 1703
vii MARY, b. about 1705; d. after 19 Sept. 1712
viii MERCY, b. about 1707; d. after 19 Sept. 1712
ix LYDIA, b. about 1709; m. Middleboro 12 June 1733, as his second wife, FRANCIS EATON, b. ca. 1700, d. before 1749; son of Benjamin and Mary (Coombs) Eaton. [See *The Francis Eaton Family*.]

References: MD 4:72; 8:250; 12:231. VR PLYMPTON. MIDDLEBORO DEATHS. MIDDLEBORO BY WESTON p. 66. GEN ADVERTISER 1:5. Plymouth Co. PR 2:113; 3:196(Fuller); 4:62(Nelson).

*The deductions made in the Middleboro Church Records that Mercy m. (2) William Eaton, and that Joseph Vaughan m. (2) Mercy Fuller (o. Wood), widow of Jabez Fuller, are in error. [See *The Edward Fuller Family*.]

5 EXPERIENCE[3] FULLER (Samuel[2-1]), b. about 1669, prob. in what is now Middleboro. She m. there 12 April 1693 JAMES WOOD, son of Henry and Abigail (Jenney) Wood.

James and Experience acknowledged on 16 April 1725 two deeds that they had signed on 5 May 1721. Both James and Experience were deceased before 21 Dec. 1728, on which date their son Jonathan was appointed administrator of James Wood's estate. The estate was settled 15 March 1736.

Children (WOOD), from settlement of James Wood's estate, as no records of births found:

| | | |
|---|---|---|
| 22 | i | LYDIA[4], b. about 1694 |
| 23 | ii | JONATHAN, (oldest son) b. about 1697 |
| 24 | iii | JAMES, b. about 1699 |
| 25 | iv | BARNABAS, b. about 1701 |
| 26 | v | BENJAMIN, b. about 1703 |
| 27 | vi | ABEL, b. about 1706 |
| 28 | vii | ICHABOD, b. about 1709 |

References: MD 13:86; 18:227; 26:36, 38. MIDDLEBORO DEATHS p. 231. Plymouth Co. PR 5:406(James Wood). Plymouth Co. LR 19:46(James Wood); 37:159(James Wood).

6 HANNAH[3] FULLER (Samuel[2-1]), b. about 1671, prob. Middleboro. She d. after 11 June 1707 and bef. 1709.

She m. sometime after 27 July 1696 ELEAZER LEWIS, b. Barnstable 26 June 1664; d. Middleboro bef. 16 June 1730; son of Edward and Hannah (Cobb) Lewis. Eleazer m. (2), by 1709, Mary -----, and had three ch. by her.

Eleazer Lewis, then of Middleboro, bought 40 acres of upland in Middleboro from William Hoskins of Taunton on 18 Jan. 1694/5. The deed, however, was not recorded until 28 April 1730. On 11 June 1707 Eleazer and his wife Hannah acknowledged a deed for sale of 1/3 part of a share of the Sixteen Shilling Purchase, "which share did formerly belong to our honoured father Mr. Samuel Fuller, deceased."

Eleazer was accepted as a townsman in Middleboro 11 June 1695; he was listed as an inhabitant there 12 Nov. 1695; and was their schoolmaster 1 March 1711.

In the settlement of Eleazer's estate, 12 May 1731, the following names were mentioned: Edward Lewis and his brothers and sisters, viz., Susanna Lewis of Middleboro; Hannah Snell, wife of Thomas Snell of Bridgewater; Elizabeth Lewis of Middleboro; Shubael Lewis of Plympton; Kezia Lewis of Middleboro; Samuel Lewis of Plympton; and, Mary Lewis of Middleboro. Kezia, Samuel and Mary were children by Eleazer's second wife.

Children (LEWIS), b. prob. Middleboro:

i EDWARD[4], b. about 1698; sold land in Middleboro on 16 June 1730 and 22 June 1731 that formerly belonged to his father; resided there in May 1732; n.f.r.
ii SUSANNA, b. about 1700; living Middleboro in May 1731
29 iii HANNAH, b. in 1703
iv ELIZABETH, b. about 1705; resided Middleboro; unm. in 1731
30 v SHUBAEL, b. about 1707

References: MD 5:72; 10:250. MIDDLEBORO BY WESTON pp. 246, 561, 563, 650. Plymouth Co. PR 6:24 (Eleazer Lewis). Plymouth Co. LR 8:83(Hannah Fuller); 25:101, 186; 30:91; 48:36(Eleazer Lewis).

7 ISAAC[3] FULLER (Samuel[2-1]), b. ca. 1674, prob. Middleboro; d. there bef. 16 Nov. 1727.

He m. Plympton 1 Sept. 1709 MARY PRATT; d. after 13 Nov. 1734.

Isaac was under 21 on 1 Oct. 1695 when John Nelson (appointed his guardian 25 Sept. 1695) signed an agreement with the widow and other heirs of Samuel Fuller. According to Thomas Weston, Isaac Fuller was an inhabitant of Middleboro, 21 years of age or older, on 12 Nov. 1695. If the latter statement is correct, the date of Isaac's birth is fixed between 1 Oct. and 12 Nov. 1674. On 16 Nov. 1727 his widow Mary was appointed administratrix of his estate.

Mary Pratt may have been the second wife and widow of Joshua Pratt, who died in Plymouth 16 Feb. 1697/98, leaving two minor children. On 13 Nov. 1734 Mary acknowledged sale of real estate that had belonged to her late husband, "Doctr Isaac Fuller." Isaac was Middleboro's first physician.

Children (FULLER), rec. Middleboro; first two also rec. Plympton:

i RELIANCE[4], b. 28 Dec. 1710; prob. d. unm.
31 ii ISAAC, b. 24 Sept. 1712
iii ELIZABETH, b. 23 July 1715
32 iv SAMUEL, b. 29 Jan. 1717/8
v MICAH, b. 31 Jan. 1719/20; reputed to have become wealthy; owned several mills and dropped dead in one of them; resided Worcester where his home was burned by Indians; removed to Hadley where he was again burned out by Indians; removed to Schenectady NY.

33 vi JABEZ, b. 7 May 1723
34 vii MARY, b. 23 Aug. 1726

References: MD 7:239-40; 16:63. VR PLYMPTON. MIDDLEBORO BY WESTON pp. 238-9, 563. Plymouth Co. LR 23:193; 29:82(Mary Fuller). FULLER GEN 2:21. Plymouth Co. PR 1:223, 224, 246, 247(Fuller); 5:358(Fuller); 1:286; 2:69(Pratt).

## FOURTH AND FIFTH GENERATIONS

8 NATHANIEL[4] FULLER (Samuel[3-2-1]), b. Plymouth 14 Nov. 1687; d. Plympton 20 April 1750 aged 62y 5m 6d.

He m. Plympton 24 Jan. 1711/2 MARTHA SAMPSON, b. there 25 Oct. 1689; d. there 8 June 1770 "N.S.," aged 80y 7m 3d; daughter of George and Elizabeth (Sprague) Sampson of Plympton. This is not a Mayflower Samson line.

Nathaniel was a housewright and mason. He made his will 16 March 1749 and it was probated 7 May 1750. He mentioned his wife Martha; eldest son Amos; son Barnabas; daughters Sarah Sturtevant and Ruth Cobb; and his grandson William Fuller and granddaughter Lydia Fuller, children of his son Nathaniel, deceased.

Children (FULLER), b. Plympton:

i SARAH[5], b. 28 Sept. 1712; d. Halifax 21 July 1763 in 52nd yr., "wife of Austin Bearse, formerly wife of Isaac Sturtevant"; m. (1) Plympton 8 April 1731 ISAAC STURTEVANT, b. there 10 Aug. 1708; d. Halifax 7 Feb. 1750/1 in 43rd yr.; son of William and Fear (Cushman) Sturtevant. [See *The Isaac Allerton Family*.] She m. int. (2) Halifax 19 Dec. 1756 AUSTIN BEARSE, b. Plympton 16 July 1714; d. Halifax 3 May 1764 in 50th yr.

Eight (STURTEVANT) ch., first b. Plympton, seven b. Halifax: Deborah b. 1731/2, Martha b. 1735, Sarah b. 1737/8, Isaac b. 1739/40, Simeon b. 1742, Samuel b. 1744/5, Jesse b. 1748, and Nathaniel b. 1750.

ii RUTH, b. 4 March 1713/4; d. bef. Aug. 1766; m. Kingston 3 April 1733 JAMES COBB JR. of Kingston, b. Plymouth 13 June 1708; d. Kingston 20 June 1793 ae. 85; son of James and Patience (Holmes) Cobb; he m. (2) Plymouth 13 Nov. 1766 Melatiah Holmes of Plymouth.

Nine (COBB) ch. b. Kingston: Ruth b. 1734/5, James b. 1754; seven d.y.

iii WILLIAM (twin), b. 20 July 1716; d. in 1716

iv ELIZABETH (twin), b. 20 July 1716; d. in 1716

v AMOS, b. 12 Feb. 1718/9; d. Plympton 31 Dec. 1790 ae. 71y 10m 8d; m. (1) Plympton 11 June 1744 ABIGAIL HARLOW, b. there 9 Aug. 1722; d. there 15 April 1755 in 33rd year; daughter of James and Hannah (Shaw) Harlow; m. (2) Plympton 25 Oct. 1759 RACHEL (STANDISH) SAMPSON, b. there 24 April 1726; d. there 13 Oct. 1809 ae. 83y 5m 8d; daughter of Moses and Rachel (Cobb) Standish, and widow of Philemon Sampson who d. Plympton 1756; and a descendant of Pilgrims Alden and Standish. [See *The Myles Standish Family*.]

Eight (FULLER) ch. b. Plympton, six by first wife, two by second wife: Mary b. 1745, Martha b. 1746, Nathaniel b. 1747, Hannah b. 1749, Sarah b. 1751, Abigail b. 1753, Amos b. 1760, and Philemon b. 1763.

vi NATHANIEL, b. 26 May 1721; d. Plympton bef. 9 April 1748 when Amos Fuller was appointed guardian to Nathaniel's two children; m. Plympton 12 June 1744 LYDIA PERRY of Plympton, b. ca. 1720-22; daughter of William and Lydia (Barnaby) Perry. [See *The Richard Warren Family*.] Nathaniel's widow m. (2) Plympton 12 May 1748 Ebenezer Dunham of Plympton, b. there 1718/9; d. there bef. 4 Aug. 1766; son of Israel and Joanna (Rickard) Dunham.

Two (FULLER) ch. b. Plympton: William b. 1744/5, Lydia b. 1746.

vii BARNABAS, b. 25 Sept. 1723; d. Hebron ME 24 March 1814 ae. 90y 6m; m. Kingston 16 March 1747/8 REBECCA CUSHMAN, b. there 9 April 1730; d. Hebron ME 6 April 1813; daughter of Robert and Mercy (Washburn) Cushman, and a descendant of Pilgrim Allerton. [See *The Isaac Allerton Family*.] Barnabas was a mariner and soldier in the Revolution.

Ten (FULLER) ch. b. Kingston: Jesse b. 1748, Barzillai b. 1751, Robert b. 1752, Martha b. 1754, Azubah b. 1756, Joshua b. 1758, Rebecca b. 1761, Ruth b. 1764, Barnabas b. 1768, Isaac b. 1771.

viii JESSE, b. 18 Feb. 1725/26; d.y.

ix SAMUEL, b. 11 Nov. 1729; d. Plympton 7 March 1742/43 ae. 13y 3m 26d.

References: MD 2:165; 3:32; 4:112; 9:152; 26:86. VR KINGSTON, PLYMPTON. HALIFAX VR p. 52. MA MARR 2:21. OXFORD ME BY KING p. 192. MSSR 6:151. Plymouth Co. PR 11:89, 91; 12:107(Nathaniel Fuller). TAG 41:180.

9 SETH[4] FULLER (Samuel[3-2-1]), b. Plymouth 30 Aug. 1692; d. Plympton after 30 March 1754 and bef. 26 Jan. 1758.

He m. (1) Plympton 12 May 1720 SARAH WRIGHT, d. there 7 June 1726; daughter of Adam and Sarah (Soule) Wright. [See *The Francis Cooke Family* and *The George Soule Family*.] Seth m. (2) Plympton 8 March 1726/7 DEBORAH (EDWARDS) COLE, widow of Samuel Cole.

No record has been found of the death of Seth's second wife. He m. (3) DEBORAH (-----) DOTEN, widow of Jacob Doten, as shown by a note given 22 Feb. 1753 by Seth Fuller and his then wife Deborah to Solomon Doten, executor of Jacob Doten's estate, for "the improvement of our thirds of the estate of Jacob Doten, late of Plympton." This note was acknowledged by Deborah Fuller on 26 Jan. 1758.

In 1735 Seth Fuller, then living in Middleboro, bought part of a sawmill in Halifax. He sold it in 1748 when he was living in Plympton. The deed of sale was acknowledged 30 March 1754.

Children (FULLER), one by first wife and two by second wife:

i ARCHIPPUS[5], b. Plympton 17 May 1721; d. Hartford VT 8 March 1811 ae. 91; bur. Christian St. Cem.; m. (1) Plympton 23 Aug. 1748 MARY PRATT; m. (2) Plymouth 26 Sept. 1753 MARIA (RIDER) CHURCHILL, b. there 2 Dec. 1724; d. Hartford VT 17 April 1798 ae. 73; daughter of Samuel and Mary (Silvester) Rider, widow of Joseph Churchill, and a descendant of Richard Warren. [See *The Richard Warren Family*.] They removed first about 1778 to Woodstock VT where they were received into full communion in Woodstock Congregational Church 5 May 1782; removed later to Hartford. Archippus was the only heir of his mother, Sarah.

Five (FULLER) ch.: Consider, Seth b. ca. 1760, Samuel b. ca. 1764, Polly, and Mariah.

ii SARAH, b. Plympton 27 Jan. 1727/8; n.f.r.*

iii SETH, b. about 1730; d. Plympton 1756; m. there 28 Sept. 1750 HANNAH DOTEN, b. there 7 May 1732; d. Carver 23 May 1764 ae. 32; daughter of Jacob and Deborah Doten. [See *The Edward Doty Family*.] On 18 July 1756 Hannah was appointed administra-

---

**The North Genealogy*, by Dexter North (1921), p. 29, errs in stating that David North, born Farmington CT 4 Aug. 1721, married Sarah Fuller. That particular David North married Sarah Tuller of Simsbury (Northington) CT, who was born there 13 Aug. 1727 and died in West Avon CT 16 Feb. 1804 ae. 76y 6m; daughter of Jacob Tuller. No evidence has been found to show that either Seth Fuller or his daughter Sarah moved to Connecticut.

trix of Seth Fuller Jr.'s estate. No known issue.

References: MD 4:240; 11:244, 245; 15:38. VR CARVER, PLYMPTON. WOODSTOCK BY DANA pp. 599, 601. Plymouth Co. LR 44:227; 47:251(Seth[4] Fuller); 64:236; 65:134(Archippus Fuller). DAR Recs. 13:116(at VT Historical Society). Plymouth Co. PR 14:74(Seth[5] Fuller).

10 EBENEZER[4] FULLER (Samuel[3-2-1]), b. Plymouth 24 March 1695; d. Kingston 2 May 1759 in 65th yr; bur. there in the old burying ground.

He m. Kingston 21 June 1721 JOANNA GRAY, b. Plymouth 29 Jan. 1695/6, d. Kingston 25 Sept. 1776 ae. 80y 7m 18d [a manuscript record, not verified]; daughter of John and Joanna (Morton) Gray, and a descendant of James Chilton. [See *The James Chilton Family*.] John Gray's will of 23 Sept. 1728 mentioned daughter Joanna Fuller.

Ebenezer's will dated 29 --- 1755, probated 1 Dec. 1772, mentioned his wife Joanna; sons Josiah (to be executor) and Ebenezer; and daughters Rebecca, Lois and Eunice.

Children (FULLER), rec. Kingston:

i JOSIAH[5], b. 15 May 1721 (1722?); d. Kingston 3 Sept. 1805 in 84th yr; m. there 21 Jan. 1746 LYDIA CUSHMAN, b. Kingston 29 Sept. 1726; d. there 3 April 1784 in 58th yr; daughter of Robert and Mercy (Washburn) Cushman, and a descendant of Isaac Allerton.
Nine (FULLER) ch. b. Kingston: Josiah b. 1748, Zephaniah b. 1750, Thankful b. 1751, Malachi and Angelina bp. 1769, Lemuel, Lydia, Joanna (b. 1762) and James, all four bp. 1769, called "ch. of Joshua."

ii SAMUEL, b. 14 Oct. 1723; d. 22 April 1724

iii REBECCA, b. 23 April 1725; a "spinster" in 1762 when she, Ebenezer Robbins and Eunice Robbins sold land in Kingston to their brother Ebenezer Fuller.

iv HANNAH, b. 8 June 1727; d. 20 Aug. 1736

v MERCY, b. 29 Aug. 1730; d. 8 Jan. 1733/4

vi LOIS, b. 16 Nov. 1733; d. Kingston 25 Feb. 1790 ae. 56; m. there 2 May 1764 NICHOLAS DAVIS, a widower, b. Kingston 12 March 1728/9; d. there 3 May 1818 ae. 89; son of Nicholas and Grace (Brock) Davis.
Four (DAVIS) ch. b. Kingston: Samuel b. 1765, William b. 1767, Lois b. 1769, and Lydia b. 1773.

vii EUNICE, b. 5 May 1736; d. Plymouth 4 June 1781 in 46th yr; m. Kingston 28 July 1760 EBENEZER ROBBINS, b. Plympton about 1730-35 (under 21 in 1740), d. Plymouth 23 June 1799; son of Jeduthan and Rebecca (Crocker) Robbins, and a descendant of John Howland. [See *The John Howland Family*.] Ebenezer m. (2) Plymouth 4 Oct. 1781 Mercy (Harlow) Doten, widow of Elisha Doten, and had four ch. by her.

Eight (ROBBINS) ch. b. Plymouth: Levi b. 1761, d.y., Ebenezer b. 1762, Thaddeus b. 1764, Consider b. 1766, James b. 1767, Ansell b. 1769, Levi b. 1771, and Joanna d.y.

viii EBENEZER, b. 16 Feb. 1737/8; d. after 11 July 1772 when he sold land to his brother Josiah. He m. (1) Middleboro 1 Dec. 1756 LOIS RIDER of Middleboro, b. Plymouth 15 Sept. 1732; daughter of Samuel and Mary (Sylvester) Rider and a descendant of Pilgrim Warren. [See *The Richard Warren Family*.] He m. (2) Plymouth 21 Oct. 1761 HANNAH RIDER. He was a mariner.

One (FULLER) ch. by first wife b. Plymouth: Ebenezer b. 1758.

References: MD 1:145; 15:38; 18:127, 128; 19:6; 23:8; 24:57; 26:40. VR KINGSTON, PLYMPTON. (PLYMOUTH) BURIAL HILL p. 53. MA MARR 2:17. Plymouth Co. PR 6:191(John Gray); 8:264(Ebenezer Robbins); 21:192(Ebenezer Fuller). Plymouth Co. LR 56:245(Rebecca Fuller; Ebenezer Fuller). PLYMOUTH CH. RECS pp. 500, 621.

11 BENJAMIN$^4$ FULLER (Samuel$^{3-2-1}$), b. Plymouth 7 March 1696; living Plympton 4 July 1755 when he sold to Samuel Fuller of Plympton, laborer, "all my homestead where I now dwell."

He m. MARY SAMSON, daughter of Samuel and Hasadiah (Eddy) Samson. Mary may have died before 4 July 1755, as she did not join with her husband in the above-mentioned deed. "Daughter Mary Fuller" was named in the will of Samuel Samson dated 31 Aug. 1744.

Children (FULLER), b. Plympton*:

i JEPTHA$^5$, b. 26 July 1720; d.y.

ii HASADIAH, b. 3 March 1721/2; d. Plympton 25 Nov. 1744; m. there 22 May 1740 JAMES STURTEVANT JR., b. there 15 Sept. 1718; d. New Braintree 8 Oct. 1796; son of James and Susanna (Cook) Sturtevant.

***The Eatonian News* (No. 9, July 1950) lists five more children in Benjamin Fuller's family. No independent evidence was found to substantiate the claim.

[See *The Francis Cooke Family*.] James Jr. m. (2) Lydia -----; d. Brookfield in 1824.

One (STURTEVANT) ch. by first wife b. Plympton: Hasadiah b. 1744.

iii SAMUEL, b. 14 May 1724; d. bef. 9 May 1758; m. Kingston 27 Oct. 1747 ANN(A) TINKHAM, b. there 6 Aug. 1726; d. after 2 Oct. 1759; daughter of John and Ann (Gray) Tinkham, and a descendant of James Chilton. Samuel's widow was appointed administratrix of his estate 9 May 1758. She sold land in Plympton 2 Oct. 1759.

Five (FULLER) ch. b. Plympton: Mary b. 1748, Ruby b. 1750/1, Benjamin b. 1752, Sylvanus b. 1755, and Anna b. 1757.

References: MD 14:37. VR BROOKFIELD, KINGSTON, NEW BRAINTREE, PLYMPTON. Plymouth Co. PR 9:338(Samuel Samson); 14:478(Samuel Fuller). Plymouth Co. LR 43:241 (Benjamin Fuller); 45:239(Ann Fuller).

12 ELIZABETH[4] FULLER (Samuel[3-2-1]), b. Plymouth 30 March 1697; d. CT, prob. Pomfret, after Aug. 1753.

She m. Plympton 30 Jan. 1723/4 JAMES RAYMOND or Raiment of Middleboro, b. Beverly 1 June 1689; d. CT, prob. Pomfret, after Aug. 1753; son of John and Martha (Woodin) Raymond. James Raymond m. (1) Mercy Tinkham; d. Middleboro 17 April 1723 ae. 31. She had two children.

Elizabeth (Fuller) Raymond was admitted to the Middleboro Church 19 July 1730. James and Elizabeth were admitted as communicants to the Abington Congregational Church, Pomfret CT, 30 Aug. 1753 on recommendation from the First Church in Middleboro.

Children (RAYMOND), b. Middleboro:

i PATIENCE[5], b. 11 Nov. 1724; d. bef. 12 Dec. 1745; m. Plympton 15 March 1743/4 JAMES BRYANT. He m. (2) Plympton 12 Dec. 1745 Abiah Wormall of Duxbury; they named their first daughter Patience, b. 1752. James and Patience had no ch.

ii ELIZABETH, b. 13 Jan. 1727/8; d. after 5 March 1798; m. Pomfret CT 14 March 1746 SILAS RICKARD, b. Plympton 26 April 1717; d. Pomfret 6 March 1802; son of Joseph and Deborah (Miller) Rickard. Elizabeth was discharged to Pomfret CT in 1749. Silas Rickard rendered patriotic service in the Revolution. His will dated 5 March 1798, and probated 1 June 1802, mentions wife Elizabeth, son Silas, and daughters Elizabeth Ashley (wife of Joseph Jr.) and Eunice Holmes (wife of Jonathan).

Five (RICKARD) ch. b. Pomfret CT: Lucy b. 1747, Hannah b. 1748, Eunice b. 1755, Silas b. 1758, and Elizabeth b. 1761.

iii MARTHA, b. 21 June 1729; m. Pomfret CT 11 May 1757 SAMUEL WINTER; d. there bef. 2 March 1772 when Martha petitioned that her brother Joshua Raymond be appointed administrator of Samuel Winter's estate in her place.

Five (WINTER) ch. b. Pomfret CT: Azuba b. 1758, Abigail b. 1760, Juvenal b. 1762, Isaac b. 1764, and Asa b. 1766.

iv RACHEL, b. 9 Sept. 1730; d. Pomfret CT 12 Dec. 1756; unm.

v BATHSHEBA, b. 18 Feb. 1731/2; m. 22 Dec. 1757 WILLIAM PLANK of Killingly CT, bp. Putnam CT 31 March 1728; d. Pomfret CT 4 July 1792 in 65th yr; son of Robert and Hannah (Cooper) Plank.

Six (PLANK) ch. bp. Thompson CT 1768: Zebediah (b. 1758), Hannah, Molly (b. 1762), Elijah, Elisha, and Elizabeth.

vi JAMES, b. 18 March 1732/3; d. Hampton CT 11 June 1807 ae. 75; m. (1) Pomfret CT 27 Nov. 1760 ABIGAIL DOWNING, b. Canterbury CT 5 June 1735; d. Hampton 13 Oct. 1788; daughter of Ichabod and Abigail Downing. She is bur. beside her husband and near her parents in the South Cemetery, Hampton. James Raymond m. (2) Hampton 13 Sept. 1789 OLIVE PARISH (or Parrish).

Three (RAYMOND) ch. by second wife b. Hampton CT: Abigail b. 1790, James b. 1792, and Asa b. 1794.

vii AMAZIAH, b. 27 May 1734; d. Pomfret CT 19 Jan. 1819 ae. 84; m. there 26 Nov. 1767 JOANNA CUTLER of Pomfret, b. Windham CT 20 March 1745/6; d. after 29 June 1815; daughter of Seth and Elizabeth (Badcock) Cutler. No rec. found of any ch.

viii JOSHUA, b. 19 March 1735/6; d. Canterbury CT between 5 Dec. 1814 and 10 April 1815; m. Pomfret CT 5 Feb. 1761 ABIGAIL SHAW, b. Windham CT 7 May 1734; d. 28 Oct. 1821 ae. 86 prob. in Canterbury; daughter of William and Elizabeth (Davis) Shaw.

Eight (RAYMOND) ch., first five b. Pomfret CT: Joseph b. 1761, Joshua b. 1763, James b. 1765, Abigail b. 1767, Lydia b. 1769, Cloe, John and Ebenezer.

ix ITHAMAR, b. 21 June 1737; n.f.r.

References: MD 4:70; 6:127; 7:241; 12:131, 132, 232; 14:84. VR BEVERLY, PLYMPTON. Middleboro Church Records. CSL Barbour Index for Pomfret,

Killingly, Canterbury, Hampton, Windham. CSL Ch Recs for Pomfret(Abington Cong.), Putnam, Thompson. CSL Hale Cem Recs for Hampton. Pomfret CT PR #3410(Silas Rickard); #4541(Samuel Winter). Canterbury CT PR #1777(Joshua Raymond). RAYMOND FAMS pp. 18-19.

13 JOHN$^{4}$ FULLER (Samuel$^{3-2-1}$), b. Plymouth 19 Dec. 1698; d. Kingston 25 Sept. 1778 in 80th year.

He m. (1) Plympton 7 Feb. 1722/3 DEBORAH RING, b. Plymouth 10 July 1698; d. Kingston 8 Nov. 1763 ae. 65y 3m 15d; daughter of Eleazer and Mary (Shaw) Ring of Plymouth, and a descendant of Pilgrim Hopkins. [See *The Stephen Hopkins Family*.]

John m. (2) Kingston 14 Nov. 1764 Mrs. MERCY (WASHBURN) CUSHMAN, b. Plymouth 21 April 1702; d. Kingston 3 May 1796 ae. 94; daughter of John and Lydia Washburn and widow of Robert Cushman, who d. Kingston 13 Sept. 1751.

John Fuller was a physician and a deacon in the Kingston Church. He made his will 31 Dec. 1761, and it was probated 5 Oct. 1778. He mentioned his sons Issachar, Ezra, Consider and Eleazer and his daughters Deborah Prince, Susanna Dingley and Hannah Bisbee. His son Issachar and his son-in-law Kimball Prince were named as executors.

Children (FULLER), by first wife, b. Kingston:

i ELEAZER$^{5}$, b. 3 Nov. 1723; d. Kingston 20 Aug. 1736

ii ISSACHAR, b. 8 July 1725; d. Carver 31 Oct. 1822 ae. 93y 3m 12d; m. (1) Plympton 19 Jan. 1747/8 ELIZABETH DOTY, b. there about 1729; d. Carver 2 July 1781 ae. 51; daughter of John and Lydia (Dunham) Doty, and a descendant of Pilgrims Cooke, Doty and Hopkins. [See *The Edward Doty Family*.] He m. (2) Middleboro 26 Dec. 1785 LUCY TINKHAM, b. 22 April 1752 "O.S.", d. Carver 30 April 1847 ae. 95y 17d; daughter of Ebenezer and Hannah (Shaw) Tinkham, and a descendant of Peter Brown. [See *The Peter Brown Family*.] Issachar served as private in a company of minutemen from Plympton.

Sixteen (FULLER) ch., eleven by first wife, first eight b. Kingston, other three b. Carver: Lydia b. 1749, Isaac b. 1751, John b. 1753, Deborah b. 1756, Noah b. 1758, Sylvia b. 1760, Issachar b. 1762, Elizabeth b. 1764, Edward b. 1768, Rebecca b. 1772, and Abigail b. 1774.

Five by second wife, b. Carver: Lucy b. 1786, Deborah b. 1788, Ebenezer b. 1789, Hannah b. 1792, and Priscilla b. 1794.

iii JOHN, b. 16 Sept. 1727; d. 30 July 1742

iv DEBORAH, b. 14 Dec. 1729; d. Kingston 4 March 1826 ae. 96; m. there 2 Nov. 1749 KIMBALL PRINCE, b. Kingston 28 April 1726; d. there 10 April 1814 ae. 88y; son of Job and Abigail (Kimball) Prince, and a descendant of William Brewster.

Nine (PRINCE) ch. b. Kingston: Christopher b. 1751, Kimball b. 1753, Sarah b. 1756, Ruth b. 1758, Deborah b. 1760, Noah b. 1763, Job b. 1765, John b. 1768, and Hezekiah b. 1771.

v SUSANNA, b. 18 Nov. 1731; d. Duxbury 17 March 1782 ae. 48 (No. Duxbury G.S. says "in 50th yr."); m. Kingston 5 April 1753 (1752 in Duxbury VR) JACOB DINGLEY JR. of Duxbury, a soldier in the Revolution; b. Marshfield 8 Jan. 1727; bp. there 25 Feb. 1727/8; son of Jacob and Mary (Holmes) Dingley, and a descendant of William Brewster. Jacob Dingley Jr. m. (1) 2 Feb. 1748 Desire Phillips, and (3) Althea (Fullerton) Joyce, widow of Ebenezer Joyce.

Seven (DINGLEY) ch. b. Duxbury: Levi b. 1756, Desire b. 1758, Susanna b. 1764, Jacob d. 1766 ae. 6w, Jacob b. 1767, Ezra b. 1770, and John b. 1773.

vi NOAH, b. 31 May 1734; d. Kingston 6 Aug. 1756; unm.

vii EZRA, b. 23 April 1736; d. Carver 24 May 1771 ae. 35y 1m 1d; m. Kingston 23 Nov. 1758 ELIZABETH WESTON, b. there 18 Sept. 1739; daughter of Jonathan and Mercy (Rickard) Weston. Ezra's will, dated 19 March 1771 and probated 5 Aug. 1771, mentions his wife and five ch.

Five (FULLER) ch. b. Kingston: Samuel b. 1759, Susanna b. 1761, Molly b. 1763, Consider b. 1765, and James b. 1768.

viii CONSIDER, b. 7 July 1738; d. possibly Maine; living Kingston 1790; m. Plympton 21 Feb. 1759 LYDIA BRYANT, b. Plympton 12 May 1741; daughter of Samuel Jr. and Tabitha (Ford) Bryant.

Eight, pos. nine (FULLER) ch., first two b. Halifax, next six bp. Kingston: Luna b. 1760, Eliphalet b. 1761, Lydia bp. 1766, John bp. 1767, Levi bp. 1767, Joseph bp. 1769, Ezra bp. 1774, and Lusanna bp. 1776; and pos. Consider b. 1780.

ix ELEAZER, b. 27 April 1740; m. Plympton 6 Jan. 1763 MARGARET HOLMES. Served in the Revolution as a minuteman, later as a sergeant. Resided in Kingston in 1778 when, with wife Margaret, he sold his land there, including a dwelling house.

Four (FULLER) ch. b. Kingston: Abigail b. 1764, Daniel b. 1765, Jenny b. 1769, and Sarah b. 1771.

x HANNAH, b. 30 April 1743; d. 20 Jan. 1831; m. Kingston 8 Jan. 1761 BENJAMIN BISBEE, b. there 9 Aug. 1736; d. 30 May 1813; son of Elijah and Eleanor (Pierce) Bisbee.

Eleven (BISBEE) ch., first three b. Plympton, first six bp. Rochester Jan. 1775: Molly 1761, Aurelia 1764, Benjamin 1766, Robert 1768, Ezra 1771, Joseph 1774, John Fuller 1777, Hannah 1780, Susan 1785, Deborah 1789, and Asa.

References: MD 1:208; 2:165; 30:156; 31:167. VR CARVER, DUXBURY, KINGSTON, PLYMPTON, ROCHESTER. 1790 CENSUS MA:170. MSSR 6:158; 163. BISBEE GEN pp. 32, 48, 86-90. Plymouth Co. PR 21:20(Fuller); 25:96(Fuller). Plymouth Co. LR 59:164; 63:13(Eleazer Fuller). Middleboro Town Rec. Middleboro Ch. Rec. FULLER GEN p. 75. MQ 41:62.

14 JABEZ$^{4}$ FULLER (Samuel$^{3-2-1}$), b. Plymouth "sometime in the beginning of June" 1701; d. Kingston in 1757.

He m. int. Kingston 13 Oct. 1733 MERCY GRAY, b. Plymouth 4 Feb. 1703/4; d. Kingston 13 Aug. 1782 in 79th year; daughter of John and Joanna (Morton) Gray, and a descendant of James Chilton. [See *The James Chilton Family*.]

Mercy Fuller, widow of Jabez Fuller of Kingston, was appointed administratrix of his estate 20 (or 29) May 1757.

Children (FULLER), b. Kingston:

i THOMAS$^{5}$, b. 31 Aug. 1734; d. Kingston 2 April 1738

ii JOANNA, b. 31 March 1736; d. bef. July 1777; m. int. Kingston 13 Sept. 1760 JAMES FAUNCE of Plympton, b. Plymouth 6 April 1719; d. Halifax bef. 5 Aug. 1782; son of Thomas and Lydia (Barnaby) Faunce, and a descendant of Richard Warren. James Faunce m. (1) 22 June 1742 Sarah Faun [Faunce or Vaughan]; m. (3) Halifax 17 July 1777 Mary Cushman. Of the children named below only Barnaby, William and Lucy were mentioned in the settlement of James Faunce's estate.

Eight (FAUNCE) ch., b. to James and Joanna, first six b. Plympton, last two b. Halifax: Molly b. 1761, Barnaby b. 1763, Desire b. 1765, Salome b. 1768, Marcy b. 1770, William b. 1771, Lucy b. 1773, and Olive bp. 1775.

iii JAMES, b. 4 Dec. 1737; d. bef. 17 Dec. 1760, on which date his mother, Mercy Fuller, was appointed administratrix of his estate.

iv JABEZ, b. 24 Feb. 1739; m. Plympton 24 April 1766 RUTH WRIGHT. Jabez a seafaring man, and his mother Mercy Fuller, widow, sold their lands in

Kingston "where we now live," on 24 Jan. 1771; Ruth, wife of Jabez, gave up her right of dower.

v JOHN, b. 29 Sept. 1742; d. Kingston 20 Oct. 1828 ae. 86; m. Plympton 28 April 1768 REBECCA ROBBINS of Carver, b. Plympton 3 March 1748; d. Kingston 16 June 1815 ae. 67; daughter of Eleazer and Rebecca (Jackson) Robbins and granddaughter of Jeduthan Robbins (see 10 vii) and a descendant of John Howland.

Eight (FULLER) ch. rec. Kingston, first five b. Plymouth: John b. 1769, Rebecca b. 1771 (d. 1772), James b. 1773, Mercy b. 1775 (d. 1775), Mercy b. 1776, Rebecca b. 1779, Eleazer Robbins b. 1784 or 1785, and Betsey b. 1787.

vi MERCY, b. 6 July 1747. Possibly she was the Mercy Fuller who m. Hardwick 23 Feb. 1777 (int. Oakham 24 Feb. 1777) EDMUND WILLIS, b. Bridgewater 24 June 1753; son of Silas and Sarah (Hayward) Willis, and a descendant of Francis Cooke. After a daughter Sally was b. Hardwick in 1783, Edmund and Mercy moved to Vermont.

References: MD 1:145; 7:50, 209; 21:62; 27:180. VR BRIDGEWATER, HARDWICK, KINGSTON, OAKHAM, PLYMPTON. HALIFAX VR p. 53. FAUNCE FAM p. 37. Plymouth Co. PR 14:238(Jabez Fuller); 16:25(James Fuller); 27:99; 28:455(Faunce). Plymouth Co. LR 56:13(Jabez Fuller).

15 MERCY[4] FULLER (Samuel[3-2-1]), b. Plymouth 3 Oct. 1702; d. after 21 Dec. 1768.

She m. Plympton 28 July 1726 EBENEZER RAYMOND of Middleboro, b. there 18 Sept. 1703; d. there bef. 5 Dec. 1768; son of John and Martha (Woodin) Raymond.

Settlement of Ebenezer's estate, ordered 5 Dec. 1768, was made 21 Dec. 1768. Named in the settlement were: widow Mercy Raymond (the order gives her name as "Mercy," the settlement reads "Mary"); son Samuel; and daughter Mercy.

Children (RAYMOND), b. Middleboro:

i SAMUEL[5], b. 26 Dec. 1732; d. Middleboro 29 Nov. 1809 in 77th yr; m. (1) there 16 Sept. 1757 DINAH WOOD, b. there 27 Dec. 1731; d. there 25 March 1766 in 34th year; daughter of Jabez and Hannah (Nelson) Wood; m. (2) Plympton 17 March 1768 JOANNA (BRYANT) (DOTY) STETSON, b. there 12 July 1739; d. Middleboro 6 Nov. 1803 in 64th yr; daughter of Deacon Samuel and Tabitha (Ford) Bryant. Joanna m. (1) Plympton 1755 Solomon Doty; she m. (2) Plympton 1763 John Stetson of Halifax.

Eight (RAYMOND) ch. b. Middleboro, three by first wife, five by second wife: Hannah b. 1758, Lucy b. 1760, Noah b. 1762, Dinah b. 1768, Joanna b. 1770, Marcy b. 1772, Tabitha b. 1773, and Samuel b. 1775.

ii MERCY, b. 1 May 1739; unm. in Dec. 1768. In the settlement of her father's estate Mercy received a piece of land, 1/4 part of a grist mill and 8 acres of woodland.

References: MD 3:83; 12:131; 14:85, 245; 15:222; 18:155; 19:174; 20:37; 23:48; 32:4. VR PLYMPTON. MIDDLEBORO DEATHS. Plymouth Co. PR 20:328 1/2(Ebenezer Raymond).

16 JAMES[4] FULLER (Samuel[3-2-1]), b. Plymouth 27 Feb. 1704; d. Attleboro bef. 24 April 1769.

He m. (1) Plympton 19 May 1725 JUDITH RICKARD, b. there 2 Sept. 1705; d. there 23 Feb. 1725/6 in 21st year; daughter of Henry Rickard and his first wife Mary -----. James m. (2) Plympton 22 May 1729 MERCY (JACKSON) PERKINS, b. Plymouth 28 Nov. 1697; daughter of Eleazer and Hannah (prob. Ransom) Jackson; widow of John Perkins, by whom she had four children.

On 29 Oct. 1738 James Fuller, bloomer, purchased a parcel of land at the new forge in Dartmouth from Stephen West. James Fuller of Dartmouth, bloomer, made his will 24 Dec. 1767, and it was probated 24 April 1769, calling him "late of Attleboro." He mentioned his wife Mercy; son Thomas; son Elkanah "in case he be alive"; daughter Judah, wife of Thomas Hauth; daughter Hannah; granddaughter Olive; and a ch. of his granddaughter Olive taken in by Thomas Hauth. He gave to sons Elkanah and Thomas land in Plymouth given to him by his father, Samuel Fuller.

Children (FULLER), one by first wife, three by second wife:

i ELKANAH[5], b. Plympton 9 Feb. 1725/6. In 1728 he inherited land from his grandfather, Henry Rickard; on 14 April 1747 Elkanah, then resident in Dartmouth, sold this land; n.f.r.

ii THOMAS, living in Dec. 1767; m. Dartmouth 2 Sept. 1762 HANNAH WASTE (or West) of Dartmouth.

iii JUDITH (Judah), m. int. Dartmouth 1 Jan. 1757 THOMAS HORTH of Tiverton.

iv HANNAH, unm. in Dec. 1767

References: MD 3:123-4; 13:205. VR DARTMOUTH, PLYMPTON. Bristol Co. PR 20:545(James Fuller). Bristol

Co. LR 28:163(James Fuller). Plymouth Co. PR 5:398; 7:392 (John Perkins); 5:491(Henry Rickard). Plymouth Co. LR 38:190(Elkanah Fuller).

17 EBENEZER[4] FULLER (John[3], Samuel[2-1]), b. 1689 prob. Middleboro; d. Halifax 27 Nov. 1786 in his 98th year; bur. there in the Thompson St. Cemetery. (The Halifax VR incorrectly gives the date of his death as 12 Nov. 1794.)

Ebenezer m. about 1715, prob. Middleboro ELIZABETH SHORT, b. Weymouth 1 Nov. 1693; daughter of Luke Jr. and Susanna Short. Ebenezer and his wife were discharged from the Middleboro Church and became original members of the Halifax Church 16 Oct. 1734.

In Ebenezer's will dated 12 July 1785 and probated 4 Dec. 1786, he mentioned his grandson Chipman Fuller, son of his son Ebenezer, deceased; granddaughters Lydia Fuller, Priscilla Fuller and Lois (elsewhere called Eunice) Fuller, daughters of his son Ebenezer; granddaughters Asenath "Kimlims" [Killam?] and Susannah Wood, to whom he gave "besides what I gave their father, Nathan Fuller, a piece of land near what John Thompson gave to his daughter Elizabeth Fuller" (see 32); grandson James Bosworth; grandson Thaddeus Thompson, "besides what I have given my daughter Elizabeth Thompson." James Bosworth of Halifax was named executor.

Children (FULLER), b. Middleboro:

i SUSANNA[5], b. 7 Dec. 1716; not mentioned in her father's will.

ii RUTH, b. 18 April 1719; d. Halifax 24 Jan. 1743 in 23rd yr; bur. there; m. 6 Nov. 1741 Deacon JOSEPH BOSWORTH; d. Halifax 1 Aug. 1769 in 50th yr; son of Ichabod Bosworth and his second wife, Mary -----, and a descendant of John Howland. [See *The John Howland Family*.] Joseph Bosworth m. (2) Bridgewater 1744 Sarah Cobb, who d. 1804 ae. 83y.

One (BOSWORTH) ch. b. Halifax: James b. 1743.

iii EBENEZER, b. 18 Oct. 1721; d. Halifax 22 Dec. 1769 in 49th yr; m. (1) Halifax 6 Jan. 1746/7 LYDIA CHIPMAN, b. there 19 Dec. 1728; d. there 22 Aug. 1766 in 30th yr; daughter of Jacob and Bethia (Thomas) Chipman, and a descendant of John Howland. Ebenezer m. (2) Kingston 7 April 1768 his cousin DEBORAH (FULLER) EATON (see 19 i), b. Plympton 23 Nov. 1727; d. Kingston 25 July 1809 ae. 81; daughter of Jabez Fuller. [See *The Francis Eaton Family*.] Ebenezer's estate was divided 5 June 1772; his heirs were: his widow Deborah; only son Chipman; daughters Ruth, wife of Elijah Leach, Lydia Fuller, Priscilla Fuller and Eunice Fuller.

Six (FULLER) ch. by first wife bp. Halifax: Ruth bp. 1748, Lydia bp. 1749/50, Chipman bp. 1755, Priscilla bp. 1758, Eunice bp. 1760, and Ichabod bp. 1766, d.y.

iv NATHAN, b. 22 April 1725; d. Halifax 26 Jan. 1761 in 36th yr; m. Middleboro 19 Sept. 1749 MARY PARLOUR, b. there 16 April 1725; daughter of Thomas and Hannah (King) Parlour. Nathan Fuller, cordwainer, in his will dated 12 Nov. 1760, probated 6 April 1761, mentioned his wife Mary and his six children.

Six (FULLER) ch., four bp. Halifax: Hannah bp. 1750/1, Lusana (Lucy) bp. 1752, Noah bp. 1754, Asenath bp. 1756, Thomas, and Susanna.

v ELIZABETH, b. 5 Aug. 1729; d. after 12 July 1785; m. int. Halifax 2 March 1760 JOHN THOMPSON 2nd, b. Plympton 18 Feb. 1725; d. by freezing 18 Jan. 1777 when returning from Plymouth to Plympton; son of John and Elizabeth (Thomas) Thompson. Division of the estate of John Thompson 2nd, late of Halifax, 6 June 1785 mentions his six ch.: Susanna, Thaddeus, Nathan, Zaccheus, Elizabeth and Stephen.

Six (THOMPSON) ch., five bp. Halifax: Susanna bp. 1761, Eliphalet bp. 1763, Nathan bp. 1766, Zaccheus bp. 1768, Elizabeth bp. 1770*, and Stephen.

vi NOAH, b. 7 Sept. 1732; d. 22 April 1749 in 17th yr.

vii LOIS, b. 22 July 1740; bp. 27 July 1740; d.s.p. before 12 July 1785

References: MD 3:159; 4:72; 9:152-3; 12:231, 240; 13:3, 4, 11, 12; 26:177; 27:27, 180, 183. HALIFAX VR pp. 6, 33, 34, 41, 48, 49, 57, 60. VR BRIDGEWATER, KINGSTON, PLYMPTON, WEYMOUTH. MA MARR 2:75(for "Nathaniel" instead of Nathan). THOMSON (JOHN) DESC p. 38. Plymouth Co. PR 16:60(Nathan Fuller); 30:45(Ebenezer Fuller); 21:148(Ebenezer Fuller); 29:305(John Thompson).

18 JOHN[4] FULLER (John[3], Samuel[2-1]), b. Middleboro 20 March 1691/2; d. Halifax 24 April 1766 ae. 74.

He m. (1) Middleboro 26 March 1719 HANNAH THOMAS, b. there 22 Feb. 1684/5, d. Halifax 20 Sept. 1760 in 75th year; daughter of David Thomas and his first wife, Abigail Wood. John and Hannah were original members of the Hali-

---

*These baptismal dates conflict with birth dates given in THOMSON (JOHN) DESC p. 38.

fax Church 16 Oct. 1734. They are bur. together in the Thompson St. Cemetery, Halifax.

John m. (2) Halifax 27 April 1762 LYDIA (ALDEN) EDDY, b. Middleboro 18 Dec. 1710; d. 11 March 1803 ae. 93y 3m; daughter of John and Hannah (White) Alden, widow of Samuel Eddy Jr., and a descendant of John Alden.

A division of John Fuller's estate, ordered 8 Sept. 1766, mentions widow Lydia; daughters Hannah Fuller and Barsheba Ellis; and grandchildren Ephraim Fuller, Thomas Fuller and Abigail Fuller. (The grandchildren were ch. of his son John, deceased.)

Children (FULLER), by first wife, b. Middleboro:

i HANNAH[5], b. 7 Feb. 1719/20; d. 8 Nov. 1769 in 50th year; bur. Halifax; unm.

ii ABIGAIL, b. 1 July 1721; d. Middleboro 17 Oct. 1723

iii JOHN, b. 5 Sept. 1723; d. Halifax 2 Aug. 1747 in 24th year; bur. there; m. there 27 Dec. 1743 JOANNA TILLSON, b. Plympton 27 Feb. 1724/5; daughter of John Jr. and Joanna (Dunbar) Tillson. Joanna m. (2) Halifax 3 Jan. 1749 Joseph Waterman of Middleboro.

Three (FULLER) ch. b. Halifax: Ephraim b. 1744, Thomas b. 1746, and Abigail b. 1747.

iv BATHSHEBA, b. 19 Jan. 1725/6; m. Middleboro 13 Dec. 1756 Ensign CHARLES ELLIS, b. there 19 June 1726; d. after 1800; son of Capt. Joel and Elizabeth (Churchill) Ellis. They moved to Woodstock VT.

Five (ELLIS) ch. b. Middleboro: Charles b. 1760, Bathsheba b. 1762, Nathaniel b. 1764, Hannah b. 1766, and Zaccheus b. 1768.

References: MD 2:201; 4:71; 12:231; 13:12; 18:156; 24:58; 26:177; 27:122. HALIFAX VR pp. 31, 33, 49, 50. MIDDLEBORO DEATHS. VR PLYMPTON. MA MARR 2:108. NEHGR 120:284. Plymouth Co. PR 19:458(John Fuller). WOODSTOCK VT BY DANA p.83.

19 JABEZ[4] FULLER (John[3], Samuel[2-1]), b. about 1698 prob. Middleboro; d. Plympton 11 or 14 Oct. 1728 in 31st year.

He m. (1) Plympton 12 Nov. 1724 DEBORAH SOULE, b. Plymouth 23 April 1702; daughter of Benjamin and Sarah (Standish) Soule, and a descendant of Pilgrims Soule, Alden and Standish. Deborah had stillborn twins in Plymouth 24 Jan. 1724/5 and d. the same day.

Jabez m. (2) Plympton 12 Jan. 1726/7 PRISCILLA SAMSON, b. Plymouth 12 Nov. 1700; living 20 March 1733/4; daughter of Isaac and Lydia (Standish) Samson, and a descendant of Pilgrim John Alden. [See *The Myles Standish Family*.] This is not a Mayflower Samson line.

Jabez' brother, Ebenezer, was appointed administrator of Jabez' estate 30 April 1729; inventory was ordered the same day and the widow Priscilla was mentioned. Five years later (20 March 1733/4) she was still a widow when the estate of her brother Josiah Samson was probated.

Child (FULLER), by second wife, b. Plympton:

i DEBORAH[5], b. 23 Nov. 1727; d. Kingston 25 July or 1 Aug. 1809 ae. 81; m. int. (1) Kingston 24 Dec. 1743 DAVID EATON, d. there 8 July 1759 in 51st year; son of Benjamin and Mary (Coombs) Eaton. [See *The Francis Eaton Family*.] Deborah m. (2) Kingston 7 April 1768 her cousin EBENEZER FULLER of Halifax (see 17 iii).
Six (EATON) ch. b. Kingston: Lot b. 1744, Jabez b. 1746, Job b. 1749, Consider b. 1752, Joshua b. 1755, and Eunice b. 1759.

References: MD 3:123; 23:161-164; 25:73. VR KINGSTON, PLYMPTON. MIDDLEBORO DEATHS. Plymouth Co. PR 5:499, 501(Jabez Fuller).

20 JOANNA[4] FULLER (John[3], Samuel[2-1]), b. ca. 1701 prob. Middleboro; d. Middleboro 9 Sept. 1771 ae. 70.

She m. Marshfield 11 Dec. 1728 THOMAS DOGGETT JR., b. there in 1706; d. Middleboro 11 Aug. 1788 ae. 82y 12d; son of Thomas and Experience (Ford) Doggett. Joanna and her husband are bur. in the Nemasket Hill Cemetery.

Thomas Doggett and his wife Joanna sold their homestead in Marshfield in March 1741. They purchased a homestead in Middleboro in May 1741 and moved there soon afterward.

Thomas Doggett of Middleboro, yeoman, in his will dated 13 Aug. 1785, probated 6 Oct. 1788, mentioned his sons Seth (executor), Jabez, and Simeon; daughters Experience Doggett and Joanna Peirce, wife of William Peirce of Taunton; and six grandchildren, William, Ephraim, Joanna, Samuel, Benajah, and Experience, ch. of William and Joanna Peirce, their shares to be given them "as they came to lawful age."

Children (DOGGETT), b. Marshfield:

i JOHN[5], b. in 1729; bp. 11 Oct. 1731; d. Middleboro 19 May 1759 ae. 29; unm.
ii THOMAS, b. in 1731; bp. 11 Oct. 1731; d.y.
iii MARK, b. in 1733; d.y.
iv JABEZ, b. 3 March 1734; d. Middleboro 17 Dec. 1816 in 83rd year; bur. Nemasket Hill Cemetery; m. (1) Plymouth 24 Jan. 1760 REBECCA RICH, b.

there 9 July 1739; d. Middleboro 1 June 1781 in 42nd year; daughter of Walter and Rebecca (Morton) Rich of Plymouth; m. (2) Middleboro 20 Oct. 1783 JAEL CASWELL, d. there 16 Nov. 1805 in 71st year; m. (3) Middleboro 25 May 1807 SARAH CASWELL. Jabez was wounded at Ticonderoga 8 July 1758 while serving in the French and Indian War under Capt. Benjamin Pratt of Middleboro.

Eight (DOGGETT) ch. by first wife, b. Middleboro: John b. 1761, Nathaniel b. 1763, Susanna (Lurana) b. 1765, Jabez b. 1766, Mark b. 1768, Rebecca b. 1770, Joanna b. 1772, and Perez b. 1776.

v SETH, b. 15 Feb. 1736; d. Middleboro 19 Aug. 1816; unm. In his will, dated 19 July 1813 and probated 16 Nov. 1816, he left a wood lot to Daniel Macomber, his executor; he mentioned his sister Experience Doggett, brother Simeon Doggett, niece Experience Peirce and Mark Doggett [nephew?].

vi SIMEON, b. 4 Jan. 1738; d. Middleboro 13 May 1823 ae. 86; m. there 28 Feb. 1760 ABIGAIL PRATT, b. North Carolina; daughter of David Pratt. Simeon was a farmer and carpenter, or "joyner." He served in the French and Indian War with his brother Jabez and was at Ticonderoga in 1758. During the Revolution he was a Tory and was restricted to the limits of his farm. His will, dated 2 April 1818 and probated 1 July 1823, mentioned sons Thomas, Simeon, and Elkanah (dec.); daughter Abigail, wife of Thomas Weston; and grandson Elkanah Doggett.

Four (DOGGETT) ch. b. Middleboro: Thomas b. 1761, Elkanah b. 1762, Simeon b. 1765, and Abigail b. 1775.

vii EXPERIENCE, b. 16 May 1740; d. Middleboro 9 May 1825 ae. 85; unm.

viii JOANNA, b. 16 March 1742; d. after 24 Jan. 1788; m. Middleboro 13 Sept. 1764 WILLIAM PEIRCE of Taunton; son of Samuel Peirce; William d. after 24 Jan. 1788, when he and his wife sold their homestead to their son William Jr. of Middleboro.

Six, pos. seven (PEIRCE) ch. b. Middleboro: William, Ephraim, Joanna, Samuel, Benajah, Experience; and pos. Abigail.

References: MD 5:237; 15:3, 41; 19:175; 22:152; 24:56; 31:170; 32:13, 14, 16, 17. MARSHFIELD VR pp. 146, 176-7. MIDDLEBORO DEATHS. GEN ADVERTISER 1:106. MA MARR 2:18. DOGGETT FAM pp. 377-378, 397, 398. Plymouth Co. PR 30:456(Thomas Doggett); 48:230(Seth Doggett); 57:116(Simeon Doggett). Plymouth Co. LR 34:93, 123(Thomas

Doggett). Bristol Co. LR 69:373(William Peirce).

21 SAMUEL$^{4}$ FULLER (John$^{3}$, Samuel$^{2-1}$), b. about 1703 prob. in Middleboro; d. bef. 27 March 1775.

He m. Middleboro 14 Nov. 1726 SILENCE SHORT, b. there 6 Feb. 1703/4; d. there 23 July 1786 ae. 83y 6m; daughter of Luke Short.

On 27 March 1775 widow Silence Fuller sold the estate given her by her brother William. Concurring in the sale were her heirs: Samuel Pratt and his wife Sarah; Mercy Potter; William Fuller; and Simeon Fuller, all of Middleboro. The deed was signed by Silence, Mercy Potter, William Fuller and Simeon Fuller, and acknowledged by Silence Fuller and Mercy Potter on 25 April 1776.

Children (FULLER), b. or bp. Middleboro:

i SAMUEL$^{5}$, bp. 10 Aug. 1729; m. DEBORAH -----.
Four (FULLER) ch.: Jabez, William, Silence, and Versalla.

ii SARAH, bp. 13 Dec. 1730; d. Middleboro 29 Nov. 1794 ae. 64; m. about 1751 SAMUEL PRATT, b. Plympton 26 Nov. 1715; d. Middleboro 20 April 1794 ae. 78; son of Daniel and Martha Pratt.

iii JABEZ, bp. 10 May 1733. Was he the Jabez Fuller who d. Middleboro 31 Jan. 1770?

iv MERCY, b. 3 Feb. 1737; living in April 1776; m. Jan. 1767 BENJAMIN POTTER ("Pattey, a transient person," in Middleboro rec.). No ch. rec. Middleboro.

v WILLIAM, b. 16 March 1739; may have d. Middleboro bef. June 1791; m. there 14 Jan. 1762 DEBORAH RIDER, b. Plymouth 18 Aug. 1741; daughter of Samuel and Mary (Silvester) Rider, and a descendant of Richard Warren. On 11 June 1770 William and Deborah sold their one-ninth part of a cedar swamp that belonged to their father Samuel Rider, late of Middleboro. William Fuller served in the Revolution as private: He marched to Marshfield on the alarm of 19 April 1775, had later enlistments, and was discharged from the last 10 Jan. 1778.
One (FULLER) ch., pos. others: Samuel b. Middleboro 1762; pos. William over 14y on 6 June 1791; still others?

vi SIMEON, b. 13 Sept. 1741; d. after 1775. On the record of his mother's deed, there is a notation, entered 15 April 1795, that Ebenezer Wood, a witness to the deed, "saw Simeon Fuller, who has absented himself for a number of years and supposed to be dead," sign the deed.

References: MD 2:24; 5:39; 15:38; 16:136; 19:142. VR PLYMPTON. MIDDLEBORO DEATHS. FULLER GEN 2:135. Middleboro TR. MSSR 6:193. Plymouth Co. LR 67:91 (Samuel Rider); 75:205(Silence Fuller).

22 LYDIA WOOD$^4$ (Experience$^3$ Fuller, Samuel$^{2-1}$), b. ca. 1694, prob. Middleboro; d. after 11 Feb. 1746.

She m. Plymouth 5 Feb. 1718/9 GEORGE HOLMES b. ca. 1690; d. Plymouth in 1746; son of John and Patience (Faunce) Holmes. George was a minor in 1700 (probably the youngest of several minor children) when his mother signed for him in the settlement of his father's estate. He was a cordwainer.

George Holmes in his will dated 11 Feb. 1746, probated 5 March 1746, mentioned his wife Lydia and his son George.

Children (HOLMES), b. Plymouth:

i GEORGE$^5$, b. 20 Jan. 1720/1; d. Plymouth bef. 5 April 1760; m. there 21 April 1741 LYDIA WEST, b. there 15 June 1725; d. after 8 Jan. 1768; daughter of Judah and Bethia (Keen) West, and a descendant of Richard Warren. On 8 Jan. 1768 Lydia acknowledged in Plymouth a deed of 10 March 1765 to her son George, disposing of her right of dower in a dwelling house and land.
Four, pos. five (HOLMES) ch., b. Plymouth: Lydia d.y., George b. 1742, Lydia d.y., Richard b. 1745; and pos. Bethia b. ca. 1746.

ii RICHARD, b. 22 Feb. 1723/4; d. bef. his father.

References: MD 13:111, 113; 14:38, 159; 15:161. Plymouth Co. PR 1:347; 10:361; 15:476; 16:287(George Holmes). Plymouth Co. LR 54:16(Lydia Holmes). (PLYMOUTH) ANC LANDMARKS p. 139.

23 JONATHAN WOOD$^4$ (Experience$^3$ Fuller, Samuel$^{2-1}$), b. about 1697 prob. Middleboro; d. Bridgewater 14 Nov. 1761.

He m. Middleboro 13 Jan. 1725/6 PERSIS ROBBINS of Plympton, b. Plymouth 27 Nov. 1699; d. after 15 Oct. 1761; daughter of Jeduthan and Hannah (Pratt) Robbins. Jonathan and Persis were mentioned as heirs in the settlement of the estate of her father, Jeduthan Robbins, 27 May 1726.

On 15 Oct. 1761 Jonathan and Persis, then of Bridgewater, made a deed of gift to their son James. In Jan. 1759 and again in Oct. 1761 they made deeds of gift to their son Jedediah.

Children (WOOD), b. Middleboro:

i JONATHAN[5], b. 13 Feb. 1726/7
ii JEDEDIAH, b. 25 May 1728; d. Macedon NY; m. Middleboro 26 Sept. 1752 KEZIA SAMSON of Middleboro; daughter of Seth and Ruth (Barrows) Samson. This is not a Henry Samson line. Jedediah Wood, cordwainer, with his wife Kezia giving up her dower, sold his homestead in Bridgewater 3 April 1775.
Six (WOOD) ch., first three b. Middleboro: Hannah b. 1753, Levi b. 1754, Lucy b. 1756, Seth b. 1758, Kezia, and Ruth.
iii ELIZABETH, b. 9 April 1730
iv JAMES, b. 12 March 1731/2; d. in 1793; m. Bridgewater 6 June 1764 ACHSAH PHINNEY, b. Plympton 28 May 1738; d. Moorefield OH; daughter of Joseph Jr. and Mary (Rickard) Phinney, and a descendant of Thomas Rogers. James Wood of Middleboro, laborer, and Achsah sold land with dwelling house in Middleboro 5 Feb. 1770. James served in the Revolution from Middleboro in 1779.
Eight (WOOD) ch.: Ichabod, Solomon, Sylvanus, Enos, Jonathan, Mary, Benjamin, and Joseph.

References: MD 2:164; 7:242; 8:250; 9:48; 18:158; 23:70. VR BRIDGEWATER, PLYMPTON. DAR PATRIOT INDEX. Plymouth Co. PR 5:148(Jeduthan Robbins); 20:372(Kezia Samson). Plymouth Co. LR 47:167, 168(James Wood); 55:160 (James Wood); 58:177(Jedediah Wood). WOOD FAM INDEX. WOOD (LEVI) DESC pp. 56, 58. MSSR 17:744.

24 JAMES WOOD[4] (Experience[3] Fuller, Samuel[2-1]), b. about 1699 prob. in Middleboro; living 13 Feb. 1772.

He m. Plymouth 21 Jan. 1735/6 DEBORAH (BARDEN) FISH of Plymouth, widow of Lemuel Fish. The int. of m. was protested 15 Jan. 1735/6 by George Holmes in the belief that Deborah's husband was still living, but the marriage took place six days later.

By a deed of gift, dated 5 May 1721, James and Experience Wood gave to their son James Wood, Jr. 45 acres in Middleboro. James Wood, laborer, signed a receipt dated 14 March 1729/30 for his "full part or portion in the estate of [his] father James Wood." He sold to Phineas Swift on 13 Feb. 1772 the "house I now dwell in and house lot and orchard...in Plymouth near the cliffs." The latter deed was acknowledged in Barnstable.

References: MD 16:254; 17:137; 18:231. Plymouth Co. LR 37:159; 55:264; 56:86(James Wood).

25 BARNABAS WOOD$^4$ (Experience$^3$ Fuller, Samuel$^{2-1}$), b. about 1701 prob. Middleboro; d. there shortly bef. 18 Dec. 1730, on which date Deacon Ephraim Wood was appointed administrator of his estate.

He m. Plympton 30 March 1726 HANNAH ROBBINS, b. Plymouth in April 1702; d. in 1734; daughter of Jeduthan and Hannah (Pratt) Robbins. Hannah Wood's brother Jeduthan Robbins was appointed administrator of her estate 20 Sept. 1734.

Barnabas Wood was a blacksmith. In the settlement of his father's estate, a paper dated 15 March 1736 reads "to the children of Barnabas Wood, late of Middleboro, deceased, who was one of the sons, £15 10s., which is their share of the estate." These children were Lydia, Rebecca and Experience. When Joseph Lucas of Plympton was appointed their guardian 5 Oct. 1736, they were all under fourteen years of age.

Children (WOOD), b. prob. in Middleboro:

i LYDIA$^5$, about 1726-7 (called Lydia Jr. at time of marriage); d. bef. 21 Dec. 1749; m. Middleboro 23 Jan. 1745 BENJAMIN SHELLY JR. of Raynham, b. Taunton 27 Sept. 1720; d. bef. 7 Sept. 1779; son of Benjamin and Alice (Goodspeed) Shelly. He m. (2) Bridgewater 21 Dec. 1749 Mary Turner. Benjamin Shelly of Raynham, yeoman, in his will dated 25 June 1778, probated 7 Sept. 1779, mentioned his wife Mary and heirs of his son Barnabas, deceased. The name of the child helps identify Lydia as daughter of Barnabas Wood.
One (SHELLY) ch.: Barnabas b. ca. 1746.

ii REBECCA, b. about 1727-8. She may have been the Rebecca Wood who m. about 1745-6 NATHANIEL COBB, and d. Carver 10 Nov. 1763 ae. 36. They had seven children.

iii EXPERIENCE, b. about 1729-30; bp. 10 May 1730; d. Raynham 8 July 1755; m. there about 1748 EBENEZER HACKETT of Raynham, b. there; d. Middleboro after 1790; son of Samuel Hackett. Ebenezer m. (2) Middleboro in 1757 Abigail Thomas of Middleboro, and m. (3) Middleboro in 1764 Betty Canedy of Middleboro. Ebenezer sold his land and dwelling house in Raynham 1 Jan. 1760. He is listed in the 1790 census in Middleboro with three males over 16 and three females in his family. No children of Experience have been found.

References: MD 2:164; 18:79; 19:174; 24:131. VR BRIDGEWATER, CARVER, PLYMPTON. Raynham VR 1:31. TAG 24:187-192. Bristol Co. PR 26:123(Benjamin Shelly).

Bristol Co. LR 46:264(Ebenezer Hackett). Plymouth Co. PR 5:805(Barnabas Wood); 7:231(Barnabas Wood); 7:54(Hannah Wood). WOOD FAM INDEX. 1790 CENSUS MA:172.

26 BENJAMIN WOOD[4] (Experience[3] Fuller, Samuel[2-1]), b. about 1703 prob. Middleboro; d. Sharon CT 16 Dec. 1760 in his 58th year.

He m. Middleboro 12 April 1733 PRISCILLA RICKARD, b. Plympton 21 Jan. 1709/10; living Sharon CT 25 March 1761; daughter of Joseph and Deborah (Miller) Rickard.

Benjamin was a house carpenter. He was of Plympton in 1729, removed about 1743 to Ashford CT, and later to Sharon. On 5 April 1744 Benjamin and Priscilla Wood, then of Ashford, sold their homestead, lying partly in Middleboro and partly in Plympton, to Robert Maxfield of Plympton. Priscilla was named administratrix of her husband's estate in Sharon 25 March 1761.

Children (WOOD), first four b. Middleboro, others b. Ashford CT:

i SAMUEL[5], b. 6 Jan. 1733/4; m. AZUBAH -----.
Two (WOOD) ch. b. Lee: Christian b. 1775, and Azubah b. 1777.

ii BARNABAS, b. 26 July 1735; d. 1808-10; m. (1) 12 Nov. 1761 SYBIL (or Sibillah) DARBEE, b. Pomfret CT 3 Jan. 1743/4; d. there 25 July 1762; daughter of Reuben and Sybil (Howard) Darbee; m. (2) 20 Oct. 1763 MARY ALWORTH, both being of Pomfret. Barnabas served in the Revolution as a minuteman "from New York."
Nine (WOOD) ch., first three b. Pomfret CT: Benjamin b. 1762, William b. 1764, Sibillah b. 1766, Barnabas, Urana, Ichabod, Parley, Erastus, and Augustus.

iii BENJAMIN, b. 6 July 1737; d. in 1820; m. Sharon CT 20 Aug. 1770 RUTH HOPKINS, both being of "Nine Partners," now Amenia NY.
Four (WOOD) ch.: Bedar b. 1770-71, Abner b. 1773, Benjamin b. 1775-6, Barnabas b. 1778.

iv PRISCILLA, b. 1 July 1739; d. Windham CT 20 Dec. 1833 ae. 92; m. Sharon CT 28 Feb. 1762 JOHN WARNER of Windham, b. Lebanon CT 22 May 1734; d. 7 June 1773 ae. 39; bur. Scotland CT; son of Ichabod and Mary (Metcalf) Warner.
Five (WARNER) ch.: Timothy b. 1763, Mary b. 1765, William b. 1768, Ichabod b. 1769, and Rosamond b. 1773.

v JOSEPH, b. 15 Aug. 1743; n.f.r.

vi EXPERIENCE, b. 30 April 1745; m. 27 Aug. 1767 PAUL JOHNSON. Res. in Amenia NY.

vii DEBORAH, b. 19 Dec. 1746; m. 23 Oct. 1765 ABNER SHEVALIER, b. Canterbury CT 22 July 1747.

viii NOAH, b. 3 Dec. 1749; m. MARY WIXON; she d. 8 Oct. 1853 ae. 95.

Three (WOOD) ch.: Rhoda b. 1780, Jemima, and Deborah.

ix SARAH, b. 2 May 1752; m. Pomfret CT 12 Aug. 1773, NEHEMIAH DODGE.

References: MD 6:127; 13:250; 14:245. VR LEE, PLYMPTON. Sharon CT PR 3496(Priscilla Wood). Plymouth Co. LR 36:172(Benjamin Wood). DAR PATRIOT INDEX. CSL Ch Rec: Hampton. WARNER (ANDREW) DESC pp. 138-139. CSL Barbour Index:Ashford, Canterbury, Pomfret, Sharon. WOOD FAM INDEX pp. 56, 58.

27 ABEL WOOD[4] (Experience[3] Fuller, Samuel[2-1]), b. ca. 1706 prob. Middleboro; d. Sharon CT 20 Jan. 1793 ae. 86. He and wife Thankful are bur. Sharon.

He m. Rochester 26 March 1736 THANKFUL LANDERS, b. there 21 July 1713; d. Sharon 16 Dec. 1760 in 46th year; daughter of Joseph and Deborah (Doty) Landers. In 1729 Abel res. in Plymouth, later in Wareham, from whence he removed in 1748 to Sharon CT.

Children (WOOD), first three b. MA, others Sharon CT:

i ELIJAH[5], b. Rochester 23 Dec. 1736; d. Salisbury CT about 1829; m. Sharon CT 15 Nov. 1764 RACHEL HURLBUT. His will made 11 Aug. 1824, probated 17 Sept. 1829, mentions sons Elijah, Abel and William; ch. of his daughters Sally and Polly; daughters Rachel and Elizabeth; and granddaughter Eunice Wood.

Eight (WOOD) ch.: Ebenezer b. Sharon CT 1767 d.s.p., Rachel, Elizabeth, Sarah, Abel, Mary (or Polly) b. 1773, William b. 1784, and Elijah.

ii EPHRAIM, b. 6 July 1740; d. 29 March 1813 pos. Bennington VT; m. 18 April 1771 RUTH PALMER of Amenia NY, d. 20 Dec. 1825 ae. 75 pos. Bennington VT.

Nine (WOOD) ch.: Isaac b. 1772, Billy b. 1774, Ephraim b. 1776, Barnabas b. 1781, Roxy b. 1785, Ira b. 1788, Silas b. 1790, Anson b. 1793, and Lillis.

iii BARNABAS, b. 20 Feb. 1743; d. Sharon CT 24 June 1820 ae. 77; m. (1) MIRIAM -----, d. Sharon 9 Nov. 1799 ae. 65; m. (2) RUTH -----, d. 10 May 1813; m. (3) Sharon in 1814 RACHEL -----. His will made 8 June 1820 mentioned wife Rachel and no other heirs.

iv DEBORAH, b. 1 March 1745; d. 14 Sept. 1745
v THANKFUL, b. 10 Sept. 1748; n.f.r.
vi MARY, b. 10 Sept. 1753; d. 16 Dec. 1760 in 8th yr.
vii LYDIA, b. 9 April 1756; d. 16 Oct. 1756
viii PHEBE, b. 11 April 1759; n.f.r.

References: VR ROCHESTER MA, SHARON CT. CSL Ch Recs: Sharon. CSL Hale Cem Recs:Sharon. Sharon CT PR 3495(Barnabas Wood); 3498(Elijah Wood). NEHGR 124:60. WOOD FAM INDEX.

28 ICHABOD WOOD[4] (Experience[3] Fuller, Samuel[2-1]), b. about 1709 prob. Middleboro; d. Richmond 12 Dec. 1798 ae. 89; bur. there in the old Center Cemetery.

He m. (1) Rehoboth 13 June 1737 CHRISTIAN WHEATON, d. there 17 June 1745; daughter of James and Mary (Shaw) Wheaton, mentioned by James Wheaton in his will of 4 Sept. 1740.

He m. (2) Rehoboth 14 Jan. 1745/6 REBECCA WOOD, b. there 23 April 1717; d. Richmond 10 Feb. 1808 ae. 92; daughter of George and Rebecca (Daggett) Wood.

Ichabod sold his property in Rehoboth 25 Jan. 1758 and probably removed to Richmond (or its predecessor town) about that time. He was a cordwainer. He made his will in Richmond 22 May 1794, mentioning his wife Rebecca; sons James, Comfort and Gideon; daughters Sybil, Joanna and Sarah. He named his daughter Sarah Wood as executrix. The estate was finally settled 3 Nov. 1807.

Children (WOOD), b. Rehoboth, five by first wife and five by second:

i ICHABOD[5], b. 1 Jan. 1737/8; d. Rehoboth 22 March 1738/9

ii JAMES, b. 1 Nov. 1739; d. bet. 22 May 1794 and 3 Nov. 1807 (settlement of his father's estate); m. Rehoboth 27 Sept. 1764 MOLLY CARPENTER, prob. the one b. there 5 Feb. 1736/37; daughter of Ebenezer and Susanna (Perrin) Carpenter. James' children are named in the probate records of his father, Ichabod.

Six (WOOD) ch.: Jonas, Ichabod, Sarah, Mary (or Polly) wife of Zachariah Comstock, Susanna wife of David Stevens, and Christina wife of Ethan Bradley.

iii LYDIA, b. 27 Aug. 1741; d.s.p. bef. May 1794

iv COMFORT, b. 14 Oct. 1743; d. Richmond 14 March 1816 ae. 72; m. HULDAH -----; d. Richmond 2 Aug. 1813 ae. 66. He was a sergeant and later a lieutenant in the Revolution; Richmond records refer to him as "Col."

Two (WOOD) ch. b. Richmond: Dennis b. 1771, and Clarinda b. 1779.

v GIDEON, b. 24 Feb. 1744/5; d. Otsego Co. NY in Nov. 1822; m. (1) Sharon CT 10 July 1768 "he of Richmond" ELEANOR HEATH, b. Sharon CT 14 July 1743; daughter of Bartholomew and Mehitable (Crippen) Heath, and a descendant of Edward Fuller. He m. (2) in Dec. 1784 MARY (SPENCER) KNEELAND, d. 19 Dec. 1839 ae. 90; daughter of Jeremiah and Abigail (Burr) Spencer, and widow of Jonathan Kneeland. Gideon removed to Otsego Co. NY after 1790, and was a goldsmith in Cooperstown NY. He was a drummer in a company of minutemen in the Revolution.

Six, prob. seven, (WOOD) ch., one by first wife; five (prob. six) by second wife: Silas b. 1774, Heath b. 1788, Jonathan, Mary, Lucy, Sabina, and prob. Jabez.

vi MARY, b. 30 Oct. 1746; d. Rehoboth 1 April 1749

vii SYBIL, b. 18 Dec. 1748; d. Richmond 12 May 1809 in 60th yr; m. THOMAS SCOTT, d. Richmond 18 Nov. 1815 ae. 69.

viii ICHABOD, b. 16 Feb. 1751; d. Richmond 22 Oct. 1764 ae. 14.

ix JOANNA, b. 26 Aug. 1754; d. Virgil NY 13 Sept. 1830 ae. 76y 17d; m. Richmond 9 May 1773 JONATHAN SKEEL JR., b. Kent CT 5 Nov. 1749; d. Virgil NY 20 July 1834 ae. 84y 9m; son of Jonathan and Abigail (Slosson) Skeel. He served in the Revolution as a private and a corporal.

One (SKEEL) ch.: Lucinda b. 1774; prob. others.

x SARAH, b. 24 Feb. 1756; d.s.p. bet. 22 May 1794 and 3 Nov. 1807.

References: VR RICHMOND MA, SHARON CT. REHOBOTH VR pp. 88, 89, 408, 409, 784, 891. Berkshire Co. PR 1967(Ichabod Wood). Bristol Co. PR 10:242(James Wheaton). Bristol Co. LR 43:93(Ichabod Wood). MSSR 14:267; 17:721, 738. CSL Ch Rec:Kent & Sharon. CARPENTER (REHOBOTH) GEN pp. 80, 140. DAR PATRIOT INDEX. WOOD FAM INDEX. Richmond Center Cem G.S. Records of Cortland Co. NY, Revolutionary Soldiers, p. 104 [MS. coll. at NYGB Society].

29 HANNAH LEWIS$^{4}$ (Hannah$^{3}$ Fuller, Samuel$^{2-1}$), b. in 1703 prob. Middleboro; d. Bridgewater 10 Feb. 1793 ae. 89y 7m.

She m. ca. 1727 THOMAS SNELL, b. Bridgewater in 1696; d. East Bridgewater 28 July 1772 ae. 76; son of Thomas Snell and his first wife, name unknown.

Children (SNELL), b. Bridgewater:

i DELIVERANCE[5], b. 18 Dec. 1727; d. East Bridgewater 4 April 1814 ae. 86; m. East Bridgewater 19 March 1767 NATHANIEL CHAMBERLAIN, b. Pembroke 24 Sept. 1722; d. East Bridgewater 26 or 27 March 1814 ae. 91; son of Freedom and Mary (Soule) Chamberlain. [See *The George Soule Family*.] Nathaniel m. (1) Sarah -----, who d. East Bridgewater 1765. Nathaniel's will, written in 1784 and probated in 1814, does not mention a daughter Deliverance.
One (CHAMBERLAIN) ch.: Deliverance bp. 1768, d. 1771.

ii THOMAS, b. 25 June 1730; bp. 21 May 1732; d. ME after 1790; m. (1) Bridgewater 30 Oct. 1755 BETHIA ALLEN, bp. East Bridgewater 13 April 1740; d. Woolwich ME in Dec. 1783; daughter of James and Bethia (Kingman) Allen; m. (2) LYDIA SLOWMAN, a widow; d. 12 Aug. 1787; m. (3) 15 Sept. 1790 SUSANNA HUTCHINSON; d. 13 Dec. 1816. Thomas Snell sold his dwelling house and land in Bridgewater 2 July 1765 to Polycarpus Snell.
Twelve (SNELL) ch., eleven by first wife, one by second wife; first three b. Bridgewater; fourth b. Georgetown ME: Rebecca b. 1756, Abigail b. 1758, Eleazer b. 1760, Hannah b. 1762, d. 1786, James b. 1764, Asa b. 1766, Barnabas b. 1768, Bethia b. 1771, Susanna b. 1773, Thomas b. 1775, Joseph L. b. 1780, and Mary b. 1787.

iii ELEAZER, b. 3 April 1732; rem. to NY; had a family.

iv JOSEPH, bp. 9 June 1734; d.s.p.

v HANNAH, b. 25 Sept. 1735; d. East Bridgewater 6 Sept. 1828 ae. 93; m. Bridgewater 23 Sept. 1756 BENJAMIN CHAMBERLAIN of Pembroke, b. there 7 Sept. 1724; d. East Bridgewater 27 March 1803 ae. 78; son of Freedom and Mary (Soule) Chamberlain. [See *The George Soule Family*.] He served in the Revolution as a private and a corporal. His will made 10 Feb. 1801, probated 5 April 1803, mentions wife Hannah; sons Lewis, Benjamin, Aaron, Arza; daughters Hannah (wife of James Lamberton), "Salvina," Chloe and Deliverance.
Eight (CHAMBERLAIN) ch., first seven b. Pembroke, last b. Bridgewater: Sylvina b. 1757, Lewis b. 1758, Hannah b. 1760, Benjamin b. 1762, Aaron b. 1765, Chloe b. 1767, Deliverance b. 1773, and Arza b. 1780.

vi POLYCARPUS, b. 24 Sept. 1737; d. East Bridgewater 29 or 30 Oct. 1806 ae. 69; m. Bridgewater 27 Nov. 1766 SUSANNA SHAW, b. there 27 April 1744; d.

East Bridgewater 2 Sept. 1817 ae. 73; daughter of Ebenezer and Mary (Read) Shaw. His will made 25 Aug. 1806, probated 1 Dec. 1806, mentions wife Susanna; sons Stephen, Lewis, Thomas and Samuel; daughters Hannah Snell and Susanna Snell.

Eight (SNELL) ch. b. Bridgewater: Lewis b. 1767, Stephen b. 1769, Thomas b. 1772, Cyrus b. 1774, Ebenezer b. 1776, Hannah b. 1779, Samuel b. 1781, and Susanna b. 1785.

vii WILLIAM, b. 2 Nov. 1740; prob. d. Tamworth NH; m. Bridgewater 1 Nov. 1774 ABIGAIL ALDEN, b. there 23 Aug. 1756; daughter of Eleazer and Sarah (Whitman) Alden, and a descendant of John Alden. William and Abigail sold their property in Bridgewater in 1786 to his brothers Barnabas and Polycarpus. Mitchell stated in 1840 that William Snell Esq. had four sons, rem. to Ware, then to Tamworth NH, and had two more sons. William is listed in the 1790 census in Ware with two males 16 or over, five males under 16, and one female in his family. He was a soldier in the French and Indian War, and lost the use of one leg.

Seven (SNELL) ch., first b. Bridgewater, first four bp. East Bridgewater: William b. 1776, bp. 1777, Seth bp. 1778, Smyrdus bp. 1780, Eleazer bp. 1784, Alden, Martin, and Thayer.

viii BARNABAS, b. 29 March 1743; d. East Bridgewater 5 Oct. 1816 ae. 75; m. (1) Halifax 25 May 1781 HANNAH HOLMES of Halifax; m. (2) Bridgewater 1 Jan. 1783 EUNICE CONANT, b. there 21 Aug. 1743; d. East Bridgewater 31 July 1795 ae. 52; daughter of Gershom and Anne (Kingman) Conant. Gershom Conant's will, made 22 Dec. 1785 and probated 6 Aug. 1792, mentions daughter Eunice Snell and her heirs. Barnabas had several periods of service in the Revolution from 1775 to 1780 as a fifer, a matross and a private. On 8 Jan. 1788 Barnabas of Pembroke sold his part of the farm in Bridgewater that he had purchased from his brother William in 1786.

One (SNELL) ch., pos. others, by second wife, b. Bridgewater: Anna b. 1785.

ix LEWIS, bp. 28 July 1745; d.s.p.

x SETH, b. 8 Aug. 1747; d. Warren RI 4 March 1823 in 77th yr.; m. HANNAH -----. He was a justice of the peace for 30 years and inspector of Customs for the Port of Warren for 16 years.

Twelve (SNELL) ch. b. Warren RI: Ruth b. 1772, William b. 1774, Hannah b. 1776, Nathan b. 1778, Mary Carr b. 1780, Seth b. 1782, Abigail b. 1784, Philip b. 1787, Thomas b. 1789, Caleb b. 1791, Deliverance b. 1793, and Betsey b. 1797.

References: MD 7:52. VR BRIDGEWATER, EAST BRIDGEWATER, PEMBROKE. RI VR 6:Warren p. 91; 23:34. Plymouth Co. PR 33:136(Gershom Conant); 38:292(Benjamin Chamberlain); 40:535(Polycarpus Snell); 45:334(Nathaniel Chamberlain). Plymouth Co. LR 52:3(Thomas Snell); 65:161 (William Snell); 113:218(Barnabas Snell). MSSR 3:262; 14:589. ALDEN MEM p. 48. BRIDGEWATER BY MITCHELL p. 297. WOOLWICH ME RECS p. 29, 30.

30 SHUBAEL LEWIS[4] (Hannah[3] Fuller, Samuel[2-1]), b. prob. Middleboro ca. 1707 (he was over 21 in 1730); d. bef. 5 Feb. 1755.

He m. Plympton 14 March 1733/4 HAZADIAH EDDY of Plympton, b. there 20 March 1711/2; daughter of Jabez and Mary (-----) Eddy. She m. (2) Middleboro 12 Feb. 1755 John Cole Jr. of Plympton.

When the estate of Shubael's father was settled in 1731, Shubael was of Plympton; he was there at the time of his marriage in 1733/4. However, Middleboro Church records for 10 May 1741 note that Shubael and Hazadiah came from Carver (which was part of Plympton until 1790).

On 5 Feb. 1755 Shubael's widow Hazadiah Lewis of Middleboro, a weaver, sold 14 acres in Middleboro to her son Eleazer of Middleboro.

Children (LEWIS), b. Plympton or Middleboro:

i ELEAZER[5], b. ca. 1734; living 21 Feb. 1765; m. Middleboro 27 Nov. 1755 MARY EDDY of Middleboro, b. Plympton 23 Dec. 1732; living 30 Sept. 1761; daughter of Jabez Jr. and Thankful Eddy. Eleazer was a cordwainer. He sold his home in Middleboro 21 Feb. 1765. This deed was not signed by his wife Mary, but a deed of 30 Sept. 1761, acknowledged 22 March 1762, was signed by her.

One (LEWIS) ch., possibly others: unnamed, d. Bridgewater 1770.

ii GIDEON, b. ca. 1736; d. Gibson PA. A Congregational minister; he resided in Claremont NH in 1771 and during the Revolution; he removed to PA. He served in Capt. Oliver Ashley's Company at Ticonderoga in May 1777.

iii JABEZ, b. ca. 1737; d. Weathersfield VT ca. 1806-7; m. ca. 1755 MARY HAYMAN (or Hinman). He resided for a while in Huntington LI NY, but removed to Warwick before the Revolution. He served in the army at the Battle of Bennington, and probably at Hubbardton.

Nine (LEWIS) ch.: Samuel b. ca. 1756, Jabez b. ca. 1757, Shubael, Wilcox b. Huntington LI NY 1768, Abner, Hannah, Jesse, Seth, and Mary d. in 1788 ae. 16.

iv SAMUEL, b. 25 May 1739; res. Claremont NH during the Revolution.

v HANNAH, b. 20 June 1740; did she m. SYMONDS?

vi AMASA, b. 16 Oct. 1741

vii ABNER, b. 25 May 1743; d. Swansea bef. 4 Aug. 1821, the date on which his will was probated. There is some confusion about his birth and death dates. *Middleboro Deaths* states that he d. 7 July 1826 at the age of 78; *Harwich by Paine* says that Abner was b. Middleboro 16 March 1745 and d. Swansea 7 July 1826 in his 82nd yr.

Abner m. (1) Bridgewater 29 Sept. 1763 MERCY HALL, b. there 26 April 1745; daughter of Reuben and Ruth (Gilbert) Hall. Abner is said to have had several wives. He m. last Harwich 23 Feb. 1808 MERCY CHASE, widow of Sylvanus Chase; bur. with Abner in North Swansea.

Abner began his preaching career in Freetown in 1774 and remained there until 1784. Subsequently he preached in Harwich, Attleboro, again in Freetown, Hyannis, Fall River (then called Troy) and lastly in the Baptist Church in Swansea until 1819. His will probated 4 Aug. 1821 mentioned his late wife, son-in-law Sylvanus Westcott, daughter-in-law Anna Westcott, granddaughter Lydia Westcott, grandniece Sophia Hood and grandniece Asenath Angell.

viii ELIZABETH, b. 24 May 1745

ix SETH, b. 8 March 1747; res. Claremont NH during the Revolution.

x MARY, b. 28 Sept. 1751; m. Deacon SHAW of East Windsor VT.

References: MD 19:47. VR BRIDGEWATER, PLYMPTON. Plymouth Co. LR 33:195(Jabez Eddy); 44:80(Hazadiah Lewis); 48:271; 50:76(Eleazer Lewis). Bristol Co. PR 63:491(Abner Lewis). EDDY GEN p. 62. LEWISIANA 5:188; 6:8, 152. MIDDLEBORO BY WESTON p. 658. MIDDLEBORO DEATHS. HARWICH BY PAINE pp. 372-3.

31 ISAAC[4] FULLER (Isaac[3], Samuel[2-1]), b. Middleboro 24 Sept. 1712; may have rem. with one of his children to Warwick MA or Winchester NH and d. there.

He m. Bridgewater 9 Nov. 1737 SARAH PACKARD, b. there 23 May 1719; daughter of Solomon and Susanna (Kingman) Packard, and a descendant of Francis Cooke.

Isaac settled in North Bridgewater (now Brockton) about 1736. He sold his property, including his house, situated in the north precinct of Bridgewater on 25 March 1777.

Children (FULLER), b. Bridgewater:

i ISAAC[5], b. 15 Dec. 1738; d. Easton 22 Aug. 1804; m. Bridgewater 24 Jan. 1765 MARY ALDEN, d. Mansfield 9 Sept. 1818. Isaac was a corporal in a company of minutemen from Easton; later in 1775 he was a lieutenant. The inventory of Isaac's estate was taken 13 Dec. 1804; Barzillai Fuller was administrator.

Ten (FULLER) ch., second b. Bridgewater, last eight b. Easton: Polly b. 1766, d. ae. 12, Lemuel b. 1768, Isaac b. 1769, Barzillai b. 1772, Alden b. 1773, Hosea b. 1775, Eunice b. 1778, Alpheus (or Aleph) b. 1779, Rufus b. 1781, and Otis b. 1785.

ii OLIVE, b. 14 Oct. 1740; m. Bridgewater 21 Oct. 1765 DANIEL EDSON, b. there 16 Oct. 1741; son of Joseph and Abigail (Forrest) Edson. Daniel and Olive sold their land in Bridgewater in 1771 to Perkins Gurney.

Two (EDSON) ch., probably others, bp. East Bridgewater: Isaiah (twin) bp. 1769, Reuben (twin) bp. 1769.

iii LEMUEL, b. 29 Sept. 1742; d. Bridgewater 25 May 1762

iv ISAIAH, b. 7 July 1744; d. Warwick 10 March 1809; m. Bridgewater 30 Sept. 1768 MARY KEYZER, b. Easton 28 Aug. 1751; d. Warwick 2 Sept. 1831; daughter of Seth and Lydia (-----) Keyzer. Isaiah was a sergeant, lieutenant, and 1st lieutenant in the Revolution, serving in companies from Bridgewater and Plymouth Co. Widow Mary's dower was ordered set off to her 6 March 1810.

Seven (FULLER) ch. (not rec. Warwick): John, Jacob b. 1776, a daughter, Henry b. 1780, Seth b. 1782, Samuel, and James b. Warwick 1793.

v SARAH, b. 23 March 1746; d. bef. Jan. 1774; m. Bridgewater 24 Jan. 1765 JOHN FREELOVE; son of John and Abigail (Washburn) Freelove. He m. (2) 4 Jan. 1774 Sarah Wood. John served as a private from Easton in the same company with his brothers-in-law Isaac and Isaiah Fuller.

One, pos. two, (FREELOVE) ch. b. to John and Sarah: one unnamed d. 1733 ae. 6 mos., and pos. Sarah (see 34 iii).

vi SUSANNA, b. 27 Nov. 1748; d. Oxford ME; m. Bridgewater 12 April 1770 ASHLEY CURTIS 2nd, bp. North Bridgewater (now Brockton) 20 April 1746; d. Oxford ME 25 Aug. 1831 ae. 85; son of Ashley and ----- (Hayden) Curtis. Ashley Curtis 2nd served as a private in a company of minutemen from Bridgewater; he also had later service in the Revolution.

Nine (CURTIS) ch., first three rec. Bridgewater: Eliphas b. 1771, Oliver b. 1773, Susanna b. 1776, Mary b. 1778, Ashley b. 1780, Sarah b. 1783, Rebecca b. 1786, Sibyl b. 1789, and Lois b. 1791.

vii LOIS, b. 13 Oct. 1751; d. 5 June 1792 in 41st yr; m. int. Bridgewater 12 Nov. 1772 SAMUEL DYKE JR., b. in Oct. 1748; d. Brockton 28 Oct. 1841 ae. 93y 7d; son of Samuel and Mary (Perkins) Dyke, who came from Ipswich. Samuel Dyke Jr. m. (2) Bridgewater 31 Jan. 1793 Mehitable (Cary) Howard.

Eight (DYKE) ch. b. Bridgewater: Lucinda b. 1773, Salmon b. 1775, Fuller b. 1778, Olive b. 1780, Rebecca b. 1782, Oliver b. 1785, Nathaniel b. 1787, and Samuel b. 1790.

viii BENJAMIN, b. 22 Sept. 1754; d. Winchester NH in 1817; m. Bridgewater 8 Sept. 1777 SARAH AMES, b. there 30 Nov. 1754; d. Winchester NH 1 April 1812 ae. 58; daughter of Daniel and Hannah (Keith) Ames, and a descendant of Francis Cooke. Benjamin served in the Revolution from Bridgewater as a private in the same company in which his brother Isaiah was a sergeant. His will dated 1 April 1812 (on file in Cheshire Co. NH), mentions his six children.

Six (FULLER) ch. b. Winchester NH: Daniel b. 1779, Lois b. 1782, Phebe b. 1787, Mehitable b. 1789, Sally b. 1791, and Benjamin b. 1792.

ix RELIANCE, b. 22 Dec. 1756; d. North Bridgewater (now Brockton) 26 June 1817 in 61st yr.; m. Bridgewater 2 April 1777 JOSIAH EDSON, b. there 31 May 1753; d. there 5 Jan. 1820 in 67th yr.; son of James and Ester (Allen) Edson, and a descendant of Francis Cooke. Josiah's will, made 10 June 1813 and probated 17 Jan. 1820, mentions son Barnabas and daughters Susanna Packard, Sarah Hayward, Zilpha Kingman, Esther Kingman, Reliance Edson and Olive Edson.

Seven (EDSON) ch. b. Bridgewater: Zilpha b. 1778, Susanna b. 1780, Sarah b. 1783, Barnabas b. 1786, Esther b. 1788, Reliance b. 1792, and Olive b. 1795.

References: VR BRIDGEWATER, BROCKTON, EAST BRIDGEWATER, EASTON, MANSFIELD, WEST BRIDGEWATER. MSSR 6:28, 152, 162, 163; 4:252. Cheshire Co. NH PR(Benjamin Fuller). Hampshire Co. PR(Isaiah Fuller). Bristol Co. PR 41:130, 361(Isaac Fuller). Plymouth Co. LR 56:176 (Daniel Edson); 59:31(Isaac Fuller). NEHGR 39:231. NORTH BRIDGEWATER BY CARY. FULLER GEN 2:136, 137. BRIDGEWATER BY MITCHELL p. 163. OXFORD ME BY KING p. 172. EDSON GEN p. 47.

32 SAMUEL[4] FULLER (Isaac[3], Samuel[2-1]), b. Middleboro 29 Jan. 1717/8; living Jan. 1768 when child baptized.

He m. Halifax 30 Sept. 1743 ELIZABETH THOMPSON, b. Plympton 7 Aug. 1726; living Jan. 1768 when child baptized; daughter of John and Elizabeth (Thomas) Thompson of Plymouth, and a descendant of Pilgrims Brown, Cooke, and Howland. Elizabeth Thompson was received into full communion in the Halifax Church 6 Feb. 1742.

Samuel and Elizabeth Fuller of Halifax sold to Ebenezer Fuller Jr. of Halifax, 2 Feb. 1752, land in Middleboro, "being part of land formerly Dr. Isaac Fuller's." They also sold to Ebenezer Fuller Jr. land in Halifax in 1757 and land lying partly in Plympton and partly in Middleboro in 1765.

The dates and places of death of Samuel and Elizabeth Fuller have not been found.

Children (FULLER), b. or bp. Halifax or Plympton:

i ZADOCK[5], b. 19 Sept. 1744; d. Lanesboro 17 Sept. 1818; m. Halifax 3 Dec. 1767 ALICE (or ELSE) PORTER of Halifax, b. about 1747; d. Lanesboro 26 Oct. 1830 in 84th yr. He served in the Revolution from Halifax as a private in 1775. In 1790 Zadock was in Lanesboro with one male over 16, three males under 16 and three females in his family.

Nine (FULLER) ch. (pos. others who died) b. Lanesboro: Sarah b. 1768, Elsie b. 1771, Jabez b. 1773, Abigail b. 1777, Samuel b. 1779, Zadock b. 1781, and Noah b. 1787.

ii ELIZABETH, b. 28 Dec. 1745; bp. 9 Feb. 1745/6

iii JOHN, b. 30 March 1748; bp. 3 April 1748; possibly the John Fuller "of Halifax, County of Plymouth," who bought land in Pelham in 1783 as noted in *Descendants of Levi Wood*, and living 1790 in Pelham with one boy and four females.

iv HULDAH, bp. 3 June 1750; d.y.

v HULDAH, b. 1 June 1752; d. Plympton 18 July 1819 N.S. ae. 67y 1m 6d; m. Halifax 28 May 1778 NEHEMIAH STURTEVANT of Plympton, b. there 19

Sept. 1749; d. there 27 Jan. 1819 N.S. ae. 69y 3m 27d; son of Noah and Susanna (Harlow) Sturtevant. Nehemiah was a private in the Revolution.

Seven (STURTEVANT) ch. b. Plympton: Abiah b. 1779, Sally b. 1781, Lucy b. 1783, Huldah b. 1785, d. 1786, Elizabeth Fuller b. 1788, Nehemiah b. 1791, and Huldah b. 1793.

vi MARTHA, bp. 25 Aug. 1754; d. Medfield 20 March 1804; m. Halifax 30 Dec. 1784 her cousin JOHN FULLER (see 33 ii).

vii LYDIA, bp. 10 Aug. 1760; d. Chesterfield 4 Nov. 1807 ae. 47; m. int. Chesterfield 26 May 1783 JOHN COWING, b. Northampton 17 March 1763; d. Jamestown NY in Aug. 1833 in 70th yr. He m. int. (2) 20 Dec. 1807 Abigail (-----) Meech, widow of Capt. Dennis Meech.

Eleven (COWING) ch. b. Chesterfield: Calvin b. 1786, John b. 1787, d. 1806, Lydia b. 1789, Sophia b. 1791, Louisa b. 1792, Charlotte b. 1794, Betsey b. 1796, Thompson b. 1798, Samuel b. 1801, Abraham b. ca. 1803, d. 1807, and Ransom b. 1803.

viii SAMUEL, bp. 20 Nov. 1763; d. Halifax 10 Nov. 1842 in 80th yr; m. Plympton 15 Dec. 1785 SARAH CUSHMAN of Plympton, b. there 7 July 1766; d. Halifax 28 April 1840 ae. 73; daughter of Benjamin Jr. and Zerviah (Sampson) Cushman, not a descendant of Henry Samson. Samuel in his will dated 22 June 1840, probated in April 1843, mentioned his sons Samuel and Isaac; daughters Polly Leach, Lucy Wood and Joanna Eddy; and grandsons (unnamed), sons of his son Benjamin, deceased.

Six (FULLER) ch. all prob. b. Halifax: Samuel, Joanna b. 1787, Mary (Polly) b. 1789, Benjamin, Isaac b. 1799, and Lucy.

ix LEMUEL (Capt.), bp. 11 Jan. 1768; d. Worthington 10 May 1842 ae. 74; m. (1) SUSANNA -----, d. there 1 Sept. 1812 in 36th yr; m. (2) Worthington 4 April 1813 ANNA SMITH, b. Chester 3 Sept. 1780; daughter of Sgt. Daniel and Keziah Smith. Lemuel's will, dated 29 June 1837 and probated Northampton 1 July 1842, mentions wife Anna; sons John, Henry, Daniel Pomeroy and Lemuel; daughters Mary Haskell, Eliza Woods, Susan Dwight Jewell, Flavia Cudworth and Nancy Haskell Atwood.

Ten (FULLER) ch., order not certain: John, Mary, Eliza b. ca. 1802, Henry, Flavey d. Worthington 1807 ae. a few mos., Flavia b. ca. 1808,

Susan Dwight bp. 1810, Nancy Haskell bp. 1812, Daniel Pomeroy, and Lemuel S. b. ca. 1816.

References: MD 13:12; 27:33, 122. VR CHESTER, MEDFIELD, PLYMPTON, WORTHINGTON. MSSR 6:145; 6:194; 15:230. THOMSON (JOHN) DESC. Plymouth Co. LR 50:246-249 (Samuel Fuller). LANESBORO BY PALMER p. 155. Plymouth Co. PR 85:164(Samuel Fuller). FULLER GEN 2:160, 161. HALIFAX VR pp. 21, 22, 30, 33, 50, 125. CHESTERFIELD HIST pp. 107, 108. WOOD (LEVI) DESC p. 70. 1790 CENSUS MA: Lanesboro, Pelham. Hampshire Co. PR(Lemuel Fuller).

33 JABEZ[4] FULLER (Isaac[3], Samuel[2-1]), b. Middleboro 7 May 1723; d. Medfield 5 Oct. 1781.

He m. Boston 12 May 1747 ELIZABETH HILLIARD (or Helyer), b. there 6 Oct. 1724; d. Medfield 22 Oct. 1801; daughter of John and Elizabeth Helyer.

Dr. Jabez Fuller was received into the Medfield Church from Bridgewater in 1747.

Children (FULLER), b. Medfield:

i JONATHAN[5], b. 3 Oct. 1748; d. Middleboro 13 March 1802 in 54th yr; m. there 1 Aug. 1775 LUCY EDDY, b. Middleboro 25 March 1758; d. there 17 Sept. 1839 in 82nd yr.; daughter of Zachariah and Mercy (Morton) Eddy, and a descendant of Stephen Hopkins. He was a physician and surgeon, and served in the Revolution as a surgeon.
Eleven (FULLER) ch. b. Middleboro: Lucy Eddy b. 1776, Jonathan Hylleir b. 1779, Thomas b. 1780, d.y., Sally b. 1781, Thomas b. 1785, Zachariah b. 1787, Betsey b. 1789, Jabez b. 1791, Seth b. 1793, John b. 1796, and Mercy Freeman b. 1798.

ii JOHN, b. 28 July 1750; d. Medfield 22 Sept. 1830 ae. 80; m. (1) Halifax 30 Dec. 1784 his cousin MARTHA FULLER, bp. there 25 Aug. 1754; d. Medfield 20 March 1804; daughter of Samuel Fuller (see 32 vi above); m. int. (2) Medfield 10 Nov. 1804 HANNAH LOVELL b. there 28 May 1766; d. there 31 Dec. 1832 ae. 67; daughter of David and Lois Lovell. John served in the Revolution in a company of minutemen from Medfield, with other periods of service in 1776.
Six (FULLER) ch. by first wife, b. Medfield: Martha b. 1785, Abigail b. 1786, Samuel b. 1788, a child d. 1791, John b. 1792, and Charlotte b. 1796.

iii ELIZABETH, b. 12 April 1752; m. Medfield 4 April 1776 STEPHEN DEXTER of Walpole, b. there 4 June 1747; son of Jeremiah and Hepzibah (Wilkinson) Dexter. Stephen served in the Revolution as a minuteman.

Four (DEXTER) ch. b. Walpole: Elizabeth b. 1777, Sarah b. 1779, Anna b. 1780, and Lorin b. 1783.

iv JABEZ, b. 26 May 1753; d. Kingston 12 April 1813 ae. 59; m. Duxbury in Aug. 1781 LUCY LORING, bp. there 19 Nov. 1758; d. Kingston 25 Oct. or 8 Nov. 1847 ae. 89y 1m; daughter of Benjamin and Anna (Alden) Loring. [See *The John Alden Family*.] During the Revolution Jabez served as a doctor in a company of Medfield militia.

In the division of Dr. Jabez Fuller's estate 13 April 1814, the widow Lucy received her dower and the remainder was divided among four surviving daughters: Lucy Fuller, Betsey Tobey wife of Silas, Sophia Fuller and Sally Fuller.

Seven (FULLER) ch. b. Kingston: Seth b. 1782, Nancy b. 1784, Lucy b. 1786, Betsey b. 1789, Polly b. 1791, Sophia b. 1798, and Sally b. 1801.

v THOMAS, b. 27 June 1755; d. bef. 27 July 1790; m. Plympton 11 June 1778 MARY HOWLAND, b. there 5 June 1758; daughter of Rev. John and Elizabeth (Lewis) Howland. [See *The John Howland Family*.] Mary m. (2) Carver 27 July 1790 Rev. Ezra Weld. Thomas was a physician; he served in the Revolution as a private in a company from Medfield.

Two (FULLER) ch.: Thomas b. 1781, d. 1799, and Betsey died Kingston 1788 ae. 2y 8m 3d.

vi MARY, b. 9 June 1758; d. Medfield 11 June 1822 ae. 64; unm.

vii CATHERINE, b. 2 April 1760; d. Medfield 2 Dec. 1831 ae. 71; unm.

viii SARAH, b. 25 Feb. 1763; m. NATHANIEL CLARK

ix EXPERIENCE, b. 1 June 1766; d. Medfield, a widow, 2 March 1800; m. Foxboro 19 Sept. 1788, as his second wife, TIMOTHY DWIGHT of Medfield, b. 7 Sept. 1750; d. bef. 2 March 1800; son of Seth and Hannah (Fisher) Dwight. Timothy was a physician.

One (DWIGHT) ch. b. Medfield: Timothy b. 1789.

References: MD 18:156; 21:126, 127; 31:138; 33:156. VR CARVER, DUXBURY, FOXBOROUGH, KINGSTON, MEDFIELD, PLYMPTON, WALPOLE. BOSTON VR 24:165; 28:245. MA MARR 2:95. MSSR 6:163, 167, 171, 191; 4:726. HALIFAX VR

p. 22. Plymouth Co. PR 45:347(Jabez Fuller). MIDDLEBORO BY WESTON p. 660. DUXBURY BY WINSOR p. 277. DWIGHT FAM 1:90. MIDDLEBORO DEATHS. FULLER GEN 2:171. MEDFIELD BY TILDEN p. 394.

34 MARY$^4$ FULLER (Isaac$^3$, Samuel$^{2-1}$), b. Middleboro 23 Aug. 1726; d. Litchfield ME 12 Jan. 1817 ae. 90.

She m. Halifax 14 Sept. 1756 SAMUEL WATERMAN, b. Plympton 11 Aug. 1718; d. Mansfield 16 Nov. 1787; son of Robert and Mary (Cushman) Waterman, and a descendant of Pilgrim Allerton. [See *The Isaac Allerton Family*.] Samuel m. (1) Halifax 16 March 1737 Mary Thompson, b. Middleboro 1718. Samuel moved to Mansfield from Halifax about 1783.

Children (WATERMAN), b. Halifax:

i ASAPH$^5$, b. 30 Sept. 1757; d. 17 Oct. 1757

ii OLIVE, b. 26 Oct. 1758; d. 14 Jan. 1759

iii OLIVER, b. 5 May 1760; d. Savoy 5 Nov. 1833; m. Mansfield 1 Feb. 1786 SARAH FREELOVE of Bridgewater; pos. daughter of John and Sarah (Fuller) Freelove (see 31 v).

Five (WATERMAN) ch., first three b. Mansfield, two b. Savoy: Oliver b. 1787, Sarah b. ca. 1790, Chloe b. ca. 1797, Robert b. ca. 1800, and Sylvanus b. ca. 1805.

iv ROBERT, b. 26 June 1762; d. 1 Feb. 1763 ae. 7m 6d

v ABIGAIL, b. 10 Nov. 1763; d. Litchfield ME 30 Oct. 1826; unm.

vi SILVANUS, b. 12 Oct. 1768; d. Litchfield ME 30 Oct. 1851; m. 6 July 1804 ABIGAIL JACKSON, b. Dresden ME 31 Dec. 1782; d. Litchfield 30 Nov. 1853; prob. daughter of William and Abigail (Tupper) Jackson. Silvanus was a physician.

Six (WATERMAN) ch. b. Litchfield ME: Granville Clifford b. 1805, Dexter b. 1807, Eliza b. 1809, Sophia b. 1811, Oliver b. 1814, and Melville Henry b. 1817, d. 1831.

References: VR MANSFIELD, PLYMPTON. WATERMAN GEN 1:38, 89, 91, 92, 179, 180. LITCHFIELD ME HIST pp. 186, 382. HALIFAX VR pp. 32, 35, 38, 46, 47. MD 27:184.

# W I L L I A M   W H I T E

of the

*M A Y F L O W E R*

Compiled by

RUTH WILDER SHERMAN, F.A.S.G.

and

ROBERT MOODY SHERMAN, C.G., F.A.S.G.

Ruth Wilder Sherman is a descendant of Pilgrim William White. She has served as Historian of the Rhode Island Mayflower Society, and is currently Secretary General of the General Society of Mayflower Descendants as well as Editor of *The Mayflower Quarterly*. In 1975 she was elected a Fellow of the American Society of Genealogists.

Robert Moody Sherman is a descendant of Pilgrims John Alden, William Brewster and Richard Warren. He has served as Governor of the Rhode Island Mayflower Society, and is presently Chairman of the Five Generations Project. He holds an S.B. degree from M.I.T. (1936). Mr. Sherman is Chairman of the Division of Science at Bristol Community College (Fall River, Mass.). In 1975 he also was elected a Fellow of the American Society of Genealogists.

Mr. and Mrs. Sherman are known for their articles on Pilgrim families, and for their transcriptions of the Marshfield and Yarmouth (Mass.) vital records. They are currently working on a second Mayflower Family--the Henry Samson Family.

## WILLIAM WHITE

Little is known about Pilgrim William White. Governor Bradford says that among the *Mayflower* passengers were "Mr. William White and Susanna his wife and one son called Resolved, and one born a-shipboard called Peregrine, and two servants named William Holbeck and Edward Thompson." In 1651 he added that "Mr. White and his two servants died soon after their landing. His wife married with Mr. Winslow.... His two sons are married and Resolved hath five children, Peregrine two, all living. So their increase are seven."

William and Susanna White left England with son Resolved. At Cape Cod, on November 11, 1620 according to the old calendar, William was one of the forty-one signers of the Mayflower Compact. Two to three weeks later son Peregrine was born, the first English birth in Plymouth Colony. Susanna was widowed in February. She became the first colony bride in May, marrying Edward Winslow, a *Mayflower* passenger who had lost his wife a few weeks before. At least four children were born to Susanna and Edward.

About 1638, the Winslows with young Peregrine and Resolved White, moved to Green Harbor, now called Marshfield. Edward Winslow rose to prominence as Governor of Plymouth Colony, became Colony representative to England, and at last was persuaded to use his diplomatic skills for Oliver Cromwell, heading up a joint commission with the Dutch to award reparations for damage caused to Danish ships. Interesting though it may be to imagine Susanna sharing those years in London with him, hostess to officials from various governments, no evidence has been found to indicate that she accompanied her husband on any of his trips to England. One of the few extant documents mentioning her by name is a "Bill of Sale" in which "Susanna Winslow wife of Mr. Edward Winslow of Marshfield and his Agent in this tyme of his Absence in England" sold for ten years the services of an Indian man. The agreement was dated 12 (11) 1647, that is 22 Jan. 1648 by our calendar.

Edward spent the last six years of his life in England. His will in 1654 as a resident of London, leaves his land in New England to son Josiah "hee allowing to my wife a full third parte thereof for her life also." If Susanna were living in London at that time, it would have been natural to provide for her there as well.

No further record of Susanna has been found. She must have died before 1675 when her son Josiah Winslow made no proviso for her in his will, although he made bequests to numerous relatives and friends. This surely refutes the claim of some that she died at Marshfield within two weeks of Josiah's death in 1680. It seems strange that this woman who was the wife of one colony governor and mother of another, first Plymouth Colony bride and mother of the famed Peregrine White, should have left no record of her passing in town, church, court or press.

*

Susanna (-----)(White) Winslow was not the sister of Dr. Samuel Fuller as is often claimed. Samuel and Edward Fuller who came on the *Mayflower* were sons of Robert of Redenhall, England. Robert had no daughter Susanna. He did have a daughter Anna, born about 1578, far too old a bride for Edward Winslow who would not be born till 1595. The will of Robert Fuller in 1614 mentions no daughter Susanna, nor a daughter married to William White. Dr. Samuel Fuller's will in 1633 mentions only one sister, Alice Bradford--actually his sister-in-law. The only positive clue to Susanna's ancestry seems to be a letter from Edward Winslow to "Uncle Robert Jackson" in 1623, in which he sent news of Susanna, her late husband, and her children. He also sent his regards to his father-in-law in England, by which time Robert Fuller was nine years dead. A cursory investigation of the Jackson family has shed no light on the subject.

*

The name White occurs too often in England to make an extensive search for William's ancestry practical. Alexander and Eleanor White of Sturton-le-Steeple, Notts, in the heart of Pilgrim country, had daughters Katherine, Bridget and Jane who married Gov. Carver, The Rev. Robinson and Randolph Thickins. They had no son William, but a nephew named William White might be worth investigation.

*

For many years genealogists have assumed that Pilgrim William White spent his early married years in Holland, marrying at Leiden in 1612 and burying children there in 1615 and 1616. A critical examination of Leiden sources casts heavy doubt on this assumption. Before 1620 there are five mentions of a William White in Leiden, but no proof that they apply to the Pilgrim. They may all apply to the William White who was still living there in 1621.

27 Jan. 1612 Betrothal of William White, woolcomber, bachelor from England, to Ann Fuller Spinster from England; Sarah Priest and Samuel Fuller witnessed

16 March 1613 William White a witness at the betrothal of Samuel Fuller to Agnes Carpenter

18 June 1615 Child of William White living at the Green Alley buried at St. Pancras

21 Dec. 1616 Child of William White living at the Uuterstegraft, buried ditto

27 Jan. 1618 Wife of William "Yten" buried in Pieterskerk

25 Oct. 1621 William White witnessed the betrothal of Godbert Godbertson to Sarah [(Allerton) Vincent] widow of Degory Priest

3 March 1623 William White tobacco merchant living in Leiden

31 March 1625 William White, Englishman, tobacco merchant, living in Leiden

8 Dec. 1628 William White tobacco merchant guaranteed for citizenship

14 Aug. 1629 Edmond White, son of William, bachelor from England, betrothed

5 Dec. 1631 William Wit buried at St. Pancras Church

Notice that the 1612 marriage is to Ann Fuller, not Susanna. White's wife is always called Susanna in New England.* The burials in 1615 and 1616 do not name the mother. Was it only coincidence that the White-Fuller marriage in 1612 was witnessed by Sarah Priest, and that she in turn had a William White witness at her 1621 marriage? Perhaps Pilgrim William was involved in neither case.

Unfortunately, the family of the William White which was still living in Leiden after the *Mayflower* sailed, is not mentioned in the incomplete 1622 poll tax return. Further research in the city archives has failed to prove that Pilgrim William ever lived in Holland. Perhaps he should be numbered among the London Contingent.

---

*An article in PN&Q disproves the theory that Pilgrim White's wife was Susanna Tilley.

References: MD 1:24-9; 4:2; 5:82, 226; 30:3. MQ 34:104; 37:56-7; 41:16-8. NEHGR 55:411, 415. LEYDEN DOCUMENTS pp. xi, xiv, xlvii, lxvii. BRADFORD'S HIST (1952) pp. 442, 445. MOURT'S RELATION p. 31. WINTHROP PAPERS, 1947, 5:196-7. DEXTER p. 649. PASTOR OF PILGRIMS pp. 17-26. PN&Q 1:1. MSS. records in the care of the Archivist at Leiden, Holland.

## FIRST GENERATION

1 WILLIAM[1] WHITE, prob. b. England; d. Plymouth 21 Feb. 1621 age and parentage unknown.

He m. SUSANNA -----, prob. b. England; d. between 1654 and 1675. There are no probate records for William or Susanna.

Susanna m. (2) Plymouth 12 May 1621 Edward Winslow of the *Mayflower*, b. England 1595; d. Barbados 1655; son of Edward and Magdalene (Oliver) Winslow.

Children (WHITE):

2 i RESOLVED[2], b. prob. about 1615 in Holland or England
3 ii PEREGRINE, b. aboard the *Mayflower* at Provincetown between 7 and 10 Dec. 1620 (new style)

References: MD 4:2; 5:82; 30:3. NEHGR 109:242; 110:182; 124:308. FAM OF PILGRIMS p. 167. WILLISON p. 480.

## SECOND GENERATION

2 RESOLVED[2] WHITE (William[1]), b. Leyden, Holland or England ca. 1615; "of Marshfield" in March 1684/5; prob. living 19 Sept. 1687.

He m. (1) Scituate 5 Nov. 1640 JUDITH VASSALL, b. England 1619; d. Marshfield; bur. 3 April 1670; daughter of William and Ann (King) Vassall. The parentage of Judith is clearly shown in a deed of 18 July 1657 in which she, as wife of Resolved White, sells land bequeathed to her as daughter of "William Vassall heretofore of Scituate, and late of Barbados deceased, by a will dated 13 July 1655."

Resolved m. (2) Salem 5 Oct. 1674 ABIGAIL (-----) LORD, b. ca. 1606; d. Salem between 15 and 27 June 1682; widow of William Lord. She seems to have had no surviving children by her first marriage.

Resolved came to Plymouth in 1620 with his parents aboard the *Mayflower*, and after 1632 moved to Marshfield with his mother and stepfather. He resided in Scituate during the period when his children were born--1640 to 1656. He and Judith, and perhaps some of their children, travelled to Barbados in 1656/7, presumably to aid in the

---

NOTE: Because *The White Family Record* by Samuel and Thomas White contains many contradictions of primary sources and many assumptions which could not be proved, this account of William White's descendants does not include any information found only in that book.

settling of the estate of her father, for on 17 March 1656/7 "Resolved White of Scituate in New Plymouth in New England, gentleman, and his wife Judith, daughter of William Vassall of this Island" deeded land in Barbados, a deed acknowledged on March 20th by "Resolved White's wife" and recorded at Barbados only four days later.

The family moved to Marshfield in 1662, and were still there in 1670 when Judith died. Resolved was in Salem from 1674 to at least 1682, being a freeman of Salem in 1680. He served in King Philip's War under Capt. Manning in 1676. He returned to Marshfield after the death of his second wife, for on 13 March 1684/5 "Resolved White of Marshfield" and sons Samuel and Josiah quitclaimed rights to an island, in return for which grantee John Branch would maintain Resolved's eldest son, William. We assume Resolved was still living on 19 Sept. 1687 when William quitclaimed his rights in the island to John Branch, mentioning his father, but not as "deceased," and mentioning the earlier deed of "my father Mr. Resolved White." The authors have found no evidence to support the claim of Pilgrim genealogist George E. Bowman that Resolved died between 1690 and 1694, nor the oft-found statement that he died in Salem.

It seems strange that there is no record of the death of Resolved, considering the fame of his brother Peregrine as the first white child born in New England; however no mention of his death has been found in records at the places where his kin were living late in the 1600's.

Approximate birth dates may be calculated for Resolved and his second wife from their depositions: He was "aged about 63" on "5:9:1678" and again in June 1679; Abigail was aged about 74 on "2:1:1679/80."

There are no probate records for Resolved or Judith White but the will of "Abigail White, wife of Mr. Resolved White of Salem" dated 26 April 1682 and proved June 1682, mentions her former husband William Lord, his kinsman William Lord and the latter's children. She left to "Resolved White my now husband," bed, bedding, chest and house furnishings.

A deed bearing the signature of Resolved White as witness was pictured in *The Mayflower Descendant* in 1915.

Children (WHITE), b. Scituate by first wife:

i WILLIAM$^3$, b. 10 or 18 April 1642; d. Marshfield 24 Jan. 1695; apparently never married; living in Marshfield with Josiah Winslow's family 2 July 1675 when Josiah made his will naming half brothers Resolved and Peregrine White, and bequeathing "kinsman William White a bed...and sheets at what time he shall leave my wife and family." On 13 March 1684/5 his brothers Samuel and Josiah and their father Resolved provided for William's care by quitclaiming an island in Marshfield to John Branch, tenant of "William White eldest son of Resolved," and in return Branch would "Maintaine the sd William White...in sickness & in health dureing the Terme of his Naturall Life." On 19 Sept. 1687 William signed a quitclaim of his rights in the island to Branch, acknowledging the act on the same day. There are no probate records for William in Plymouth County.

ii JOHN, b. 11 March 1644; living in 1650 (BRADFORD'S HIST); may have d.y. or gone to live in Barbados with some of his mother's siblings; but it seems likely that he died before 1684/5, when two of his living brothers (but not he) quitclaimed land to provide for William.

4 iii SAMUEL, b. 13 March 1646

iv RESOLVED, b. 12 Nov. 1647; bur. Marshfield 27 March 1670 "[worn] White Jr.," a week before the burial of his mother.

5 v ANNA, b. 4 June 1649

6 vi ELIZABETH, b. 4 June 1652

7 vii JOSIAH, b. 29 Sept. 1654

viii SUSANNA, b. Aug. 1656; n.f.r. Claims that she might have married Uriah Johnson, son of John of Sudbury, or that she married Uriah Johnson, grandson of the first settler of Woburn (WHITE FAM REC) prompted an investigation of these two families. Resolved White's associations with a Humphrey Johnson of Hingham have also been checked with no clue found to any Susanna, wife of a Johnson. Resolved White of Marshfield deeded to Humphrey Johnson of Hingham all right, title, etc. in his common lands at Scituate 21 April 1669. Humphrey was warned out of Scituate in 1673; on 28 Oct. 1684 he was involved in a suit for land as "assigne to Mr. Resolved White of Marshfield."

References: MD 1:16; 5:82; 17:1; 33:98-9. PN&Q 5:87-8. TAG 17:200f. MARSHFIELD VR p. 10, 19. VR SALEM, SCITUATE. Plymouth Co. LR 9:272(Resolved White). Plymouth Col. LR 4:1:130(White to Johnson). PLYMOUTH COL RECS 5:142; 7:284. MA BAY RECS 5:539.

3 PEREGRINE[2] WHITE (William[1]), b. aboard the *Mayflower* in Cape Cod Harbor at what is now Provincetown between 7 and 10 Dec. 1620 N.S.; d. Marshfield 20 or 22 July 1704 ae. 83y 8m.

He m. before 6 March 1648/9 O.S. SARAH BASSETT, d. Marshfield 22 Jan. 1711 "widow of Peregrine White"; daughter of William and Elizabeth (-----) Bassett. On 16 June

1656 "William Bassett Senior of Duxburrow now liveing Att Bridgwater" gave his Scituate lands to his "two sonnes there liveing viz Perigrine White and Nathaniell Bassett."

Peregrine moved to Marshfield sometime after 1632 with his mother and stepfather, and apparently resided there all his life except for a brief period around 1656 when the above deed from his father-in-law places him in Scituate.

On 7 June 1636 Peregrine White, then about 16, was one of the "voluntaries" to join with those of Massachusetts Bay and Connecticut to fight the Pequot Indians. On 23 Oct. 1643 when he was "of Marshfield," he sold to Mannasses Kempton of Plymouth land at Eel River given him the previous year by his stepfather Edward Winslow, a deed witnessed by his brother Resolved. Peregrine and Resolved both received land from the Plymouth Colony Court in Feb. 1664 "Leiftenant Perigrine White" having lot four on "Pochade Necke near Namassaskett."

Recognition of Peregrine as the first English child born in New England was given on 11 Oct. 1655 when "in Respect that hee was the first of the English that was borne in these ptes;...The Court have graunted unto him two hundred Acrees of Land Lying and being att the Path that goes from Bridgwater to the bay adjoyning to the Bay line."

When his eldest son was to be married, Peregrine not only deeded to "son Daniel White of Marshfield in consideration of his intended marriage my dwelling, barn, outhouses and lands in Marshfield and a share of the enlargement recently granted, from the day of my decease," but he also provided for his own wife and daughters: "except I die before Sarah my wife, she may enjoy the new end of my dwelling...Daniel shall pay to my two daughters Sarah and Mercy White £20 each when they are 18 or marry." The deed was dated 19 Aug. 1674 and acknowledged the same day.

The next year Josiah Winslow made his will naming his (half) "Brother Peregrine White" who was to have his Spanish rapier and buff belt with silver clasps.

Peregrine White fought not only the Pequot Indians but also the advances of the church, until at the age of 78 he was admitted to the Marshfield Church: "Capt. Peregrine White the first born Child of New England born November 1620 was admitted into this Church May 22 1698 In the 78th year of his age. Mat. 20.6.7."

The Marshfield vital records note the death of "Capt. Perigrine White" on "July ye 20:1704" and the *Boston Newsletter* of Monday July 31, 1704 gives the following obituary: "Marshfield, July, 22 Capt. Peregrine White of this Town, Aged Eighty three years, and Eight Months; died the 20th Instant. He was vigorous and of a comly Aspect to the last; Was the Son of Mr. William White and Susanna his Wife; born on board the *Mayflower*, Capt. Jones Commander, in Cape Cod Harbour, November, 1620. Was the First Englishman born in New-England. Altho' he was in the former part of his Life extravagant; yet was much Reform'd in his last years; and died hopefully." The place of his burial and that of most other *Mayflower* passengers is unknown.

The will of Peregrine White (owned by and displayed at Pilgrim Hall in Plymouth), dated 14 July 1704 and proved 14 Aug. of the same year, states: "Peregrine White of Marshfield ... Being aged and under many Weaknesses and Bodily Infirmities" devised to his wife Sarah everything not otherwise disposed of by the will; to his "eldest son Daniel my great table, my joynworke bedstead and cupboard" and half of his Middleboro land; to daughters Sarah and Mercy each one painted chair and a cushion; to son Jonathan his rapier [perhaps the one he had received under the will of Josiah Winslow?]; and to sons Peregrine and Jonathan, the other half of his Middleboro land. At least three autographs of Peregrine have been identified (and were pictured in *The Mayflower Descendant* in 1911), but his will was signed with the initials PW "The mark of Peregrine White" who was then aged almost 84 years.

Children (WHITE):

8 i DANIEL[3], b. ca. 1649
ii -----, b. ca. 1650/1; d.y.
9 iii JONATHAN, b. Marshfield 4 June 1658
10 iv PEREGRINE, b. ca. 1660
11 v SARAH, b. Marshfield Oct. 1663
12 vi SYLVANUS, b. Marshfield bef. 1667
vii MERCY, b. ca. 1670; d. Marshfield 12 June 1739 ae. 69 "wife of William Sherman." She m. Marshfield 3 Feb. 1697 WILLIAM SHERMAN, b. there 19 April 1672; d. there 26 Feb. 1739 ae. 67; son of William and Desire (Doty) Sherman.
William's will proved 7 April 1740, names his two grandchildren John and Mary, "children of my daughter Thankful Polden, deceased"; son-in-law Adam Hall and his wife Sarah; daughters Mary and Abigail Sherman. [See *The Edward Doty Family* for further information on Mercy's daughters and their families.]

References: MD 1:29; 3:119; 5:82; 10:25; 13:1-2; 18:33; 25:133; 26:100; 30:145-6; 31:145; 34:81. MARSHFIELD VR p. 23, 24, 32, 33, 43, 44, 408. YARMOUTH VR p. 126. PN&Q 5:83. Plymouth Col. LR 6:83(Peregrine to Daniel White). PLYMOUTH COL RECS 2:183(m. date of Peregrine and Sarah). TAG 17:202.

## THIRD GENERATION

4 SAMUEL[3] WHITE (Resolved[2], William[1]), b. Scituate 13 March 1646; d. bet. 20 Sept. 1720 and April 1731.

He m. REBECCA ----- , b. ca. 13 March 1646; d. Rochester 25 June 1711 in 65th year; prob. the daughter bp. to Thomas Lapham at Scituate 15 March 1645/6, the very same day as the bp. of Samuel.

Samuel White was in Sandwich as early as 20 May 1667 when Maj. Josiah Winslow of Marshfield, half brother of Samuel's father, deeded "for love and good will to my kinsman Samuel White now of Sandwich." He was still in Sandwich 8 June 1671 when he and his wife Rebecca deeded land, acknowledged 8 June 1677. In 1679 he was listed as one of the proprietors of Rochester.

Children (WHITE), b. Sandwich and Rochester, but all rec. Rochester:

13 i JOHN[4], b. 24 Aug. 1669
14 ii SAMUEL, b. 22 July 1671
iii ELIZABETH, b. 4 March 1673; n.f.r.
15 iv MELATIAH, b. 14 Feb. 1676
v JUDEE, b. 30 April 1678; n.f.r.
vi HESIKIAH, b. 5 April 1682 (twin); living 3 Aug. 1733
16 vii SUSANNA, b. 5 April 1682 (twin).
17 viii PENELOPE, b. 12 March 1687
ix WILLIAM, b. 6 June 1690; n.f.r.

References: FAM OF PILGRIMS p. 161. MD 9:218; 12:97. VR ROCHESTER, SCITUATE. Plymouth Col. LR 4:246 (Winslow). TAG 17:201. NEHGR 5:88; 36:19; 115:83-5. Plymouth Co. LR 41:228(Hezekiah White).

5 ANNA[3] WHITE (Resolved[2], William[1]), b. Scituate 4 or 5 June 1649; d. Concord 25 May 1714 ae. 64 "wife of John Hayward."

She m. Concord 2 June 1671 JOHN HAYWARD (also spelled Heyward, Haywood, Howard or Haward), b. Concord 20 Dec. 1640; d. there 22 Nov. 1718 ae. 78; son of George and Mary (-----) Hayward.

There are no probate records for John or Anna, but on 1 March 1702/3 John gave to "eldest son George Haywood of Concord...the west end of my dwelling house..." and on 12 Feb. 1711/2 to John Hayward Jr. of Concord the rest of the dwelling house, barn and land in Concord "said John to provide for me and my wife Anna...and to pay my daughter Judith Goss...my daughter Mercy Browne...my daughter Anna Allen...and my daughter Sarah Allen...." Every Middlesex

Co. deed involving John and Anna has been searched, but no provision has been found for daughter Mary.

Children (HAYWARD), b. Concord:

18 i MARY[4], b. 5 Dec. 1671
19 ii GEORGE, b. 20 July 1673
20 iii JUDITH, b. 9 April 1675
21 iv MARCY (or Mercy), b. 13 May 1677
22 v JOHN, b. 7 July 1680
23 vi (H)ANNAH, b. 30 Aug. 1682
24 vii SARAH, b. 16 June 1689

References: FAM OF PILGRIMS p. 161. CONCORD VR pp. 2, 16-8, 20, 24-5, 31, 435. VR SCITUATE. Middlesex Co. LR 14:518(John Hayward); 16:44-5; 17:175(John Hayward). NEHGR 87:115-8. HAYWARD (JAMES) GEN p. 20.

6 ELIZABETH[3] WHITE (Resolved[2], William[1]), b. Scituate 4 June 1652.

She m. Concord 17 July 1672 OBADIAH WHEELER, b. Concord ca. 1650; son of Obadiah Wheeler.

On 28 March 1712 Obadiah Wheeler Sr. of Concord sold land to his son Obadiah with his wife Elizabeth releasing her dower. They acknowledged the deed 10 March 1712/3. No other land or probate evidence has been found to connect them with their children, and no further mention has been found for Elizabeth and Obadiah in the following sources: land and probate records of Barnstable, Middlesex, Plymouth, Worcester or Suffolk Counties; *Essex Institute Historical Collections;* or *Massachusetts Bay Acts & Resolves*.

Children (WHEELER), b. Concord:

25 i OBADIAH[4], b. 21 Sept. 1673
26 ii JOSIAH, b. 22 Oct. 1675
27 iii URIAH, b. 13 April 1678
28 iv SAMUEL, b. 23 Jan. 1680/1
29 v JONATHAN, b. 28 July 1683
30 vi ELIZABETH, b. 7 Feb. 1685
31 vii JOSEPH, b. 7 March 1690/1
32 viii BENJAMIN, b. 29 Sept. 1693
33 ix JOSHUA, b. 9 April 1696

References: FAM OF PILGRIMS p. 161. CONCORD VR p. 16, 17, 19, 21, 24, 26, 28, 34, 38, 41. VR SCITUATE. Middlesex Co. LR 17:467(Obadiah Wheeler). NEHGR 87:115-8. WHEELER (OBADIAH) GEN p. 6. WHEELER FAM 1:353.

7 JOSIAH[3] WHITE (Resolved[2], William[1]), b. Scituate 29 Sept. 1654; d. Boxford bet. 3 March and 5 June 1710.

He m. before 30 Dec. 1680 REMEMBER READ, bp. Salem 26 April 1657; living at Salem 20 May 1721 when she acknowledged a deed; daughter of Thomas Read. The parentage of Remember is shown through two Essex Co. deeds: On 23 Dec. 1713 Samuel Stacey and others, including Remember White "daughter of Thomas Read, widow of Josiah White and joint administrator with her son Joseph" deeded land; and on 20 July 1720 when Joseph White of Salem, joiner, sold land, Remember White signed off on 20 May 1721. The same Remember acknowledged the deed on 20 May 1720 (*sic*) as "relict of Josiah White late of Salem and mother to the within Joseph."

Josiah was a house carpenter and lived in Boxford and Topsfield. His will, dated 3 March 1710 and proved 5 June 1710, names his wife Remember; sons Josiah, Joseph and Samuel who was under 21; daughters Sarah White and Hannah White who was under 18. The wives of his three sons are named in various deeds.

Children (WHITE), four bp. Salem Village (now Danvers):

34 i JOSIAH[4], bp. 20 May 1705 "adult"
ii MARY, bp. 20 May 1705 "adult"; presumed to have d. bef. 3 March 1710, as she is not mentioned in her father's will.
35 iii JOSEPH
iv SARAH, bp. 26 July 1713 "adult"; n.f.r.
36 v SAMUEL, b. Salem 4 Sept. 1696
vi HANNAH, bp. 1 Nov. 1713 "daughter of Remember"; n.f.r.

References: MD 8:165. FAM OF PILGRIMS p. 161. VR SALEM, SCITUATE. Essex Co. PR 310:244(Josiah White). Essex Co. LR 45:174(Joseph White); 75:178(Samuel Stacey et al). TAG 17:202. ESSEX INST HIST COLL 62:384.

8 DANIEL[3] WHITE (Peregrine[2], William[1]), b. ca. 1649; d. Marshfield 6 May 1724 ae. 70 (VR) or 75 (G.S.).

He m. Marshfield 19 Aug. 1674 HANNAH HUNT, last known to be living 25 May 1721. The probate and land records of Plymouth Colony and Plymouth County shed no light on her identity.

The will of Daniel White of Marshfield, yeoman, dated 25 May 1721 and proved 28 May 1724, names wife Hannah; sons John and Joseph; five youngest sons Thomas, Cornelius, Benjamin, Eleazer and Ebenezer. There is no probate record for Hannah.

Children (WHITE), b. Marshfield:

37 i JOHN[4], b. 26 April 1675
38 ii JOSEPH, b. 1 March 1677/8
iii THOMAS, b. 8 May 1680; d. Hanover 31 March 1762; m. Pembroke 16 April 1719 MARTHA BISBEE, b. Marshfield 13 Oct. 1688; daughter of John and Joanna (Brooks) Bisbee. No probate or land records are available for John or Joanna which connect them with Martha or give us a clue as to what happened to her. No record of Martha's death has been found, nor any children to Thomas. Thomas served in Queen Anne's War in 1710 and was taken care of for many years by his nephew Benjamin White, son of his brother Cornelius.
39 iv CORNELIUS, b. 28 March 1682
40 v BENJAMIN, b. 12 Oct. 1684
41 vi ELEAZER, b. 8 Nov. 1686
42 vii EBENEZER, b. 3[torn] Aug. 1691

References: MD 2:180; 6:19; 7:119; 13:133; 20:61; 30;154; 31:122. FAM OF PILGRIMS p. 163. TAG 17:202; 48:72f. VR PEMBROKE. HANOVER FIRST CH p. 189. MA BAY ACTS & RESOLVES 11:124; 17:212. MARSHFIELD VR pp. 8, 25, 31, 32, 86, 413.

9 JONATHAN[3] WHITE (Peregrine[2], William[1]), b. Marshfield 4 June 1658; d. Yarmouth bet. 14 July 1736 and 22 Feb. 1737.

He m. (1) Yarmouth 2 Feb. 1682/3 HESTER NICKERSON, b. there the last week of Oct. 1656; d. there 8 Feb. 1702/3; daughter of Nicholas and ----- (-----) Nickerson. On 14 May 1706 there was an agreement bet. the children of Mary Nickerson, late of Yarmouth, widow deceased, and Jonathan White who had married one of her daughters.

Jonathan m. (2) ELIZABETH ----- , d. Yarmouth 12 April 1718 "wife of Jonathan White."*

Jonathan was in Yarmouth by 21 Oct. 1677 when he was a witness.

---

*The authors have found no evidence to support the claim of Roscoe R. White in *White Family Record* (1939) pp. 22-25, that Jonathan White married 8 August 1708 Margaret Elizabeth Alexander, b. ca. 1670, and had two children: Alexander, b. 8 Sept. 1709, and Margaret. Alexander is said to have died at Greenwich NJ in Sept. 1776, having had ten children, including one named Peregrine. When Roscoe White submitted this lineage to the Mayflower Society, the only evidence offered was a record in a family Bible printed in 1870, with all entries in the same hand. The Society does not accept this lineage.

The will of Jonathan White, yeoman of Yarmouth, dated 14 July 1736 and proved 22 Feb. 1737, names eldest son Jonathan; 3rd son Joseph; son Ebenezer; daughter Elizabeth White, single; daughters Esther Drake, Sarah White and Mary Russell; and grandson Jonathan Dell, under age.

Children (WHITE), prob. b. Yarmouth:

i ELIZABETH[4], living single 14 July 1736 when her father made his will.
43 ii ESTHER, b. ca. 1685
iii SARAH, may have been the Sarah White bur. Yarmouth 22 Nov. 1762, or she may have m. Bernard Lumbart as his second wife, int. Barnstable 18 March 1741/2 and also int. Yarmouth 22 March 1741/2. He was b. Barnstable April 1668; son of Jabez and Sarah (Derby) Lumbart. No children found. Nothing was found on this Sarah in Barnstable County probate records or in the *MA BAY ACTS & RESOLVES*.
44 iv JONATHAN, "oldest son" in father's will.
45 v EBENEZER, b. 9 Aug. 1698
46 vi JOSEPH, b. ca. 1702
47 vii MARY, prob. b. before 1703

References: MD 2:207-9; 9:122; 33:166, 169. FAM OF PILGRIMS p. 163. TAG 17:202-5. YARMOUTH VR pp. 153, 180. NICKERSON GEN pp. 1-2. Barnstable Co. PR 5:304(Jonathan White); 3:14(Mary Nickerson). Barnstable VR 1:397; 2:418. LUMBERT-LOMBARD pp. 1, 4. NEHGR 79:441-2.

10 PEREGRINE[3] WHITE (Peregrine[2], William[1]), b. Marshfield ca. 1660; bp. Boston 16 Feb. 1723/4 "aged 62"; d. Boston 20 Nov. 1727 "aged 66."

He m. (1) ca. 1684 SUSANNA ----- . He m. (2) before 9 June 1696 MARY ----- , d. after 13 March 1755. Mary m. (2) 1728 Cornelius Judevine.

Peregrine was a blacksmith and lived at Weymouth from 1685 to 1696; he was in Boston Dec. 1696, Concord by 1710, and back in Boston by 1718.

The will of Peregrine White of Boston, blacksmith, dated 27 Oct. 1727 and proved 18 Dec. 1727, left all his property to his wife Mary who was his executrix, and to her heirs.

Child* (WHITE), b. Weymouth:

*In the 1930's the Mayflower Society accepted a claim that Peregrine[3] had a son Mark White. An article appeared in 1958 tending to refute this claim [TAG 34:129-35]. After an extensive review of all available material, including an intensive but fruitless search for Mark's ancestry, we conclude that the claim was based solely on family tradii BENONI[4], b. 26 Jan. 1685; he and his father were involved with the law in a matter of counterfeiting in 1704, when Benoni successfully engraved a plate for the printing of money; n.f.r.; the probate and land records have been searched in Suffolk, Middlesex and Worcester Counties.

References: FAM OF PILGRIMS p. 163. VR WEYMOUTH. (BOSTON) GRANARY BUR GD p. 245. TAG 17:203; 20:91; 34:129. Suffolk Co. PR 26:47 and #5547(Peregrine White). NEHGR 30:438. NGSQ 61:243-8.

11 SARAH[3] WHITE (Peregrine[2], William[1]), b. Marshfield in Oct. 1663; d. Scituate 9 Aug. 1755 in 92nd yr., "widow of Thomas Young."

She m. Scituate in Jan. 1688/9 THOMAS YOUNG, b. there 5 Nov. 1663; d. there 25 Dec. 1732 ae. 69y 1m 20d; son of George and Hannah (Pinson) Young.

Administration on the estate of their father Thomas Young, late of Scituate, was granted 19 March 1732 to George and Thomas Young, both of Scituate. On 23 Jan. 1737 Joseph Young and Joshua Young signed for their share of their father's estate.

Children (YOUNG), b. Scituate:

48 i GEORGE[4], b. 30 Nov. 1689
ii JOSEPH, b. 3 Oct. 1692; d. Scituate Aug. 1699
iii SARAH, b. 12 Sept. 1695; d. Scituate Aug. 1699
iv THOMAS, b. 29 Sept. 1698; d. Scituate Aug. 1699
49 v THOMAS, b. 18 May 1700
50 vi JOSEPH, b. 10 Oct. 1701
vii EBENEZER, b. 1 April 1703; d. before 23 Jan. 1737 when the estate of his father was divided among his four sons.
51 viii JOSHUA, b. 27 Sept. 1704
ix ISAAC, b. 20 Sept. 1706; d. before 23 Jan. 1737

References: MD 8:118; 24:129. BOSTON NEWSLETTER 29 Aug. 1755(death of Sarah Young). FAM OF PILGRIMS

---

tion--not today acceptable evidence. Three impartial referees independently agreed [MQ 39:45].

Copies of the data gathered in our review and search repose in the libraries of the NEHG Society in Boston, and the General Society of Mayflower Descendants in Plymouth. A summary of the data was published in 1973 [NGSQ 61:243-8]. We surmise that Mark White was an immigrant.

The Society no longer accepts new members through Mark White; however, those who have already joined are encouraged to retain membership.

p. 163. VR SCITUATE TAG 17:205. NEHGR 4:192. Plymouth Co. PR 6:323; 7:368(Thomas Young). Plymouth Co. LR 28:13 (George and Joseph Young). SAVAGE 4:671.

12 SYLVANUS[3] WHITE (Peregrine[2], William[1]), b. Marshfield before 1667; d. Scituate before 29 June 1688.

He m. DEBORAH ----- , d. after 30 June 1688. It is likely that she was the daughter of Richard and Elizabeth (Warren) Church, b. 27 Jan. 1657 in Hingham.

Administration on the estate of Sylvanus was granted to his father Peregrine White, Esq. 30 June 1688; Deborah White swore to the inventory of her husband on that same day. No further record of Deborah has been found in Plymouth County records.

A well reasoned article by the late George A. Moriarty presents evidence to prove Sylvanus was father of William[4] White. An Obadiah White was baptized in Marshfield 26 July 1697, who may possibly have been another child of Sylvanus. No further record of him has been found in Plymouth or Marshfield.

Child (WHITE):

52 i WILLIAM[4], b. ca. 1683

References: MD 11:37. TAG 17:195-206; 40:101. Plymouth Co. PR 1:20(Sylvanus White). FAM OF PILGRIMS p. 163.

## FOURTH AND FIFTH GENERATIONS

13 JOHN[4] WHITE (Samuel[3], Resolved[2], William[1]), b. Rochester record 24 Aug. 1669; d. there bet. 29 June and 9 Nov. 1748.

He m. MARTHA ----- , d. after 1748; prob. Martha Dotey, b. ca. May 1672 to Thomas and Mary (Churchill) Dotey.

John went to Sandwich after his marriage and then returned to Rochester. The will of John White of Rochester, yeoman, dated 29 June and proved 9 Nov. 1748, names wife Martha, son Silvenus, daughter Mary, sons Thomas and Justice, daughters Elizabeth and Deborah, and "grandson Nathaniel son of my daughter Jedidah." There are no papers on file for the estate and none of the recorded papers indicate whether Jedidah was living at the time of the will. Son John was probably omitted from the will because he had been given land by his father in 1725.

Children (WHITE):

i JOHN[5], d. Rochester 5 Sept. 1777 ae. 88; m. Barnstable 23 Dec. 1718 MERCY JENKINS, b. there 5 Jan. 1695; d. Rochester 15 May 1769 in 76th yr., "wife of John"; daughter of Thomas and Experience (Hamblin) Jenkins.

Six (WHITE) ch. b. Rochester: William b. 1721, Thomas b. 1722, Ebenezer b. 1724, Malatiah b. 1727, Joseph b. 1731/2, and Marcy b. 1733.

ii MARY, d. Barnstable bef. 18 Feb. 1763; m. (1) Rochester 23 May 1723 NATHAN ELLIS, b. ca. 1698; d. Middleboro or Rochester bef. 16 March 1731/2; son of William and Lydia (-----) Ellis. Mrs. Mary Ellis of Middleboro was named administrator of the estate of her deceased husband Nathan 16 March 1731. John White of Rochester was named guardian of two ch. of the dec. Nathan 1 Aug. 1733. Mary m. (2) Rochester 6 July 1738 JOSIAH JENKINS, b. Barnstable 16 April 1702; d. there bet. 29 Dec. 1749 and 6 Feb. 1749/50; son of Thomas and Experience (Hamblin) Jenkins. The will of Josiah Jenkins of Barnstable, dated 29 Dec. 1749 and probated 6 Feb. 1749/50, gives his estate to his wife and his siblings. The will of Mary Jenkins of Barnstable, widow, dated 21 Nov. 1755 and proved 18 Feb. 1763, names her "only son William Ellis, and only daughter Mariah Jenkins wife of Nathaniel Jenkins," and her two granddaughters.

Two (ELLIS) ch. b. Rochester: William b. 1725 and Mariah b. 1729/30.

iii THOMAS, b. Rochester 15 Feb. 1701; living 29 June 1748 when he was named in his father's will; m. Barnstable 19 April 1727 HOPE JENKINS, b. there 5 July 1704; daughter of Thomas and Experience (Hamblin) Jenkins.

Four (WHITE) ch. b. Rochester: Thomas, Jr. b. 1727, John b. 1729, Jedidah b. 1732 and Hopeful b. 1735.

iv JEDIDAH, b. Rochester 29 Jan. 1703. No m. record discovered, but a ch. is recorded in Rochester: "Nathaniel White, born Ju[-] the 6th, 1722 to Jedidah." Nathaniel was named in his grandfather's will.

One (WHITE) ch. b. Rochester: Nathaniel b. 1722.

v ELIZABETH, b. Rochester 16 Jan. 1704/5; living 29 June 1748 when her father made his will.

vi JUSTIES (or Justus), b. Rochester 28 Feb. 1707; living in 1758 (birth of last child); m. Rochester 20 June 1745 JANE SHERMAN, b. there

2 Oct. 1716; living 17 Oct. 1758 (birth of last child); daughter of John and Sarah (Baker) Sherman. On 6 June 1753 Justis and Silvanus White of Rochester sold a mansion house and farm that was "our father John White's," late of Rochester deceased. "Jean," wife of Justus, and Anna, wife of Silvanus, surrendered dower 7 June 1753; on 13 Sept. of that year Anna acknowledged her signature.

Five (WHITE) ch. b. Rochester: Resolved b. 1746, Edward b. 1748, Justus b. 1751, Major b. 1753 and Jane b. 1758.

vii SALVENUS, b. Rochester 9 Feb. 1709; living in 1768; m. Rochester 16 Nov. 1752 ANNA WILLIAMS, who was living at Rochester 29 Sept. 1768 (birth of last child). No Williams probate record in Plymouth Co. mentions a daughter Anna who could have m. Sylvanus.

Eight (WHITE) ch. b. Rochester: Martha b. 1753, Deborah b. 1755, Cornelius b. 1757, Elizabeth b. 1761, Silvanus b. 1764, twins Jonathan and David b. 1766 and Lusanna b. 1768.

viii EBENEZER, b. Rochester 15 Feb. 1711; d. there 15 March 1710/1 in his first year.

ix DEBORAH, prob. d. Tisbury in April 1801 unnamed "wife of Samuel"; m. Rochester 12 April 1739 SAMUEL LEWIS, b. there ca. 1718; d. Tisbury 5 Jan. 1804 ae. 86. Samuel was a blacksmith.

Five (LEWIS) ch. bp. Rochester: Martha b. 1740, Susanna bp. 1742, Deborah b. 1744, Micah bp. 1745/6 and Susanna bp. 1747.

References: MD 6:236; 9:219; 12:97-8; 14:227; 22:156-160; 33:28, 170. FAM OF PILGRIMS p. 82. VR ROCHESTER, TISBURY. Barnstable VR 1:389; 6:236. Plymouth Co. PR 11:153; 19:125(John White); 6:139,387(Nathan Ellis). Barnstable Co. PR 9:230(Mary Jenkins). Plymouth Co. LR 44:9(Justus and Silvenus White). TAG 17:202; 36:4. NEHGR 5:88; 115:83-5; 120:118-9. BARNSTABLE FAMS pp. 96-7. JENKINS DESC pp. 13-14. SHERMAN DESC pp. 68-9. MARTHA'S VINEYARD BY BANKS 3:179, 235, 237, 274.

14 SAMUEL$^{4}$ WHITE (Samuel$^{3}$, Resolved$^{2}$, William$^{1}$), was b. Rochester record 22 July 1671; living at Tiverton RI 4 March 1734/5 when he acknowledged a deed.

He m. (1) MARY ----- . Did he marry at Barnstable in 1719 SUSANNA GOODSPEED? He m. Dartmouth 11 May 1731 MARY CHASE.

Samuel was last known to be living in Rochester 12 April 1731. (He is not the Samuel who m. Weymouth 6 Dec.

1687 Anna Bingley; that Samuel was son of Joseph and Lydia (Rogers) White; he and Anna had children in Weymouth from 1689 to 1702.)

Children (WHITE), recorded Rochester, first seven by first wife, one by Mary Chase:

i REBECCA[5], b. 2 April 1699; n.f.r.

ii JUDEE, b. 24 Aug. 1701; living 10 Feb. 1771 when she and other subscribers agreed not to request an inventory of the estate of her husband. She m. Tiverton RI 6 May 1727 EBENEZER ANDREWS (Anderson in some records); b. Plymouth 5 May 1704; d. Dartmouth bet. 15 March 1770 and 10 Feb. 1771; son of John Andros. Ebenezer d. bef. 10 Feb. 1771 when there was an agreement not to inventory his estate. Ebenezer's will, dated 15 March 1770 and proved 25 Feb. 1771, names wife Judeath, eldest son John, grandson Peter Creapo, daughter Sary Peckham, daughter Susannah Samson, and sons Ebenezer and Stephen.

Six (ANDREWS) ch. (no birth rec.): John, Sarah, Susanna, Stephen, Ebenezer and Mary (who m. Rochester, Amos Crapo).

iii SAMUEL, b. 28 Jan. 1703/4; d. Rochester 14 Oct. 1762 in 60th yr.; m. there 14 March 1733/4 ELIZABETH ASHLEY, prob. his cousin who was b. Rochester 23 July 1711; daughter of Abraham and Susanna (White) Ashley [see #16 iv]. He may have m. int. (2) Dartmouth and Rochester 5 April 1746 ELIZABETH JACKSON; d. Rochester 26 Jan. 1776 in 60th yr., "widow of Samuel." The will of Samuel White of Dartmouth, yeoman, dated 25 Aug. 1762 and proved 2 Nov. 1762, names wife Elizabeth, son William, and four daughters Rebecca, Betty, Jemima and Mary.

Eight (WHITE) ch., six rec. Dartmouth, three by first wife, three by second: William b. 1734, Amasa b. 1736, Rebecca b. 1738, Samuel b. 1746/7, Edward b. 1748, Elizabeth b. 1750, Jemima and Mary.

iv JOSIAH, b. 17 July 1706; n.f.r.

v MARTHA, b. 5 May 1709; m. int. Rochester 1 Aug. 1734 ROBERT JONES, poss. the one b. Sandwich 28 Aug. 1700 to Adam and Mary (-----) Jones. He m. (1) Rochester 28 Feb. 1722/3 Mary Stuart. Nothing further was located in probate records at Barnstable, Bristol, Middlesex, Plymouth or Suffolk Counties.

vi MAREY, b. 18 Nov. 1711; n.f.r.

vii MALATIAH, b. 24 Aug. 1713; m. Tiverton RI 28 April 1737 JEAN COOMBS, b. Rochester as Jane Coms 29

March 1710; daughter of Anthony Coms. No record found of this family later than 1752. Nothing further located in probates of Barnstable, Bristol, Plymouth or Suffolk Counties.

Four (WHITE) ch. bp. Rochester: Caleb bp. 1743, Josiah bp. 1743, Anthony bp. 1752 and Mary bp. 1752.

viii SUSANNAH, b. 16 Dec. 1731; n.f.r.

References: MD 4:114; 9:219-220; 12:98; 14:227; 30:61. VR DARTMOUTH, ROCHESTER. RI VR 6:Tiverton. Bristol Co. PR 18:14 and original papers(Samuel White); 21:520 and original papers(Ebenezer Andrews). NEHGR 5:88; 36:19. TAG 17:198. BOSTON TRANSCRIPT 24 March 1938 #6956.

15 MALATIAH[4] WHITE (Samuel[3], Resolved[2], William[1]), was b. Rochester record 14 Feb. 1676; d. there 21 Aug. 1709 in 39th yr. (Printed and original VR both state this age, although it does not agree with birth record.)

He m. MERCY WINSLOW, b. Yarmouth ca. 1676; d. Rochester before 16 July 1755; daughter of Kenelm and Mercy (Worden) Winslow. Mercy m. (2) bet. Dec. 1712 and Dec. 1715 Thomas Jenkins of Barnstable.

Administration on the estate of Malatiah White late of Rochester, deceased, was granted to his widow Mercy 21 Sept. 1709; her account of 18 Dec. 1712 names eldest son Meletiah White, eldest daughter Judah, 2nd daughter Mercy, 3rd daughter Margaret. On 22 Dec. 1715 a further accounting by Marcy, late widow of Meletiah White and now wife of Thomas Jenkins of Barnstable, mentions her four children by Meletiah, the eldest of whom was not ten when his father died. An administrator on the estate of Marcy Jenkins, late of Rochester widow, was appointed 16 July 1755.

Children (WHITE), b. Rochester:

i JUDE[5], b. 17 July 1699; d. Barnstable 27 April 1729 "wife of Ebenezer." She m. as "Judith" at Barnstable 9 Nov. 1721 EBENEZER JENKINS, b. there 5 Dec. 1697; d. June 1750; son of Thomas and Experience (Hamblin) Jenkins. He m. (2) Barnstable 25 July 1732 Elizabeth Tupper and had four ch. The will of Ebenezer Jenkins, dated 19 June and proved 5 July 1750, names his wife Elizabeth and all ch. by both marriages.

One (JENKINS) ch. b. Barnstable to Ebenezer and Judith: Thomas b. 1725/6.

ii MERCY, b. 22 July 1702; living 18 Dec. 1712 according to an account of her father's estate.

iii MARGARET, b. 13 March 1703/4; d. bef. 17 June 1783 (not mentioned in husband's will); m. Barnstable 19 Sept. 1727 EDWARD MORSE, b. Plymouth 25 July 1704; d. Rochester bet. 17 June 1783 and 8 Sept. 1784; son of Joshua and Elizabeth (Dotey) Morse, a descendant of Pilgrims Cooke, Doty and Hopkins. The will of Edward Morse of Rochester, dated 17 June 1783 and proved 8 Sept. 1784, names sons Joshua, Edward, Benjamin, John and Ebenezer, and grandson Ebenezer Morse.

Ten (MORSE) ch. b. or bp. Rochester: Joshua b. 1728, Edward b. 1730, Marcy b. 1732, Malletiah b. 1733, Marcy b. 1735/6, John b. 1738, Benjamin b. 1740, Benjamin b. 1742, Ebenezer b. 1746 and Ebenezer b. 1747.

iv MALATIAH, b. 17 March 1706/7; living 18 Dec. 1712 according to an account of his father's estate.

References: MD 2:163; 6:236; 12:98; 14:89; 22:156-158; 32:55; 33:28; 34:18-20. VR ROCHESTER. Barnstable VR 1:333, 389; 2:355, 425. Plymouth Co. PR 13:488, 523 & #11412(Mercy Jenkins); #22592(Malatiah White); #22593(gdns. for ch. of Malatiah); #14187(Edward Morse). Barnstable Co. PR 8:114(Thomas Jenkins); 8:254(Ebenezer Jenkins). TAG 17:201. NEHGR 5:88. NORTH BROOKFIELD BY TEMPLE p. 787. BARNSTABLE FAMS 2:95-96. WINSLOW MEM 1:74-78. JENKINS DESC p. 13. HAMLIN FAM 1:101. MORSE GEN 1:24,46. MORSE MEM(1896) pp. 39, 98.

16 SUSANNA[4] WHITE (Samuel[3], Resolved[2], William[1]), b. Rochester 5 April 1682; d. bef. 1733.

She m. Sandwich 9 Sept. 1703 ABRAHAM ASHLEY, b. Rochester 28 July 1682; d. there bef. 5 Nov. 1759. He m. (2) Rochester 22 Nov. 1733 Elizabeth Rogers.

No probate was found for Susanna, but the inventory of the estate of Abraham Ashley, late of Rochester, was sworn to by his widow and administratrix, Elizabeth, 5 Nov. 1759.

Children (ASHLEY), b. Rochester:

i REBECCA[5], b. 30 March 1704; n.f.r.

ii MERCY, b. 5 Oct. 1708. She was prob. the one who m. Rochester 12 Feb. 1732/3 WILLIAM ASHLEY, prob. her cousin who was b. Rochester 12 Dec. 1708; son of Joseph and Elizabeth (Percival) Ashley. He is prob. the William Ashley who d. at Freetown bef. 23 Dec. 1783 (date of inventory of his estate). He may have m. int. (2) Tiverton RI 31 May 1746 Elizabeth (Macomber) Rounseville and had three ch. No probate was found for his first wife. An account of his estate 5 March 1793 mentions his widow, unnamed, and administrator Levi Rounsvell. A William Ashley of Freetown deeded to son Abraham of Dartmouth 18 Jan. 1771, and to son Jepthah of Freetown 15 Aug. 1776, some of his land in Freetown.

Two (ASHLEY) ch. prob. b. to William and Mercy: Abraham and Jephthah b. 1743.

iii WILLIAM, b. 17 May 1710; n.f.r.

iv ELIZABETH, b. 23 July 1711; prob. the one who m. Rochester 14 March 1733/4 SAMUEL WHITE, prob. her cousin (see Samuel #14 iii).

References: MD 30:60. VR ROCHESTER. RI VR 6:Tiverton p. 7. Plymouth Co. PR 15:410(Abraham Ashley. Bristol Co. PR 28:245; 32:237(William Ashley). Bristol Co. LR 53:370; 56:88; 58:224(William Ashley). TAG 17:202.

17 PENELOPE[4] WHITE (Samuel[3], Resolved[2], William[1]), b. Rochester 12 March 1687; d. bef. 23 Nov. 1738.

She m. Rochester 31 May 1704 PETER CRAPO, b. poss. Bordeaux, France; d. Rochester bet. 20 Feb. and 1 May 1756. He m. (2) Rochester 23 Nov. 1738 Ann Luce.

Tradition says that as a lad Peter was shipwrecked on Cape Cod about 1680 and given the name of Pierre Crapeau; he lived with Francis Coombs in Middleboro. The will of Peter Crapo of Rochester, yeoman, dated 20 Feb. 1756 and proved 3 May 1756, names his wife Ann; sons Frances (*sic*), Peter, John and Hezekiah "they to provide for their mother-in-law [stepmother] my widow," and sons Nicholas and Seth; four daughters Susannah Demeranville, Mary Spooner, Elizabeth Luke (*sic*) and Rebecca Matthews. Receipts of heirs name the husbands of his daughters: James Lake, Louis Demaranville, Jonathan Spooner and John Matthews.

Children (CRAPO), b. Rochester by first wife:

i FRANCIS[5], b. 14 Oct. 1705; d. after 1759 when he received property from his father's estate and before his wife's death; m. Dartmouth 13 Feb. 1734/5 PATIENCE SPOONER, b. there 20 March 1717/8; d. Rochester 11 April 1794 "the widow Patience"; daughter of Nathan and Patience (-----) Spooner.

Eight (CRAPO) ch. b. Rochester: Francis b. 1738, Penelope b. 1739, Jonathan b. 1742, Mary b. 1744, Jeremiah b. 1746, Rest b. 1748, William

b. 1750 and Spooner b. 1753.

ii SUSANNA, b. 5 Nov. 1707; d. after 28 Dec. 1757, when she received property from her father's estate, and bef. her husband's death; m. Rochester 8 Dec. 1730 LOUIS DEMARANVILLE, who came to Dartmouth from Paris, France; he d. Dartmouth bef. 28 Sept. 1772. The will of Louis D'Marainville of Dartmouth, yeoman, dated 26 June 1772, was disallowed 6 Oct. 1772. The final distribution of the estate 9 April 1775 names ch.: Chaumont, John, Charles, Mary Demoranville, Frances Demoranville, Susannah Spooner, Gabriel Demoranville, heirs of Elizabeth Simmons deceased, Thankful Demoranville, Stephen and Louis.

Eleven (DEMARANVILLE) ch.: Chaumont b. 1730, John, Mary b. 1735, Frances (or Francoise), Susannah b. ca. 1739, Gabriel, Elizabeth, Thankful, Charles b. ca. 1744, Stephen b. 1750 and Louis.

iii PETER, b. 20 Nov. 1709; living at Rochester 29 July 1762 when he sold land there; m. Dartmouth 24 May 1734 ELEANOR TABER, b. there 28 March 1713; daughter of Joseph and Elizabeth (Spooner) Taber. The will of Joseph Taber of Dartmouth dated 20 Dec. 1748 and proved 6 Feb. 1753, names his daughter Eleanor Crapo. Peter Crapo prob. m. (2) Rochester 13 Feb. 1755 Hannah Axdill of Middleboro. No evidence was found to support the claim that Eleanor (Taber) Crapo d. before 1738. This seems to be based on the assumption that $Peter^5$ m. Ann Luce in 1738, whereas it was his father $Peter^4$ who m. Ann, and she is named in her husband's will. On 1 May 1756 Peter sold land bounded by land owned by his father at his death; Hannah, wife of Peter, released her dower.

One (CRAPO) ch. b. Rochester: Amas b. 1735.

iv JOHN, b. 22 Feb. 1711/2; d. Rochester after 16 May 1783 when he acknowledged a deed; he m. Rochester 7 Nov. 1734 SARAH CLARK, b. there 18 March 1714/5; d. after 24 Dec. 1776, when she and her husband John sold land; daughter of John and Mary (Tobey) Clark. The estate of John Clark of Rochester was ordered to be divided bet. his wife and ch., including daughter Sarah Crapo; she and husband John Crapo signed receipts 5 May 1760.

Eleven (CRAPO) ch. b. Rochester: Consider b. 1735, Elnathan b. 1737, John b. 1739, Sarah b. 1740, Peter b. 1743, Joshua b. 1746, Rest b. 1748, Jean b. 1750, Rest b. 1753, Mary b. 1755, John b. 1758.

v MARY, b. 27 Sept. 1713; living 28 Dec. 1757 when she received her portion of her father's estate; m. Rochester 31 Dec. 1733 JONATHAN SPOONER, b. Dartmouth 26 Nov. 1711; son of Nathan Spooner; prob. living 28 Dec. 1757 when "Mary, wife of Jonathan Spooner" received her portion of her father's estate. Jonathan was a farmer. No land or probate record was found for this family in Plymouth or Barnstable Cos.

Seven (SPOONER) ch. b. Dartmouth: Barnabas b. 1735, Thomas b. 1737, Nathan b. 1740, Bigford b. 1743, Lazarus b. 1747, Patience b. 1749 and Jonathan b. 1755.

vi ELIZABETH, d. Dutchess Co. NY after 2 March 1759 when she received her share of her father's estate; m. Rochester 31 Oct. 1734 JAMES LAKE, b. Tiverton or Little Compton RI 18 July 1710; d. Poughkeepsie NY 1771/2; son of John and Susanna (Case) Lake. No further record on this family was found in Plymouth or Barnstable County land or probate records.

Four (LAKE) ch. b. Little Compton RI: Crapo b. 1735, Susanna b. 1736, Alice b. 1740 and Merebah b. 1742.

vii REBECCA, b. 22 March 1717/8; d. Rochester 30 Jan. 1791 in 73rd yr., "widow of John"; m. there 5 Jan. 1743 JOHN MATTHEWS, who was living 5 July 1774, a cordwainer. He was not the son of John and Hannah Matthews b. 29 March 1717. Nothing further was located on this couple in Plymouth or Barnstable County land or probate records.

viii HEZEKIAH, b. 12 March 1719/20; d. Rochester 11 March 1795 unm. Administration on the estate of Hezekiah Crapo of Rochester was granted 23 March 1795 to Nicholas and Philip Crapo of Rochester. On the day of his death Hezekiah deeded to nieces Bethia and Rebecca Crapo, singlewomen, "for kindness and favors received," various livestock and the right to dwell in his house.

ix NICHOLAS, b. 5 Dec. 1721; d. Rochester 3 Oct. 1793 in 73rd yr., "son of Pero"; m. Rochester 14 Sept. 1749 ALICE BLACKWELL, b. there 19 May 1725 (rec. as Alse); d. there 23 Sept. 1800 in 78th yr., "widow of Nicholas"; daughter of Caleb and Bethia (Tabor) Blackwell. [See *The Richard Warren Family* for Alice's ancestry.] The will of Caleb Blackwell of Rochester, dated 9 Nov. 1762 and proved 28 April 1763, names "son-in-law Nicholas Crapo" as executor; and in a deed of 1752 Nicholas Crapo of Rochester sold land to his "father Caleb Blackwell" and mentioned his father Peter Crapo. The will of Nicholas Crapo of Rochester, dated 26 Sept. 1793 and proved 20 Nov. 1793, names wife Alice, sons Nicholas and Philip, daughter Alice wife of William Crapo, and daughters Bethiah and Rebecca "both unmarried."

Seven (CRAPO) ch. b. Rochester: Bethia bp. 1752, Bethia b. 1753, Allice b. 1756, Michah b. 1759, Rebecca b. 1761, Nicholas b. 1765 and Philip b. 1767.

x SETH, b. 19 May 1722; d. Ballston NY bef. 10 Nov. 1810; m. int. Freetown 20 July 1751 ABIGAIL PALMER, b. Dartmouth 17 Dec. 1729; living 16 April 1794 when Seth made his will; daughter of William and Hester (-----) Palmer. The will of William Palmer of Freetown, dated 1774 and proved 1775, names his wife Esther, son-in-law Seth Crapo and daughter Abigail Crapo. Seth and Abigail were in Rochester as late as 21 May 1779 when he deeded land. Seth is listed in Ballston in the 1790 census. The will of Seth Crapo of Ballston, Saratoga Co. NY dated 16 April 1794 and admitted to probate 10 Nov. 1810, names wife Abigail, daughter Esther wife of Isaac How, daughter Eunice wife of David How, sons Seth, Thomas, Hezekiah and Samuel.

Six (CRAPO) ch.: Esther b. 1755, Eunice, Seth, Thomas, Hezekiah and Samuel.

References: MD 9:220; 12:97; 13:224. VR DARTMOUTH, ROCHESTER. RI VR 6:Little Compton, Tiverton. Freetown VR 1:16. MIDDLEBORO DEATHS p. 47. TAG 12:23. Bristol Co. PR 22:347; 23:594(Louis Demarainville); 23:433 (William Palmer); 13:289(Joseph Taber). Plymouth Co. PR 14:146; 16:468(Peter Crapo); 34:23; 35:405(Hezekiah Crapo); 48:263(Nicholas Crapo); 16:420, 430(Caleb Blackwell); 33:480, #5194(Nicholas Crapo). Plymouth Co. LR 53:147 (Peter Crapoo); 56:238(John, Peter & Hezekiah Crapo); 46:164(John Clark); 60:150; 75:15(John Crapo); 52:81(Peter, John and Hezekiah Crapo); 83:154(William Crapo); 48:192(John Mathas); 58:83(John Mathes); 58:170(John Matthews); 77:222(Hezekiah Crapo); 42:167(Nicholas Crapo); 62:111(Seth Crapo). 1790 Census NY:18(Seth Creps). FOWLER HIST pp. 479-80. Aspinwall Papers (birthdates of Nicholas and Seth Crapo). MATTHEWS FAM. DEMARANVILLE GEN. Saratoga Co. Surrogate 2:233(will of Seth Crapo). LITTLE COMPTON FAMS pp. 393, 394, 648. CRAPO GEN 1:74. SPOONER DESC 1:42, 74, 81-2. POULTNEY VT BY JOSLIN p. 305. TABER GEN (1952) pp. 8, 13. NEHGR 117:192-3.

18 MARY HAYWARD[4] (Anna[3] White, Resolved[2], William[1]), b. Concord 5 Dec. 1671; in all probability d. bet. 20 Nov. 1727 when a Mary Willard rendered an account on the estate of her husband, and 9 March 1729 when an administrator was appointed on the "estate of John Willard...unadministered by his widow Mary, lately also deceased."

She almost certainly m. Concord 31 Oct. 1698 JOHN WILLARD, b. there 12 Feb. 1656/7; d. there 27 Aug. 1726 "husband to Mary"; son of Simon and Mary (Dunster) Willard.

In a decree for settlement of the estate of John Willard late of Concord, dated 25 Sept. 1732, sons Jonathan and Simon were to pay their brother David and sister Mercy Willard. Present at the reading of the decree were Simon Willard, "William Wheeler Jr. who married a daughter," and Joseph Wright, guardian to the eldest son "non-compos."

Although the Mary Hayward who married John Willard as detailed above appears to be the daughter of John and Anna[3] (White) Hayward, lack of mention of her in family records gives some cause for doubt. There are no estates for either John Hayward or his wife Anna, but John deeded to his eldest son George and his other son John. The latter deed states that George and John are brothers. The deed of John Hayward the father, to John[4] the son, of almost everything he owned, provided that the son care for his father and mother, and after their deaths pay certain amounts to sisters Judith Goss, Mercy Brown, Sarah Allen and Anna Allen: No mention is made of a sister Mary. In 1715 John[4] Hayward deeded to John Willard a saw mill etc., a consideration being that he care for "my father John Hayward" and after the latter's death, pay to the same four sisters mentioned above: Again no mention of Mary.

However, a month later John[4] Hayward sold his own house and other property received from his father to the same John Willard; and in 1717 John Willard paid off a mortgage of John[4] Hayward. Further, the *Willard Memoir* indicates that it was Mary, daughter of John[3] Hayward, who married John Willard. Since there are no deeds which connect John Willard with any other Hayward family, it seems almost certain that he did marry the Mary whose father he promised to care for. The Mayflower Society accepts this line for purposes of membership.

Children (WILLARD), b. Concord:

i DAVID[5], b. 9 Sept. 1699; living unm. in Concord 1757; on 8 Dec. 1727 the court requested inquiry into his condition, his brother Jonathan saying that he was of weak understanding; on 9 March 1729 a guardian was appointed for David Willard "non-compos" of Concord, son of John Willard deceased. By 17 Jan. 1757 bond was given by William Wheeler of Concord and Nathaniel Wheeler of Acton to "support and bury" William's brother [in-law] David Willard.

ii JONATHAN, b. 28 April 1701; living in Sheffield in 1753 (birth of last child); m. (1) in 1722 SARAH ----- , who d. Concord 16 Jan. 1729/30 "wife of Jonathan"; m. (2) Sheffield Oct. 1740 ABIGAIL YOUNGLOVE, perhaps daughter of Samuel and Abigail (Smith) Younglove who were m. in Haverhill. Jonathan Willard, carpenter, bought land in Sheffield in Jan. 1743/4 on which he built a house, but sold the house and acreage in July 1744. From 1756-63 Jonathan Willard, millwright of Sheffield and later Great Barrington, bought and sold land in those towns. This could be either Jonathan[5] or his son.

Ten (WILLARD) ch., three b. Concord by first wife: Jonathan b. 1723, John b. 1725, Josiah b. 1727/8; seven b. Sheffield by second wife: David b. 1741, Daniel b. 1742, Mary b. 1744, Susanna b. 1746, Mercy b. 1748, Samuel b. 1750 and Catherine b. 1753.

iii MERCY, b. 4 June 1704; d. Concord 17 Feb. 1760 "wife of William"; m. WILLIAM WHEELER b. Concord 9 Jan. 1693/4; d. there bef. 6 Oct. 1769 (date of bond on administrator of his estate); son of William and Sarah (Fletcher) Wheeler. The distribution of his estate on 23 April 1770 named eldest son William Willard (born as Willard), youngest son Oliver, eldest daughter Mary Walker, 2nd daughter Catherine Wheeler and youngest daughter Marcy Kingsman.

Seven (WHEELER) ch. b. Concord: Mary b. 1729, Catherine b. 1730/1, William b. 1732, Willard b. 1734, Mercy b. 1737/8, Wareham b. 1740 and Oliver b. 1742.

iv SIMON, b. 2 Aug. 1708; d. Sheffield 19 Oct. 1766 in his 60th yr., "born Concord 7 Aug. 1706 (*sic*) removed to Sheffield in 1729"; m. Sheffield 28 Nov. 1744 ZERVIAH (NASH) BEALES, widow of John; b. Northampton 2 Nov. 1713; living 30 June 1767, date of her appointment as administratrix of Simon's estate; daughter of Daniel and Experience (Clark) Nash.

Six (WILLARD) ch. b. Sheffield: Dubertus b. 1745, Simon b. 1746/7, Lewis b. 1749, Rufus b. 1751, Anna-Mary b. 1755 and Frederick.

References: VR HAVERHILL. CONCORD VR pp. 8, 16, 38, 46, 48, 51, 61, 72, 108, 115, 118, 121-22, 125, 133, 137, 146, 150, 155, 205. LANCASTER VR p. 451.

Sheffield VR(typescript NEHG Soc.) pp. 18, 43, 46. Middlesex Co. PR #24944(John Willard); #24380(William Wheeler); #24938(David Willard). Middlesex Co. LR 16:45(John Hayward); 17:110, 352, 355(John Hayward Jr.). Berkshire Co. LR 1:6-7; 2:222(Jonathan Willard). Berkshire Co. PR #796 (Simon Willard). NASH FAM pp. 37-8, 54-5. WILLARD MEM pp. 376-7. Hampden Co. LR 0:104, 322; Y:669; 1:790(Jonathan Willard). HARVARD GRADS 13:681. WHEELER FAM 2:1024, 1062. GREAT BARRINGTON BY TAYLOR pp. 103, 132-3.

19 GEORGE HAYWARD[4] (Anna[3] White, Resolved[2], William[1]), was b. Concord 20 July 1673; d. Brookfield 5 July 1725.

He m. Concord 17 Jan. 1695/6 HANNAH CHADWICK, b. perhaps in England bef. 1673; living in Brookfield 9 Aug. 1734 when she purchased land; daughter of John and Sarah (-----) Chadwick. The will of John Chadwick of Watertown, dated 31 Jan. 1710 presented 5 May 1710, names wife Sarah and daughter Hannah Haward.

George was a miller in Brookfield starting in 1718. The settlement of the estate of George Howard late of Brookfield 25 April 1727 names widow Hannah; Ephraim Howard, eldest son; Edward Walker in his wife's right; Judith, Hannah, Experience, Mercy, Jonas and Sarah Howard. A second settlement 24 May 1727 names Edward Walker and his wife Elenor, and Experience Howard.

Children (HAYWARD), b. Concord:

i SIMON[5], b. 2 June 1696; d. Concord 19 July 1696.

ii EPHRAIM, b. 26 July 1697; living in Western (now Warren) 19 April 1756 when the court granted his petition; m. Brookfield 28 June 1726 JOANNA WHEELER (see #28 iii), b. Concord 13 Aug. 1708; d. after 14 Nov. 1745 (birth of last child). Ephraim was a blacksmith. No probate record was located for him in Worcester Co., nor any Worcester Co. deeds after 1754, but the family is found in Onslow N.S. ca. 1760.
Nine (HAYWARD) ch. b. Brookfield and Warren: Mary b. 1727, Abigail b. 1729/30, Martha b. 1731, Anna b. 1733/4, George b. 1735, Lucy, Mary b. 1743, Thankful b. 1745 and Joanna.

iii ELENER, b. 1 Nov. 1699; d. Brookfield bef. 29 July 1778, the date of the bond on the administrator of her estate; m. Brookfield 4 April 1723 EDWARD WALKER, b. Charlestown 25 May 1690; d. Brookfield 12 Sept. 1754; son of Edward and Elizabeth (Dean) Walker. He m. (1) Dorothy ----- by whom he had one son in Brookfield. The division of the estate of Lt. Edward Walker late of Brookfield dated 22 Dec. 1755 names widow Eleanor Walker, Silvanus Walker, Adonirum Walker,

Edward Walker (son of 1st wife), Ephraim Walker, Gideon Walker, Dorothy Walker, Elizabeth Walker, Zebulon Walker and Solomon Walker. Widow Eleanor's part of the estate was divided 6 April 1779 among: heirs of Edward Walker Jr. deceased, heirs of Ephraim Walker deceased, Phineas Upham in the right of Silvanus Walker, Adonirum Walker, Gideon Walker, Solomon Walker, Zebulon Walker, Ithar Wright in the right of his wife Elizabeth daughter of deceased, and Dorothy Walker daughter of deceased.

Nine (WALKER) ch. b. Brookfield to Edward and Elener: Ephraim b. 1723, Dorothy b. 1726, Silvanus b. 1728, Elizabeth b. 1730, Hannah b. 1732, Adoniram b. 1734, Gideon b. 1737, Zebulon b. 1740 and Solomon b. 1744.

iv JUDITH, b. 31 March 1701; d. Warren 7 March 1786 in 86th yr., "wife of Hezekiah"; m. Brookfield 23 April 1734 HEZEKIAH MARKS, a blacksmith, b. there; d. Warren 6 Sept. 1788 in 84th yr.; son of Joseph and Mary (-----) Marks. The will of Hezekiah Marks of Western, husbandman advanced in age, dated 12 April 1786 and filed 28 Oct. 1788, names son Adonijah, daughters Eunis Rice, Mary Burbanks, children of daughter Martha Talmadge deceased, and daughter Miriam Davis.

Five (MARKS) ch. b. Warren: Adonijah b. 1734, Eunice b. 1737, Mary b. 1740, Martha b. 1744 and Miriam.

v JOHN, b. 12 Feb. 1702/3; drowned Concord 22 July 1706.

vi EXPERIENCE, b. 9 Feb. 1704/5; d. Brookfield Jan. 1791 ae. 86; m. there 28 June 1726 BENJAMIN WALKER*, b. Charlestown 9 Jan. 1697/8; d. Brookfield 23 March 1763 "husband of Exsperance"; son of Edward and Elizabeth (Dean) Walker. The will of Benjamin Walker of Brookfield, gentleman, dated 9 March 1763 and allowed 29 March 1763, names wife Experience, sons Silas, Benjamin Jr., daughters Lois and Eunice Walker, grandchildren Silas Rice and Levi Rice, children of daughter Thankful Rice deceased, friend and Kin Sarah Walker, wife of Ephraim; and Sarah Wakefield.

Nine (WALKER) ch. b. Brookfield: Lois b. 1726, Gideon b. 1728, Silas b. 1730, Eunice b. 1732, Exsperance b. 173[?], Thankful b. 1738, Benjamin b. 1740, Lois b. 1742 and Eunice b. 1745.

vii HANNAH, b. 2 April 1707; d. Conway 16 Jan. 1805

---

*The claimed marriage of Experience Hayward, granddaughter of Anna$^3$ White, to James Dunbar of Bridgewater has been disproved. [See *TAG* 47:42-4.]

ae. 96y 9m "widow of Jonathan, formerly of Brookfield"; m. (1) Brookfield the 13th of an unknown month in 1731 EBENEZER JENNINGS, b. there 24 Jan. 1707/8; d. there 25 March 1770 in 63rd yr.; son of Stephen and Mary (-----) Jennings. Hannah m. (2) Brookfield 21 Nov. 1782 JONATHAN RICHARDSON, d. bef. 1 May 1801 when Hannah Richardson, widow in Conway, deeded land. A distribution of the estate of Ebenezer Jennings late of Brookfield, gentleman, dated 6 Oct. 1770, names widow Hannah and daughters Mary Brewer, Hannah Jennings, Persis Nelson, Zilpah Jennings and Lydia Gould.

Five (JENNINGS) ch. b. Brookfield: Mary b. 1732, Hannah b. 1739, Persis b. 1742, Zilpha b. 1744 and Lida (or Lydia) b. 1746/7.

viii AMOS, b. 10 March 1708/9; d. Concord 23 March 1708/9.

ix MARCY, b. 25 Sept. 1710; d. Warren 5 Oct. 1769 in 58th yr., "wife of John"; m. Brookfield 24 May 1737 JOHN BLAIR, b. Ireland in 1710; d. Warren 10 May 1796 in 86th yr.; son of Robert and Isabella (Rankin) Blair. He m. (2) Palmer 19 Nov. 1771 Katherine Shaw. The estate of John Blair was ordered settled 4 Oct. 1796 with one-third to Katherine Blair, and residue divided among Francis Blair, Molly Brown, Ezekiel Blair, Robert Blair, Sarah Glezen, Timothy Blair and Samuel Blair.

Seven (BLAIR) ch. b. Warren: Francis b. 1737, Molly b. 1740, Ezekiel b. 1742, Robbard b. 1744, Sarah b. 1746, Timothy b. 1749 and Samuel b. 1752.

x JONAS, b. 5 Feb. 1712/3; d. Warren 3 Jan. 1756; m. Brookfield 21 Aug. 1734 DEBROTH (or Deborah) GILBERT, b. there 7 July 1714; d. Heath 28 Jan. 1805 ae. 92; daughter of Ebenezer and Deborah (-----) Gilbert. She m. (2) in 1764 David Jones of Wilbraham. On 23 May 1757 the estate of Jonas Hayward, late of Western yeoman, was settled among the widow Deborah and the ch.: Jonas, John, George, Moses, Solomon, Sarah, Mary, Deborah, Zerviah, Hannah and Marcy. On 16 Dec. 1767 Deborah Jones of Wilbraham was called widow of Jonas Hayward, in the sale of her inheritance.

Eleven (HAYWARD) ch. b. Warren: Jonas b. 1735, John b. 1736, George b. 1738, Sarah b. 1740, Mary b. 1742, Deborah b. 1743, Moses b. 1745, Solomon b. 1747, Zerviah b. 1749, Hannah b. 1750/1 and Marcy b. 1754.

xi SARAH, b. 7 Aug. 1715; living 24 May 1727. Did she m. and have daughter Sarah Wakefield b. ca. 1747? Benjamin Walker of Brookfield was appointed guardian to a Sarah Wakefield ae. 14 daughter of ----- Wakefield, late of Boston mariner, 26 Sept. 1761.

References: VR BROOKFIELD, CONWAY, HEATH, WARREN(called Western until 1834). CONCORD VR pp. 17, 41, 42, 44, 48, 51, 54, 57, 62, 67, 69, 72, 75, 81, 86. Hampshire Co. PR Box 74 #33(George Howard); Box 79 #37 (David Jones). Worcester Co. PR #61259(Edward Walker); #61264(Eleanor Walker); #38764(Hezikiah Marks); #61228 (Benjamin Walker); #61114(Gdn. Sarah Wakefield); #33050 (Ebenezer Jennings); #5828(John Blair); #28623(Gdn. of Hannah Hayward); #28658(Jonas Hayward). Middlesex Co. PR #4105(John Chadwick). Worcester Co. LR 8:46-7; 35:A269 (Ephraim Hayward); 93:369(Hezekiah Marks et al); 158:283 (Reuben Hendrick et al); 168:270(Ezra Torry and Zilpha). Middlesex Co. LR 14:518; 17:175(John Hayward). HAYWARD (JAMES) GEN pp. 20-1. CHARLESTOWN BY WYMAN 2:991. BLAIR FAM pp. 31, 41. GILBERT (THOMAS) DESC p. 121. NORTH BROOKFIELD BY TEMPLE pp. 177, 597, 650, 680, 767. TAG 31:65-8; 47:42-4. WATERTOWN BY BOND p. 151. WHEELER FAM 2:1060. Correction Bk. 3 p. 59, NEHG Soc.(2nd m. and d. Deborah Gilbert). MA BAY ACTS AND RESOLVES 15:753(Ephraim Hayward). Onslow Nova Scotia Town Clerk.

20 JUDITH HAYWARD$^4$ (Anna$^3$ White, Resolved$^2$, William$^1$), b. Concord 9 April 1675; d. Brookfield 18 April 1748 in 74th year, "widow of Capt. Philip."

She m. Concord 30 Aug. 1699 PHILIP GOSS, bp. Roxbury 16th day, 12th month, 1678/9*; d. Brookfield 13 Sept. 1747 in 70th year, "Capt. Philip, husband of Judith"; son of Philip and Hannah (Hopkins) Goss. This is not a Mayflower Hopkins line.

Thomas Goss of Bolton, clerk, was appointed administrator of the estate of Judith Goss, late of Brookfield widow, 1 May 1748. The distribution of the estate of Philip Goss, late of Brookfield gentleman, in Aug. 1748, names Mrs. Judith Goss, his widow; 2nd son John; [grandson] Philip Goss, son of eldest son Philip deceased; son Rev. Thomas Goss; heirs of eldest son Philip Goss deceased; Judith Gilbert, wife of Thomas Jr.; Hannah Rich, wife of Experience; Thankful White, wife of John; and Mary Walker, wife of Daniel.

Children (GOSS) were:

i JUDITH$^5$, d. bef. husband wrote will 24 Aug. 1779; m. Brookfield 2 Dec. 1718 THOMAS GILBERT, b.

**Hartford Times* gives his birth at Roxbury 16 Dec. 1676.

there ca. 1695; d. there 13 Feb. 1781; son of Henry and Elizabeth (Beldin) Gilbert. The will of Thomas Gilbert of Brookfield, dated 24 Aug. 1779 and filed 5 March 1781, names sons Lemuel and Philip, daughters Anna, Elizabeth, Thankful and Judith, sons Abner, John, Thomas, and ch. of sons Seth and Jedidiah.

Thirteen (GILBERT) ch. b. Brookfield: Thomas b. 1719/20, Abner b. 1721, John b. 1723, Anna b. 172[5], Seth b. 1727/8, Jedediah b. 1730, Elizabeth b. 1732, Philip b. 1734, Thankful b. 1737/8, Thomas b. 1739, Jedediah b. 1742, Judith b. 1745 and Lemuel b. 1747.

ii PHILIP, d. Brookfield bef. 17 Sept. 1742 (date of inventory of his estate); m. there 25 Nov. 1723 KEZIAH COOLEY, b. Springfield 29 Oct. 1702; d. Brookfield bef. 4 Feb. 1745; daughter of Benjamin and Margaret (Bliss) Cooley. Did widow Keziah Goss m. Brookfield 18 April 1744 Timothy Brown [see #21 ii]? In the settlement of the estate of Philip$^5$'s father Capt. Philip Goss, Keziah$^6$ Goss and her husband Zachariah Haskell gave up rights to her grandfather Philip Goss' property. This clears up some of the errors and confusion resulting from the multiplicity of Philip Gosses. An inventory of the estate of Philip$^5$ Goss of Brookfield was made 17 Sept. 1742. The bond on Philip$^6$ Goss is dated 4 Feb. 1745 to administer his father's estate "which was formerly committed to his widow now deceased." The settlement on 4 March 1745/6 orders Philip Goss, eldest son, to pay his brothers and sisters as follows: Thomas Haskell for wife Hanna; Zachariah Haskell for wife Keziah, Thomas Goss, minor, and Judith Goss, minor.

Seven (GOSS) ch. b. Brookfield: Philip b. 1724, Hannah b. 1726, Ebenezer b. 1728, Keziah b. 1730, Judith b. [1731], Nathaniel b. [1733] and Thomas b. 1734/5.

iii HANNAH, d. after 19 Dec. 1770, the date of her husband's will; m. Brookfield 27 May 1723 EXPERIENCE RICH, b. there; d. Western (now Warren) bet. 19 Dec. 1770 and 18 Jan. 1771; son of Thomas and Mary (Taylor) Rich. The will of Experience Rich of Western, yeoman, dated 19 Dec. 1770 and filed 18 Jan. 1771, names wife Hannah, daughters Mehitable Smith, Hannah Cowens and Mary Rich, sons Moses, John, David and Luther and granddaughter Sarah Rich daughter of son Philip dec.

Ten (RICH) ch., first seven b. Brookfield: Submit b. 1727 or 172[8], Moses b. 1730, Philip b. 1732, Elijah b. 1734, John b. 1736, Hannah b. 173[8], David b. 17[40], Mehitable, Mary and Luther.

iv JOHN, b. Brookfield 10 Jan. 1710/1; d. there bef. 26 Feb. 1759 (bond on wife as administratrix of his estate); m. Brookfield 27th day of an unknown month in 1730 MARY GILBERT, b. there 8 March 171[-]; d. bet. 26 Feb. 1759 and 7 March 1760; daughter of Thomas and Martha (Barnes) Gilbert. Bond on the widow Mary as administratrix of the estate of John Goss of Brookfield was dated 26 Feb. 1759. Bond on [son-in-law] Ebenezer Wright as administrator of the estate of John Goss, left unadministered by Mary the widow, now dec., was dated 7 March 1760. An order to divide John's estate on 7 April 1763 named Thankful Wright wife of Ebenezer, Eunice Shelden, Meriam Wright, and the guardian of Comfort Goss.

Nine (GOSS) ch. b. Brookfield: Thankful b. 1726, Mary b. 1731, Samuel b. 1733, Miriam b. 1737, Samuel b. 1739, Eunice b. 1741, Miriam b. 1744, John b. 1747 and Comfort b. 1749.

v THANKFUL, b. Brookfield 13 Dec. 1713; d. Chester 9 Feb. 1780 "widow"; m. Brookfield 20 June 1732 JOHN WHITE, b. Concord 3 July 1708; d. Chester "fore part of 1779"; son of John and Prudence (Hayward) White. This is not a Mayflower White line. The account of Elijah White, administrator of the estate of his father John White of Murrayfield (Chester) dated 26 April 1782, lists as debts, "cost of my father's...(and)...my mother's last sickness, and keeping my mother 11 months after my father's death." Elijah had been appointed administrator 10 Jan. 1782.

Seven (WHITE) ch. b. Brookfield: Prudence b. 1733, Lucy b. 1735, John b. 1738, Varsel (son) b. 1740, Thankful b. 1747, Nathan b. 1748 and Elijah b. 1750.

vi MARY, d. Brookfield 27 Sept. 1751 "wife of Daniel"; m. there 13 Dec. 1728 DANIEL WALKER, b. Charlestown 17 June 1700; d. Brookfield in Oct. 1777; son of Edward and Elizabeth (Dean) Walker. He m. (2) Worcester 29 Nov. 1753 Mary (-----) Lovell. The will of Daniel Walker of Brookfield, aged, dated 14 June 1776 and filed 25 Nov. 1777, names wife Mary "whose former husband was Michael Lovell," sons Daniel, Abraham and Isaac, grandson Jason Walker, daughters Mary Carter, Thankful Shays, Sarah Belknap and Judah

Hall.

Ten (WALKER) ch. b. Brookfield to Daniel and Mary (Goss): Mary b. 1729/30, Samuel b. 1731, Daniel b. 1732, Sarah b. 1734, Abraham b. 1736, Isaac b. 1738, Jacob b. 1740, Thankful b. 1742, Sarah b. 1747 and Judith b. 1750.

vii THOMAS, b. Brookfield 6 July 1716; d. Bolton 17 Jan. 1780 ae. 63 "Pastor of the church in Bolton for over 39 years"; m. Medford 3 Dec. 1741 ABIGAIL WADE, b. there 28 July 1717; d. Amherst NH 15 July 1791 "widow"; daughter of Samuel and Lydia (Newhall) Wade. Thomas graduated from Harvard in 1737. The will of Thomas Goss of Bolton, "clerk" (minister) dated 10 Dec. 1779 and filed 8 Feb. 1780, names wife Abigail, son Ebenezer Handen Goss, grandchild Mary Winship, daughters Abigail Atherton, Elizabeth Newhall, Mary Hemenway, Salomy Goss, sons Thomas and Samuel Goss.

Eight (GOSS) ch. b. Bolton: Ebenezer b. 1743, Judith b. 1745/6, Abigail b. 1749, Thomas b. 1751, Samuel b. 1754, Mary b. 1757, Elizabeth b. 1760 and Salome b. 1763.

References: VR BOLTON, BROOKFIELD, CHESTER, MEDFORD, ROXBURY, WORCESTER. CONCORD VR pp. 18, 50, 77. LANCASTER VR p. 451(Marr. of Philip Goss' father). Worcester Co. PR #23741(Thomas Gilbert); #24894(John Goss); #24898 & #24899(Judith Goss); #24905(Philip Goss); #24906 (Philip Goss Jr.); #24910, #24911(Thomas Goss); #50044(Experience Rich); #61243(Daniel Walker). Hampshire Co. PR Box 159 #4(John White). Middlesex Co. LR 16:45(John Hayward Sr.); 17:352(John Hayward Jr.). NEHGR 16:260; 34:388. HARTFORD TIMES 1 Aug 1942 A709. NORTH BROOKFIELD BY TEMPLE pp. 168, 596-8, 604, 605, 767. HAYWARD (JAMES) GEN pp. 20-1. GILBERT (THOMAS) DESC pp. 88, 113, 121. COOLEY GEN p. 458. MIDDLEFIELD BY CHURCH-SMITH p. 643. LONGMEADOW CENT p. 49. CHARLESTOWN BY WYMAN 2:991. COLONIAL CLERGY p. 94. HARVARD GRADS 10:175. GOSS FAM. RICH GEN.

21 MERCY HAYWARD[4] (Anna[3] White, Resolved[2], William[1]), b. Concord 13 May 1677; d. Brookfield 26 April 1762 "widow of Thomas."

She m. Concord 3 or 6 April 1706 THOMAS BROWN*, d. Brookfield bef. 16 Aug. 1751 when his estate was divided; son of Jabez and Deborah (-----) Brown. Jabez' widow Deborah and eldest son Thomas were named to administer his estate 28 Sept. 1692. (Possibly Deborah's maiden name was Gove as John Gove states that he will sign her bond and

---

*VR STOW list the marriage of Thomas Brown and Nancy Hayward; we believe Nancy to be an error for Marcy.

calls her "my sister Brown."

Thomas was prob. in Stow as early as Dec. 1693 and was still there in 1723 when he signed a deed with his brother; he was in Brookfield by Oct. 1729. His estate divided 16 Aug. 1751 names son Timothy eldest and son Abner; daughter Silence Hamilton, wife of Jonas; "our mother Mercy Brown."

Children (BROWN):

i SILENCE[5], prob. d. bef. husband as she is not named in his will or the partition of his estate; m. Brookfield 28 June 1733 JONAH HAMILTON, d. there bef. 24 April 1771 when there was a warrant for appraisal of his estate; he was prob. son of John and Hannah (-----) Hamilton. A partition of the estate of Jonah Hamilton dated 11 July 1774 set off all land to "Jabez, only surviving son" who was to pay heirs of his brother Timothy dec., heirs of brother Obed dec., sister Marcy Spring wife of Henry, sister Dorothy Aldrich wife of Benjamin, and sister Thankful Hamilton.

Nine (HAMILTON) ch., first seven b. Brookfield: Amos b. 1737, Marcy b. 1739, Aaron b. 1741, Thankful b. 1743, Timothy b. 1745, Jabish b. 1747, Dorothy, Israel and Obed.

ii TIMOTHY, m. (1) THANKFUL ----- ; m. (2) Brookfield 18 April 1744 KEZIAH GOSS. [Could she have been Keziah (Cooley) Goss, widow of Philip[5] (see #20 ii)?] Timothy was in Brookfield early in 1735 when he deeded land and his wife Thankful released her dower. The only other record naming Timothy's first wife is the birth of their children.

Six (BROWN) ch. b. Brookfield by first wife: Anna b. 1730, Mabel b. 1732/3, Ephraim b. 1734/5, Silence b. 1737, Ruth b. 1739 and Timothy b. 1742.

iii ABNER, b. Stow 4 March 1714; d. Chesterfield 12 June 1790 in 77th yr. "Lieutenant"; m. (1) MARTHA GILBERT, b. Brookfield 27 Feb. 1714; d. there 10 Aug. 1746 "wife of Abner"; daughter of Thomas and Martha (-----) Gilbert. He m. (2) Sherborn 14 April 1748 DORCAS GREENWOOD, b. there 17 July 1717; d. Brookfield 23 Jan. 1760 "wife of Abner"; daughter of William and Abigail (-----) Greenwood. Abner Brown and wife Dorcas were among those who conveyed title to real estate of "our father William Greenwood, late of Sherborn" on 15 Dec. 1756.

Abner Brown m. int. (3) Brookfield and Warren 26 April 1760 MEHITABEL (LINCOLN) RUSSELL, widow of John of Brimfield; Mehitabel d. Chesterfield 24 Jan. 1801. Abner and Mehitabel Brown of Brookfield were guardians of children of John Russell, late of Brimfield deceased, in a petition to sell land 12 June 1762, "she in debt over years to support them." Abner and Mehitabel were admitted to Chesterfield Church from Brookfield and Western 7 Jan. 1770. The will of Abner Brown of Chesterfield, gentleman, dated 19 May 1790 and proved 3 Aug. 1790, names wife Mehetibel, son Thomas, daughter Sarah Rice, 2nd daughter Martha Cutler, daughter Thankful Brewer, sons Daniel and Greenwood, grandson Joseph Brown, son of Joseph deceased, daughters Abigail Brown and Elizabeth Bannister, son Josiah, daughter Mehitabel Bannister, daughter Dorcas Brown and daughter Persis Curtis.

Sixteen (BROWN) ch. b. Brookfield, by first wife: Sarah b. 1737, Samuel b. 1739, Thomas b. 1740, Martha b. 1742, Thankful b. 1744, Hannah b. 1746; by second wife: Daniel b. 1749, Abigail b. 1750, Josiah b. 1752, Elizabeth b. 1753, Jonas b. 1754, Joseph b. 1756, Greenwood b. 1758; by third wife: Mehitabel b. 1761, Dorcas b. 1764 and Perces b. 1767.

References: VR BROOKFIELD, SHERBORN, STOW, WARREN. CONCORD VR pp. 20, 66. Chesterfield VR (on cards at NEHG Soc.) Worcester PR #8360(Thomas Brown); #26689(Jonah Hamilton). Worcester Co. LR 41:54-5(Timothy Brown); 73:336(Abner Brown). Hampshire Co. PR Box 20 #49 (Abner Brown). Middlesex Co. LR 16:45; 17:352(John Hayward); 18:139, 165; 22:466; 36:352(Thomas Brown); 58:4 (William Greenwood et al). Middlesex Co. PR #3042 and 8:9 (Jabez Brown). HAYWARD (JAMES) GEN pp. 20-1. NORTH BROOKFIELD BY TEMPLE p. 613. HAMILTON, HOUSE OF p. 144. CHESTERFIELD HIST p. 60-1.

22 JOHN HAYWARD[4] (Anna[3] White, Resolved[2], William[1]), b. Concord 7 July 1680; living 14 April 1715 when he acknowledged two deeds.

He m. Concord 17 Feb. 1708/9 SUSANNA DAKIN, b. there 17 May 1689; living 14 April 1715 when she acknowledged the above deeds; daughter of John and Sarah (Woodis) Dakin.

John went from Concord to Brookfield in 1703; in 1710 he was given a grant for a saw mill; and in 1714 returned to Concord. In 1714 John Hayward of Concord, millwright, and wife Susanna mortgaged property, a debt which was paid "by the hands of John Willard" (his brother-in-law?) on 8 May 1717. On 25 March 1715 John Hayward deeded to John Willard of Concord for good cause and consideration, his corn mill and saw mill, if Willard would "support and care for my father John Hayward" and after the latter's death would "pay my sisters Judith Goss, Marcy Brown, Anna Allen and Sarah Allen." On the same day he deeded to John Willard "my house lot formerly my father John Hayward's." John and his wife Susanna acknowledged both deeds 14 April 1715. These are the latest records found about this family.

Children (HAYWARD), b. Concord:

i JOHN[5], b. 10 July 1710; n.f.r.
ii TIMOTHY, b. 8 Jan. 1711/2; n.f.r.
iii HENRY, b. 18 April 1714; n.f.r

References: CONCORD VR pp. 24, 31, 72, 75, 79, 83. Middlesex Co. LR 17:110, 355(John Hayward); 17:352(John Hayward Jr. to John Willard). HAYWARD (JAMES) GEN pp. 20-1. NORTH BROOKFIELD BY TEMPLE pp. 164, 177. DAKIN DESC p. 14.

23 ANNA HAYWARD[4] (Anna[3] White, Resolved[2], William[1]), b. Concord 30 Aug. 1682; poss. she was the Ann Allen, widow, admitted in 1743 to Presbyterian Church at Morristown NJ and a member there until 1756.

She m. 23 Nov. 1706 Concord MA and Suffield CT rec. SAMUEL ALLEN, b. ca. 1679; d. Hanover NJ 28 Nov. 1730; son of Edward and Sarah (Kimball) Allen of Ipswich who went to Suffield CT about 1678. Confirmation that Anna (Hayward) had indeed married an Allen is contained in deeds of John Hayward (1712) mentioning wife Anna and daughter Anna Allen; and of John Hayward Jr. (1715) naming his sister Anna Allen.

Samuel was a weaver; he moved from Suffield to Hanover NJ where he was a deacon.

Children (ALLEN), b. Suffield CT:

i SAMUEL[5], b. 3 Sept. 1707; n.f.r.
ii JOB, b. 20 Nov. 1709; d. Rockaway NJ 5 Nov. 1767; m. ca. 1736 CHRISTIANA -----, who d. after 10 Nov. 1767 when she renounced her right to administer Job's estate.

Nine (ALLEN) ch. b. Rockaway NJ: Anna b. 1737, Eunice b. 1738, Christiana b. 1742, Elizabeth b. 1743, Deborah b. 1746, Lois b. 1748, Job b. 1750, Jane b. 1751 and Mary b. 1758.

iii ANNA, b. 4 April 1712; bp. "Hannah" 11 May 1712; n.f.r.

iv MARTHA, b. 19 Sept. 1714; bp. 14 Nov. 1714; n.f.r.

v JONAH, b. 20 Jan. 1716/7; d. Rockaway NJ ca. Nov. 1756 "of Pequanock township"; m. Morristown NJ 30 Jan. 1752 SARAH MUIR, who joined the Morristown Church 19 March 1758.
Three (ALLEN) ch. bp. Morristown NJ in 1758: Amos, Elizabeth and Jonah.

and probably:

vi EBENEZER, b. Hanover NJ; a freeholder in Morris Co. in 1752; last mentioned in 1754 in a suit marked "discontinued." No record of a family.

References: CONCORD VR pp. 25, 66. CSL Barbour Index: Suffield. Middlesex Co. LR 16:45; 17:352 (John Hayward). NJ ARCH 32:10; 33:13. SUFFIELD CT CONG CH REC pp. 25, 27, 28. NJ GEN MAG 15:36, 37, 39, 40; 16:60-2; 17:38. ROCKAWAY NJ RECS pp. 4, 193-7. HAYWARD (JAMES) GEN pp. 20-1. DEERFIELD BY SHELDON 2:11. BOSTON TRANSCRIPT 20 June 1921 #8950.

24 SARAH HAYWARD$^4$ (Anna$^3$ White, Resolved$^2$, William$^1$), b. Concord 16 June 1689; d. prob. in NJ bef. 1748.

She m. (1) Concord 27 Jan. 1708/9 JOHN GROSVENOR, bp. Roxbury 6 June 1675; killed by Indians in Brookfield 20 or 22 July 1710; son of John and Hester (Clarke) Grosvenor. The estate of John Grosvenor was appraised 29 Aug. 1710, and on 8 May 1711 the widow Sarah was administratrix. It is interesting to note among the debts owed by the estate, money due to one Peregrine White and a receipt for "money due my husband" signed by Prudence White. It is stated that John Grosvenor's estate was settled in 1724 by his brothers Leicester and Ebenezer of Pomfret CT. No children were found for this marriage.

Sarah m. (2) Suffield CT 29 Nov. 1711 DAVID ALLEN, (int. in that town 25 Oct. call him Richard Allen); b. Ipswich 1 Feb. 1675/6; d. Hanover NJ after 1752; son of Edward and Sarah (Kimball) Allen. In 1696 Edward Allen of Suffield bequeathed his dwelling house to his son David. Confirmation that Sarah (Hayward) Grosvenor had indeed married an Allen is contained in the deeds of John Hayward (1712) mentioning his wife Anna and daughter Sarah Allen, and of John Hayward Jr. (1715) naming his sister Sarah Allen.

Children (ALLEN):

i DAVID$^5$, b. Suffield CT 9 Feb. 1712/3; prob. m.

ANNA -----; lived in Mendham and Rockaway NJ; both were living in 1792.

ii ADONIRUM, b. Suffield CT 8 March 1714/5; prob. d.y.

iii JOHN, b. Suffield CT 15 March 1716/7; d. Hanover NJ bet. 12 April and 20 May 1762, date and probate of his will. He m. (1) Morristown NJ 6 Aug. 1751 TABITHA (-----) LYON, who d. 1752/3. He m. (2) Morristown NJ 30 Sept. 1753 SARAH (BALDWIN) FORD, widow of Samuel, b. Newark NJ about July 1709; d. Morristown NJ 22 April 1789 ae. 79y 9m; daughter of Jonathan and Susanna (Kitchell) Baldwin. Sarah m. (3) in 1763 Solomon Boyle.

John Allen was a weaver. He went to NJ with his parents in 1717/8, lived at Mendham NJ after his first marriage, and later at Hanover NJ. In his will dated 12 April 1762 and proved 20 May 1762, John Allen of Hanover, weaver, divided his estate bet. his wife and his son Daniel, with a contingent bequest to his wife's children.

One (ALLEN) ch. by first wife: Daniel bp. 1753.

iv HANNAH, b. NJ about 1726; d. Bridport VT 22 Dec. 1800 ae. 74, "wife of Samuel"; m. about 1742 SAMUEL SMITH, d. Bridport VT 11 Nov. 1798 ae. 78. Samuel was the second permanent settler of Bridport; he went from NJ to Panton VT about 1770 and to Bridport in Nov. 1773. In 1778 he moved to Pittsford VT because of an Indian raid.

Two (SMITH) ch.: Nathan b. 1752, and Marshall, both captured by Indians and taken to Quebec, but eventually returned to VT.

Other ch. are said to have been born in NJ to Sarah and David Allen, but only Hannah has been positively identified.

References: VR BROOKFIELD, IPSWICH, ROXBURY. CONCORD VR pp. 31, 72. CSL Barbour Index:Suffield. Bridport VT VR (MSS. at NEHG Soc.) p. 96. VT VR:Bridport. Middlesex Co. LR 16:45; 17:352(John Hayward). Hampshire Co. PR Box 65 #6(John Grosvenor). NJ ARCH 33:13. NEHGR 72:141. WOODSTOCK CT BY BOWEN 6:264. GROSVENOR ANCY p. 13. MA HIST BY BARBER p. 561. NJ GEN MAG 15:35-8; 16:61. HAYWARD (JAMES) GEN pp. 20-1. DEERFIELD BY SHELDON 2:11. ADDISON CO VT HIST pp. 381, 385. Suffield CT PR 3:24 (Edward Allen).

25 OBADIAH WHEELER[4] (Elizabeth[3] White, Resolved[2], William[1]), b. Concord 21 Sept. 1673; m. Concord 25 March 1702 HANNAH FLETCHER, prob. the one b. there 24 Oct. 1674;

daughter of Francis and Elizabeth (Wheeler) Fletcher. On 29 June 1715 he acknowledged a deed of his dwelling house and barn, his property at Fairhaven and Concord, meeting-house pew, etc. with his wife Hannah giving up her dower. He prob. went to Lebanon CT and was the one who received land there 2 April 1717 from Joseph Bradford. The latest record found of this Obadiah is an indenture of 25 Nov. 1718. Obadiah of Concord was a tailor; Obadiah of Lebanon was a husbandman.

Children (WHEELER), b. Concord:

i HANNAH[5], b. 5 April 1703; she was possibly the one who m. Lebanon CT 5 Feb. 1735/6 JAMES BETTIS, who d. there 7 Sept. 1793 ae. 77. "The widow Bettis" d. Lebanon CT 27 March 1795 "aged." James is known to be of Lebanon from 1735 to 1738 and Hannah was bp. in and admitted to the Lebanon Church 5 Nov. 1738.

Three (BETTIS) ch., first two bp. Lebanon: Hannah bp. 1739, James bp. 1742, and poss. Mary who m. Caleb Lyman.

ii JOSIAH, b. 8 March 1704/5; poss. d. Pomfret CT 23 Oct. 1782 ae. 74; might be the one who m. Pomfret CT 14 Dec. 1735 ANNA GROSVENOR, b. there 27 May 1719; d. there 30 April 1804 ae. 84 "wife of Joshua" (*sic*); daughter of Leicester and Mary (-----) Grosvenor. The will of Josiah Wheeler of Pomfret, blacksmith, dated 11 Sept. 1782 and proved 7 Jan. 1783, names wife Anna, sons Josiah, John, Lemuel and William, and daughters Sarah Whiting and Anna Wheeler. The will of Anna Wheeler of Pomfret, dated 7 May 1797 and proved 8 May 1804, left whole estate to daughter Anna Jackson.

Ten (WHEELER) ch. b. Pomfret: Mary b. 1735/6, Josiah b. 1737/8, John b. 1740, Lemuel b. 1742, Leicester b. 1745, Sarah b. 1747, Mary b. 1749/50, Anna b. 1752, William b. 1754 and Anna b. 1757.

iii PHINEAS, b. 23 Oct. 1707; prob. d. Lebanon CT bet. Dec. 1769 and Nov. 1772; prob. the one who m. Lebanon CT 30 April 1740 MARY GILLETT, who was living at Lebanon in Sept. 1782 when she sold part of her dower land; daughter of John and Eunice (-----) Gillett. The will of Phineas Whealor of Lebanon CT, dated 23 Dec. 1769 and proved 15 Feb. 1773, names wife Mary, and daughter Mary wife of Ephraim Carpenter; the inventory was dated 10 Nov. 1772.

One (WHEELER) ch. bp. Lebanon: Mary bp. 1745.

iv PEREGRINE, b. 23 Jan. 1709/10; n.f.r.

References: CONCORD VR pp. 17, 18, 54, 59, 63, 67, 73. CSL Barbour Index:Pomfret. CSL CH Recs: Lebanon. CT MARR 2:40-1. Middlesex Co. LR 16:399, 591; 17:465(Obadiah Wheeler). Lebanon CT LR 3:147(Obadiah Wheeler); 3:206(Belcher to Obadiah Wheeler); 3:35(Joseph Bradford to Obadiah Wheeler); 7:2(Marsh to Phineas Wheeler); 8:28(John Gillet et al); 10:403(Marsh to Bettis); 14:162(Mary Wheeler). Pomfret CT PR #4346(Josiah Wheeler); #4341(Anna Wheeler); #4102(Phineas Whealor). CSL Hale Cem Recs:Pomfret. NEHGR 31:294, 296. WHEELER FAM 1:19, 21, 354; 2:1084.

26 JOSIAH WHEELER[4] (Elizabeth[3] White, Resolved[2], William[1]), b. Concord 22 Oct. 1675; d. Bolton 8 Dec. 1738 "in 64th year"; bur. in Lancaster.

He m. MARTHA PRESCOTT, b. ca. 1680; d. Lancaster 21 May 1748 "in 69th year, wife of Capt. Peter Joslyn, formerly wife of Mr. Josiah Wheeler"; prob. daughter of John and Sarah (Hayward) Prescott.

Josiah Wheeler and his wife were admitted to the Lancaster Church from the Concord Church 9 April 1710. The will of Josiah Wheeler of Bolton, dated 5 Dec. 1738 and proved 6 Feb. 1738/9, names wife Martha, daughters Martha Wilder, Experience Pollard, Thankful Fairbanks, Dinah Stearns, and granddaughters Sarah, Copia and Patience Broughton. A petition for partition 27 March 1739 was signed by widow Martha Wheeler; James Wilder, husband of eldest daughter; William Pollard, husband of second daughter; Jonas Fairbanks, husband of third daughter; Benjamin Stearns, husband of fourth daughter; and James Wilder, guardian to Sarah, Copia and Patience Broughton. On 21 Feb. 1743 the petition of Thomas White and his wife Sarah, formerly Broughton, and James Wilder, guardian to Copia and Patience Broughton, minors, to sell real estate from their grandfather Josiah Wheeler, deceased, was granted.

Children (WHEELER):

i MARTHA[5], d. Lancaster 19 March 1774 "wife of Major James Wilder"; she m. (1) EDWARD BROUGHTON, perhaps the one b. Boston 12 Oct. 1673; son of George and Perne (Rawson) Broughton. He was a schoolmaster and merchant. She m. (2) Lancaster 24 Dec. 1734 JAMES WILDER, bp. Lancaster 30 April 1710; d. there 15 or 16 Jan. 1780 "Major"; son of James and Abigail (Gardner) Wilder. James was a merchant of Boston and later of Lancaster. The will of James Wilder, Esq. of Lancaster, dated 1 Dec. 1779 and filed 9 Feb. 1780, names granddaughter Martha Wilder, heirs of daughter Abigail Ball, sons Josiah and Asaph,

daughter Susannah Prescott, and son James.
Three (BROUGHTON) ch. b. Lancaster: Sarah b. 1722/3, Copia b. 1724 and Patience b. 1726/7.
Seven (WILDER) ch. b. Lancaster: Josiah b. 1735, Martha b. 1737, Abigail b. 1739, James b. 1741, Josiah b. 1744, Aseph b. 1749 and Susannah b. 1751.

ii EXPERIENCE, bp. Lancaster 28 Nov. 1708; d. Bolton 18 May 1785 ae. 77 "widow of William." She m. Lancaster 23 Nov. 1726 WILLIAM POLLARD, b. Billerica 3 Aug. 1698; d. Bolton 28 May 1762 ae. about 65; son of Thomas and Sarah (Farmer) Pollard. Papers in the estate of William Pollard, cooper, late of Bolton deceased, dated 1763 and 1764, name widow Experience, sons Oliver, John, William, Jonas, Thomas, Abijah, daughters Lois Pollard and Experience Howe. Papers in the estate of Experience Pollard late of Bolton dated in 1785 name all above sons except Jonas, and add Eunice Rice daughter of Lois Rice deceased who was daughter of Experience Pollard.
Twelve (POLLARD) ch., first five b. Lancaster and last seven b. Bolton: Oliver b. 1727, John b. 1729, William b. 1731, Jonas b. 1733, Lois b. 1736, twins Patience and Prudence b. 1739, Experience b. 1741, Thomas b. 1744, Abijah b. 1747, twins Mary and Sarah* b. 1751.

iii THANKFUL, bp. Lancaster 30 Sept. 1711 (twin); d. there 13 May 1795 ae. 81 "wife of Jonas"; m. Lancaster 8 April 1731 JONAS FAIRBANKS, bp. there 1708; d. there 4 Nov. 1792 in 89th yr.; son of Jabez and Mary (Wilder) Fairbanks. Jonas served in the French and Indian Wars, and is referred to as "gentleman" in deeds. Jonas deeded land to sons Elijah, Josiah, Abijah, Cyrus and Jonas from 1761-74.
Eleven (FAIRBANKS) ch. b. Lancaster: Martha b. 1731/2, Josiah b. 1734, Elijah b. 1734 (*sic*), Cyrus b. 1737, Rhoda b. 1739, Mary b. 1741, Jonas b. 1743, Sarah b. 1745, Abijah b. 1748, Elizabeth b. 1750 and Manasseh b. 1753.

iv EBENEZER, bp. 30 Sept. 1711 (twin); n.f.r.

v DINAH, bp. Lancaster 30 June 1717; d. Bolton 21 Dec. 1771 in 55th yr., "widow Dinah"; m. Lancaster 11 Sept. 1738 BENJAMIN STEARNS, b. Concord 8 Nov. 1714; d. Bolton 5 Jan. 1755; son of John and Mercy (Davis) Stearns. Benjamin was a cordwainer who moved from Bedford to Bolton. Dinah was bonded as administratrix of Benjamin's estate 31 Jan. 1755. The will of Dinah Stearns of Bolton, widow, dated 10 May 1759 and filed 27 Jan. 1772, names children Samuel, Donnel,

*Descent through their youngest daughter Sarah has been disproved. [See TAG 46:12-3.]

Mercy, Martha, Sarah and Asa Stearns.
Seven (STEARNS) ch. b. Bolton: Josiah b. 1740, Samuel b. 1741, Daniel b. 1743, Marcy b. 1745, Martha b. 1750, Sarah b. 1751 and Asa b. 1754.

References: VR BILLERICA, BOLTON. CONCORD VR p. 19. LANCASTER VR pp. 22, 24-27, 54-57, 59, 61-63, 77, 159-160, 271, 273-275, 284, 288, 297, 326, 328, 330, 410. BOSTON VR 9:126. Worcester Co. PR #63439(Josiah Wheeler); #47255(William Pollard); #47217(Experience Pollard); #7829(Copia Broughton's gdn.); #65610(James Wilder); #55576(Benjamin Stearns); #55621(Dinah Stearns). Worcester Co. LR 45:253; 72:667(Jonas Fairbanks). Middlesex Co. LR 23:403; 27:214(Josiah Wheeler to E. Broughton). NEHGR 37:299. TAG 46:12. WILDER GEN pp. 3, 11. FAIRBANKS GEN pp. 50-2, 71. WHEELER FAM 1:354. WATERTOWN BY BOND p. 454. MA BAY ACTS AND RESOLVES 13:327. STEARNS GEN.

27 URIAH WHEELER[4] (Elizabeth[3] White, Resolved[2], William[1]), b. Concord 13 April 1678; d. Sudbury 9 Dec. 1753 ae. 76y 8m.

He m. Watertown 28 Dec. 1704 ABIGAIL RICE, b. Sudbury 27 Nov. 1687; d. there 10 Jan. 1754 "in 67th yr., wife of Mr. Uriah"; daughter of John and Tabitha (Stone) Rice. On 13 Jan. 1720/1 Abigail and Uriah and a number of her siblings sold to their "elder brother John Rice, all right, title and interest...of our father John Rice or our mother Tabitha."

Uriah was a carpenter living in Sudbury in Jan. 1701/2 and 1723. The will of Uriah Wheeler of Sudbury, advanced in age, dated 1 Feb. 1748/9 and the heirs consented 20 Dec. 1753, names wife Abigail, son Elisha, daughters Thankful wife of Isaac Gibbs of Sudbury, and Abigail wife of Zephaniah Smith, son-in-law Samuel Eaton "now living with and providing for me," and daughter Millicent wife of Samuel Eaton.

Children (WHEELER), b. Sudbury:

i URIAH[5], b. 12 June 1705; d. Sudbury 28 Aug. 1705.
ii URIAH, b. 10 June 1706; d. Sudbury 28 July 1706.
iii THANKFUL, b. 7 Aug. 1707; m. Sudbury 1 Oct. 1725 ISAAC GIBBS, b. there ca. 1700; son of John and Sarah (Cutler) Gibbs. A petition for appointment of a guardian for Isaac Gibbs of Sudbury, non-compos, aged, was drawn 5 July 1785 and signed by several of his children or their spouses, mentioning their "aged parents." A counter petition signed by Isaac and Thankful (the parents) was presented the same year.

Eleven (GIBBS) ch. b. Sudbury: Hepsebeth b. 1726, Isaac b. 1728/9, Hepzibah b. 1730/1, Abigail b. 1732, Sarah b. 1735, Thankful b. 1737/8, Jonas b. 1740, Anna b. 1742, Uriah b. 1744, Asa[el] b. 1748 and Millicent b. 1754.

iv ABIGAIL, b. 26 Jan. 1708/9; d. Sudbury bef. 13 March 1794, date of the bond on the administrator of her estate; m. Sudbury in May 1732 ZEPHANIAH SMITH, b. Sudbury 29 Oct. 1705; d. there bef. 13 March 1782; son of Thomas and Elizabeth (-----) Smith. The bond on Asa(el) Smith to administer the estate of Zephaniah Smith late of Sudbury, deceased, was dated 13 March 1782. Settlement of the estate on 3 Sept. 1783 names eldest son Asahel Smith, his brother Abel, and his sisters Sarah Rice, Eunice Balcom and Olive Willis.

Seven (SMITH) ch. b. Sudbury: Asal b. 1735, Silas b. 1736/7, Eunice b. 1741, Sarah b. 1743, Abel b. 1746, Olive b. 1747 and Jeduthan b. 1749.

v ELISHA, b. 1 Feb. 1710/1; d. Sudbury 17 July 1785; m. 30 Nov. 1731 MARY LORING, b. Sudbury 1716; d. 22 Jan. 1801; daughter of Rev. Israel and Mary (Hayman) Loring. The will of Israel Loring of Sudbury, dated 10 Oct. 1770 and presented 14 April 1772, names daughter Mary Wheeler. Elisha and Mary Wheeler signed a receipt for her portion of her father's estate 6 Sept. 1773. Elisha was a farmer and tavern keeper, and served in the Revolution.

On 16 Sept. 1785 Asahel Wheeler, gentleman, gave his bond as administrator of the estate of Lt. Elisha Wheeler late of Sudbury deceased; sureties were Israel and Elisha Wheeler. Dower was set off to widow Mary Wheeler 13 Sept. 1786; her reverted dower was reported sold 15 March 1802.

Fourteen (WHEELER) ch. b. Sudbury: Mary b. 1733, Sarah b. 1734, Abigail b. 1737, Elizabeth b. 1739, Asahel b. 1741, Ann b. 1743, Israel b. 1745, Uriah b. 1747, Sarah b. 1749, Elisha b. 1750, Abigail b. 1752, Jonas b. 1755, Caleb b. 1757 and Heyman b. 1760.

vi HEPSIBAH, b. 23 May 1713; d. Sudbury 13 Aug. 1713.

vii ASAHEL, b. 23 Nov. 1714; prob. d. Sudbury 17 Nov. 1729.

viii JONAS, b. 1 April 1719; d. Sudbury 11 Dec. 1729.

ix MILLICENT, b. 7 Nov. 1731, living Holden 31 Dec. 1784; m. Sudbury 18 April 1748 SAMUEL EATON of Worcester; b. in 1722; son of Samuel and Ruth (-----) Eaton. This is not a Mayflower Eaton line. He was in Sudbury as late as April 1773 with wife Millicent, and was prob. the Samuel who was in Holden until at least April 1785. (Three of Samuel's children married in Holden.) A Samuel Eaton and his wife were dismissed from Sudbury First Church to Worcester 14 Sept. 1746.

Ten (EATON) ch. b. Sudbury: Elizabeth b. 1751, Lucy b. 1753, Uriah b. 1755, Nabby b. 1757, Millicent b. 1761, Samuel b. 176[ ], Abel b. 1766, Rebecca b. 1769, Jeduthan b. 1771 and Jesse Moore b. 1777.

x URIAH, b. 28 Sept. 1733; d. Sudbury 22 Oct. 1740 in 8th yr. [He is not the one who m. Sudbury 15 March 1768 Ann Smith.]

References: VR SUDBURY, WAYLAND, WORCESTER. CONCORD VR p. 21. Middlesex Co. PR #24373(Uriah Wheeler); #9059(Isaac Gibbs Gdn.); #20791(Zephaniah Smith); #20555(Abigail Smith); #24256(Lt. Elisha Wheeler); #14349 (Israel Loring). Middlesex Co. LR 75:125(Elisha Wheeler); 28:183(Edward Rice, Uriah Wheeler et al). Worcester Co. PR #18646(Samuel Eaton). Worcester Co. LR 73:303; 93:198; 94:438; 96:119(Samuel Eaton of Holden). Sudbury First Church Rec (NEHG Soc.) p. 242. NEHGR 7:326; 61:125-6. TAG 25:162. BOSTON TRANSCRIPT 23 May 1932 #2887. WHEELER FAM 1:354-6. RICE GEN p. 17. SUDBURY GS pp. 19-20. BRAINERD-BRAINARD pp. 123-4.

28 SAMUEL WHEELER[4] (Elizabeth[3] White, Resolved[2], William[1]), b. Concord 23 Jan. 1680/1; d. prob. Brookfield after 17 Oct. 1761 when he was to be provided for by son-in-law Thomas Banister.

Samuel m. Concord 23 Nov. 1704 JOANNA WALCOTT, b. Newbury 22 Jan. 1686/7; d. Brookfield 4 July 1751 "wife of Samuel"; daughter of John and Joanna (Emerson) Walcott.

Samuel apparently went to Brookfield about 1710 after the birth of daughter Joanna and before the birth of Elizabeth.

Children (WHEELER):

i JONATHAN[5], b. Concord 14 Sept. 1705; living at Brookfield 10 Dec. 1755 when brother Josiah promised to support him.

ii MARY, b. Concord 18 Oct. 1706; d. after 4 May 1746 when she gave bond as widow and administratrix of John's estate; m. Brookfield 8 Jan. 1724/5 JOHN HAMILTON, b. Concord 26 Aug. 1699; d. Brookfield bef. 4 May 1746; son of John and Hannah (-----) Hamilton. John is called "gentleman" in probate.

Seven (HAMILTON) ch. b. Brookfield: Reuben b. 1726, John b. 1728, Levi b. 1730, Hannah b. 1733, Silas b. 1735/6, Mary b. 1739 and Marcy b. 1743.

iii JOANNA, b. Concord 13 Aug. 1708; m. EPHRAIM HAYWARD (see #19 ii).

iv ELIZABETH, b. Brookfield 19 Jan. 1711; d. there 19 Feb. 1717.

v RUTH, b. Brookfield 23 July 1712; living 9 Oct. 1780; m. Brookfield 23 June 1732 NATHAN HAMILTON, still of Brookfield in 1794 when he mortgaged land, and was prob. the "old Mr. Hamilton" who d. New Braintree 14 Feb. 1795; son of John and Hannah (-----) Hamilton. Nathan was a private in the Revolution. There are no probate records for Nathan or Ruth in Worcester Co.

Seven (HAMILTON) ch. b. Brookfield: Ezra b. 1733, Mary b. 1734/5, Elisha b. 1739, Moses b. 1744, John b. 1747, Hannah b. 1749 and Ruth b. 1752.

vi SAMUEL, b. Brookfield 23 Oct. 1714; living Greenwich 25 Feb. 1774; m. HEPZIBAH -----. On 8 Nov. 1745 they were in Western, and moved to New Salem in 1762. Hepzibah was living at New Salem 25 Oct. 1768 when she released her dower. Samuel was of New Salem when he bought land in Greenwich 25 Oct. 1768, and was living in Greenwich 25 Feb. 1774.

Six (WHEELER) ch., first four b. Brookfield: Solomon b. 1737, Rezinah b. 1739, Meriam b. 1742 and Amos b. 1746; two b. Warren: Thankful b. 1747/8 and Hepzibah b. 1750. They may also have had a son Samuel.

vii JOSIAH, b. Brookfield 26 July 1716; d. 22 March 1806; m. (1) Brookfield 6 June 1740 ZERUIAH RICE, b. there 23 Sept. 1721; d. there 21 March 1740/1 ae. 20 "wife of Josiah"; daughter of Azariah and Hannah (Bartlett) Rice. The parentage of Zeruiah is shown by the will of Azariah Rice dated 8 July 1772 consent given by heirs 6 July 1779, which names his granddaughter Zeruiah Sandford. Josiah m. (2) bet. 1741 and 1748 HANNAH ADAMS, b. Pomfret CT 25 March 1724; d. Warren 25 Dec. 1809 ae. 86 "the widow Hannah"; daughter of Richard and Mary (Cady) Adams.

Three (WHEELER) ch., first b. Brookfield by first wife: Zeruiah b. 1740; two b. Warren by second wife: Rice b. 1749 and Hannah b. 1753.

viii MERCY, b. Brookfield 18 Oct. 1718; d. there 27 March 1819 ae. 100 "wife of Thomas"; m. THOMAS BANISTER, b. Brookfield 15 June 1715; d. there 11 Aug. 1791 in 76th yr.; son of Joseph and

Sarah (-----) Banister.
Eight (BANISTER) ch. b. Brookfield: Anna b. 1742, Marcy b. 1743/4, Abigail b. 1746, Lazarus b. 1748/9, Silas b. 1751, Jesse b. 1754, Thomas b. 1759 and Andrew b. 1762.

ix LYDIA, b. Brookfield 5 Aug. 1720; d. Warren 25 March 1805 ae.83 "widow of Josiah"; m. Warren 13 Jan. 1740/1 JOSIAH PUTNAM, b. Salem 3 March 1718/9; d. Warren 4 Feb. 1795 ae. 76; son of Josiah and Ruth (Hutchinson) Putnam. Josiah was at the Lexington Alarm and served as a captain in the Revolution.
Six (PUTNAM) ch. b. Warren: Asa b. 1742, Lydia b. 1744/5, Thankful b. 1747, Josiah b. 1749, Ruth b. 1752 and Mary b. 1757.

x THANKFUL, b. Brookfield 5 July 1722; d. there 11 Dec. 1745, unm.

References: VR BROOKFIELD, NEW BRAINTREE, NEWBURY, SALEM, WARREN(called Western to 1784). CONCORD VR pp. 24, 48, 62, 65, 66, 72. CSL Barbour Index:Pomfret. Worcester Co. PR #49486(Azariah Rice); #26687(John Hamilton). Worcester Co. LR 12:50; 17:347; 32:120; 39:252 (Samuel Wheeler); 21:69(Samuel Wheeler Jr.); 124:126(Nathan Hamilton); 123:40(Josiah Putnam); 40:362(Josiah Wheeler); 44:453(Thomas Banister). Hampden Co. LR 10:626 (Samuel Wheeler); 4:369, 893; 12:739-742(Samuel Wheeler). NEHGR 123:282-3. TAG 23:144; 25:247. WHEELER FAM 1:354-355; 2:597, 617, 1061+. NORTH BROOKFIELD BY TEMPLE pp. 157, 194, 503-4, 613-615, 792. HAMILTON, HOUSE OF p. 1044. HAMILTON FAM pp. 16, 22. PUTNAM FAM pp. 127, 189.

29 JONATHAN WHEELER[4] (Elizabeth[3] White, Resolved[2], William[1]), b. Concord 28 July 1683; d. bef. 24 April 1747 when his estate was divided.

Jonathan m. MARY FLETCHER, d. Bolton 19 Feb. 1738/9 "wife of Jonathan"; daughter of Samuel and Hannah (Wheeler) Fletcher. The will of Samuel Fletcher of Chelmsford, dated 1713 and presented 1726, names wife Elizabeth and son Samuel who is to pay his sister Mary Wheeler. Heirs' citation of same date was "read to Jona. Wheeler (who married Mary, a daughter of the deceased)."

On 24 April 1747 Jonathan Moore and his wife Mary, and Jonathan Wheeler, all of Bolton, sold to Obadiah Wheeler of that town, blacksmith, part of the "estate of our father Jonathan Wheeler dec."

Children (WHEELER), first three bp. Lancaster:

i MARY[5], b. 1st day, 2nd mo. 1710; d. Bolton 20 July 1795 in 86th yr. "wife of Jonathan"; m.

Lancaster 19 April 1727 JONATHAN MOORE, b. there 4th mo. 30th day, 1704; d. Bolton 10 Dec. 1795 in 92nd yr. "husband of Mary"; son of Jonathan and Hannah (-----) Moore. Jonathan's will, dated 12 Sept. 1794 allowed 2 Feb. 1796, mentions his brothers and sisters and the Friends Meeting. They apparently left no children.

ii HANNAH, bp. 24 May 1713; not mentioned in division of father's estate in 1747.

iii OBADIAH, b. 22nd day, 12th mo. 1716; d. Bolton 11 March 1805 "husband of Hannah"; m. (1) King's Chapel, Boston 4 June 1739 (int. 19 May 1739) ELEANOR MALONY; m. (2) Swansea 7th day, 2nd mo. 1748 HANNAH BAKER, b. 16th day, 11th mo. 1718; d. Bolton 23 March 1790 "wife of Obadiah"; daughter of Abraham and Mehitabel (Sherman) Baker. He m. (3) 4th day, 8th mo. 1791 HANNAH (GIRDLER) GASKILL, widow of Ebenezer; daughter of George Girdler of Salem. She outlived Obadiah and was one of those consenting to his will. The will of Obadiah Wheeler of Bolton, advanced in years, dated 30 June 1794 and filed 23 March 1805, names wife Hannah, oldest son Obadiah, 2nd son Abraham, 3rd son Moses, 4th son Asa, oldest daughter Dinah Baker, heirs of 2nd daughter Miriam Fry deceased, and daughter Phebe McBride; codicil dated 10 Aug. 1798 names John McBride son of daughter Phebe. Obadiah was a Quaker and a blacksmith. On 24 April 1747 he and Jonathan Wheeler of Bolton deeded to their sister Mary Moore of Bolton part of the estate of "our father Jonathan Wheeler dec."

Ten (WHEELER) ch. b. Bolton, by first wife: Margaret b. 1737, Mary b. 1740, Dinah b. 1741, Miriam b. 1743 and Obadiah b. 1744; by second wife: Abraham b. 1750, Moses b. 1752, Hannah b. 1754, Phoebe b. 1758 and Asa b. 1761.

iv JONATHAN, b. Shrewsbury 22 June 1720; d. Bolton 10 Aug. 1791; m. Swansea 9th day, 3rd mo. 1751 THANKFUL BAKER; not mentioned in her husband's will; daughter of Abraham and Mehitabel (Sherman) Baker. Jonathan was a glazier and brickmaker. The will of Jonathan Wheeler of Berlin, yeoman, advanced in years, dated 13 June 1790 and accepted 4 Oct. 1791, names oldest son Jonathan and his son Jonathan, 2nd son Stephen and his son Jonathan, 3rd son Peregreen, 4th son Levi, oldest daughter Mary Watson, 2nd daughter Dinah Aldrich, and 3rd daughter Thankful Baker; son Levi and son-in-law Thomas Watson, executors.

Seven (WHEELER) ch. b. Berlin, except Thankful: Jonathan b. 1752, Mary b. 1754, Stephen b. 1756,

Peregrine b. 1759, Dinah b. 1761, Thankful and Levi b. 1768.

References: VR BERLIN, BOLTON, CHELMSFORD, MENDON, SHREWSBURY. CONCORD VR p. 26. LANCASTER VR pp. 24, 273-276. BOSTON VR 28:231, 330. RI VR 7:176, 278. Middlesex Co. PR #7920(Samuel Fletcher). Worcester Co. PR #41431(Jonathan Moore); #63508(Obadiah Wheeler); #63422 (Jonathan Wheeler). Worcester Co. LR 23:154(Jonathan Moore et al); 23:155(Obadiah and Jonathan Wheeler); 51:485 (Obadiah Wheeler). NEHGR 57:303. WHEELER FAM 1:355, 357. MOORE ANCY p. 326. WHEELER (OBADIAH) GEN p. 24. Robert Fletcher of Concord by W. L. Holman, MS. at NEHG Soc., Boston MA, 1930, p. 74.

30 ELIZABETH WHEELER[4] (Elizabeth[3] White, Resolved[2], William[1]), b. Concord 7 Feb. 1685.

She m. Concord 10 Feb. 1707/8 ELISHA RICE, b. Sudbury 4 Dec. 1679; d. there bef. 19 Oct. 1761 when an administrator was appointed for his estate; son of Thomas and Mary (King) Rice.

Elisha lived in Sudbury, received land in Worcester in 1718, and lived there for some time before returning to Sudbury by 1722. On 19 Oct. 1761 Eliakim Rice was appointed administrator of the estate of Capt. Elisha Rice late of Sudbury, deceased. All of Elisha's children were involved in a deed on 22 Jan. 1762 when Eliakim Rice and Elisha Rice, both of Sudbury, Elijah Rice of Westboro, Zebulon Rice of Lancaster, and Jonas Livermore and his wife Elizabeth of Leicester sold a farm to Silas Rice of Westboro.

Children (RICE), b. Sudbury, except Silas:

i ELIAKIM[5], b. 27 Feb. 1[709]; m. Weston 14 May 1730 MEHITABEL LIVERMORE, b. there 15 March 1712/3; daughter of Daniel and Mehitabel (Norcross) Livermore. Eliakim was of Sudbury in his marriage rec., but later of Worcester, for his children were recorded there; and he was back in Sudbury again from 1754 to 1762, the last records found.

Five (RICE) ch. b. Worcester: Mehitabel b. 1731, Daniel b. 1733, Eliakim b. 1736, Ezekiel b. 1742 and Elizabeth b. 1748.

ii ELISHA, b. 27 May 1711; living Sudbury 15 March 1769 when he acknowledged a deed.

iii ELIZABETH, b. 3 Nov. 1713; d. Leicester 29 March 1799, widow; m. Sudbury 28 Nov. 1735 JONAS LIVERMORE, b. Weston 13 May 1710; d. Leicester bet. 2 April 1773 and 28 Nov. 1775; son of Daniel and

Mehitabel (Norcross) Livermore. The will of Jonas Livermore of Leicester, yeoman, dated 2 April 1773 and assented to probate 28 Nov. 1775, names wife Elizabeth, sons Jonas and David, daughters Mary Scott and Elizabeth Tucker, sons Elisha and Micah, and daughters Beulah and Lydia both under 21.

Eight (LIVERMORE) ch. b. Leicester: Jonas b. 1736, Micah b. 1738, Mary b. 1742/3, twins Elizabeth and David b. 1745, Elisha b. 1751, Beulah b. 1753 and Lydia b. 1755.

iv JULIA, b. 20 March 1715/6; non compos mentis.

v SILAS, b. Worcester 28 April 1719; d. Northboro 24 March 1800 ae. 79; m. int. (1) Lancaster 10 March 1744/5 COPIA BROUGHTON, b. there 28 Oct. 1724; d. Northboro 4 May 1769 in 45th yr. "wife of Silas"; daughter of Edward and Martha (Wheeler) Broughton (see 26 i). Silas m. (2) Bolton 20 Sept. 1770 LOIS POLLARD, b. Lancaster 4 April 1736; d. Northboro 19 March 1778 in 42nd yr. "wife of Silas"; daughter of William and Experience (Wheeler) Pollard (see 26 ii). Silas m. (3) Northboro 3 or 4 Dec. 1784 MEHITABEL GOODNOW; d. there 1 June 1790 in 52nd yr. "wife of Silas."

Nine (RICE) ch., eight by first wife, first six b. Westboro, last three b. Northboro: Lucy, b. 1745, Copiah b. 1747, Silas b. 1748, Relief b. 1753, Timothy b. 1755, Ezekiel b. 1757, Lucy b. 1765, Timothy b. 1766 and Eunice b. 1771.

vi ELIJAH, b. 5 March 1721/2; d. Holden in March 1818 in 97th yr.; m. Shrewsbury 23 Nov. 1748 HULDAH KEYES, b. there 19 April 1727; d. Holden in March 1799; daughter of Ebenezer and Tamar (Wheelock) Keyes. The will of Elijah Rice of Holden, gentleman, dated 8 April 1799 and filed 19 Feb. 1818, names granddaughter Abigail Stickney; and six ch. Elijah, Ebenezer, Lois formerly wife of Edward Goodnow dec., Zerviah wife of Thaddeus Colburn, Lettice wife of Thomas Davis, and Huldah wife of Asa Raymond.

Eight (RICE) ch., first four b. Shrewsbury: Elijah b. 1749, Lois b. 1751, Ebenezer b. 1756, Zerviah b. 1760, twins Joseph and Tryphena bp. either 1753 or 1758, Lettuce bp. 1764 and Huldah (named only in her father's will).

vii ZEBULON, b. 5 June 1725; d. Boylston 26 Dec. 1799 in 75th yr.; m. Sudbury 7 Dec. 1749 SUSANNA ALLEN, b. there 22 Jan. 1731/2; d. Ashburnham 17 Dec. 1823 in 92nd yr.; daughter of Zebediah and Mary (Hoar) Allen. The will of Zebediah Allen of Sudbury, dated 7 July 1767 and presented 22 July 1777, names wife Mary and daughter Susannah Rice.

Seventeen (RICE) ch. b. Lancaster: Josiah b. 1750, Zebulon b. 1752, Jonas b. 1754, Eliakim b. 1756, Reuben b. 1757, Susanna b. 1759, Elisha b. 1760, Benjamin b. 1761, Molly b. 1762, John b. 1764, Luke b. 1765, Stephen b. 1766, Simeon b. 1768, Joseph b. 1769, David b. 1772, Elizabeth b. 1774 and Dolly b. 1776.

References: VR BOLTON, LEICESTER, NORTHBOROUGH, SHREWSBURY, SUDBURY, WAYLAND, WESTBOROUGH, WESTON, WORCESTER. CONCORD VR pp. 28, 70. LANCASTER VR pp. 31, 54, 63, 107, 166. Middlesex Co. PR #363(Zebediah Allen); #18699(Capt. Elisha Rice). Middlesex Co. LR 66:10(Eliakim Rice et al); 66:12; 69:616(Elisha Rice); 52:506(Eliakim Rice). Worcester Co. PR #37551(Jonas Livermore); #49589 (Elijah Rice). Worcester Co. LR 36:428(Eliakim Rice); 117:521(Eliakim Rice of Ashburnham). MA MARR 1:89. NEHGR 77:17, 20. ALLEN (PHINEAS) DESC Walter:9. RICE GEN pp. 6, 31, 73, 74, 135-136[several errors]. WHEELER FAM 1:353-4. LIVERMORE FAM pp. 18, 26. WATERTOWN BY BOND p. 340.

31 JOSEPH WHEELER[4] (Elizabeth[3] White, Resolved[2], William[1]), b. Concord 7 March 1690/1; d. Lancaster 29 Feb. 1780.

He m. (1) Cambridge 2 March 1726/7 ABIGAIL BUTTERFIELD, b. there 11 May 1702; d. 2 Oct. 1764; daughter of Jonathan and Ruth (Wright) Butterfield. In a decree dated 18 March 1754 for settlement of the estate of Jonathan Butterfield, late of Cambridge deceased, cordwainer, Abigail Wheeler was named among his children.

Joseph m. (2) Lancaster 15 Aug. 1766 SARAH ALLEN, b. Weston 7 June 1718; d. Lancaster 14 April 1789 ae. 71 widow; daughter of Ebenezer and Sarah (Waight) Allen. The will of Sarah Wheeler, widow of Joseph of Lancaster, dated 11 April 1789 and filed 4 May 1789, mentions her brother John Allen and other relatives.

Joseph lived in Concord, where all of his children were born, until about 1742 when he went to Lancaster. The will of Joseph Wheeler of Lancaster, dated 15 Aug. 1778 and proved 6 March 1780, names his wife Sarah, and his four ch. Joseph Jr., Phoebe Wilder, Rachel Wheeler and Abigail Conqueret.

Children (WHEELER), b. Concord by first wife:

i PHOEBE[5], b. 11 Jan. 1727/8; d. in 1806; m. Leominster 3 March 1746/7 JOTHAM WILDER, b. Lancaster in 1710; d. Brattleboro VT 25 May 1801; son of Thomas and Sarah or Susannah (Hunt) Wilder. Jotham fought in the Colonial Wars and at Bunker Hill. Nothing further found in VT VR or VT PR.

Eight (WILDER) ch. b. Lancaster: Stephen b. 1747, Titus b. 1749, Phoebe b. 1752, Susanna b. 1756, Jotham b. 1759, Reuben Wheeler b. 1761, Abigail b. 1765 and Sarah b. 1768.

ii REUBEN, b. 3 Dec. 1729; d. in Ireland 29 July 1763, in the service of King George III.

iii RACHEL, b. 15 Sept. 1731; d. Lancaster 15 May 1790, unm.

iv JOSEPH, b. 13 March 1734/5; d. Worcester 10 Feb. 1793; m. (1) Bolton 21 Oct. 1760 MARY GREENLEAF, b. there 3 July 1742; d. Worcester 27 Aug. 1783 "wife of Joseph"; daughter of Daniel and Silence (Nichols) (Marsh) Greenleaf. Joseph m. (2) 20 May 1784 MARGUERITA (OLIVIER) (COOLIDGE) JENNISON, b. Annapolis, Nova Scotia 8 Nov. 1726; d. Boston 25 Oct. 1816 ae. 90; bur. King's Chapel; daughter of Antoine and Mary (Sigourne) Olivier. Joseph was a Harvard graduate in 1757; a minister at the Town of Harvard from 1761-8; member of the Provincial Congress 1774-5; representative to the General Court 1775; Registrar of Probate for Worcester County from 1781 until his death. He marched to Lexington in the Revolution. A division of the estate of Joseph Wheeler late of Worcester, Esq., dated 12 Nov. 1794 names nine ch.: Mary Weld, wife of Ezra; Joseph; Daniel G.; John; Moses; Clarissa Wheeler; Abigail Wheeler; Sophia Wheeler; the widow Margaret; and oldest son Theophilus.

Eleven (WHEELER) ch. by first wife, first ten b. or bp. Harvard: Elizabeth b. 1761, Mary b. 1763, Theophilus b. 1764, Joseph b. 1766, Daniel Greenleaf b. 1768, John b. 1770, Moses b. 1772, Clarissa b. 1774, Abigail b. 1776, Levi bp. 1779 and Sophia b. Worcester 1782.

v ABIGAIL, b. 13 May 1737; d. Lancaster 23 or 24 Oct. 1817 ae. 80 "Mrs. Abigail Rogers wife of Mr. Joseph"; m. (1) Lancaster 23 July 1758 LOUIS CONQUERET who went to sea in 1758 and was not heard from thereafter. She m. int. (2) Lancaster 18 Sept. 1780 JOSEPH ROGERS of Lancaster; still living there in 1803 when he and Joel Osgood partitioned property. It is probably this Abigail who filed intentions at Lancaster 8 April 1779 with Ebenezer Smith of Ashby, although they did not marry.

One (CONQUERET) ch. b. Lancaster: Mary, prob. the one born 1759 to Louis and Mary *(sic)*, who d. unm. in 1840.

References: VR BOLTON, CAMBRIDGE, HARVARD, LEOMINSTER, WESTON. CONCORD VR pp. 34, 120, 124, 129, 149. LANCASTER VR pp. 31, 39, 73, 74, 79, 80, 82, 88, 90, 100, 139, 140, 189, 297, 304, 306, 328, 330, 359, 375. Middlesex Co. PR #3726(Jonathan Butterfield). Worcester Co. PR #63433; #63434(Joseph Wheeler); #63451(Sarah Wheeler). Worcester Co. LR 149:590; 240:490(Joseph Rogers). MA BAY ACTS AND RESOLVES (1896) 6:209. WHEELER (OBADIAH) GEN p. 7. WHEELER FAM 1:355, 357-365. NEHGR 44:36. WATERTOWN BY BOND pp. 5+. WILDER GEN pp. 6, 395. BRATTLEBORO ANNALS p. 158. HARVARD BY NOURSE p. 197. GREENLEAF FAM pp. 205-209. HARVARD GRADS 14:234. (BOSTON) KING'S CHAPEL p. 189. WORCESTER SOC COLL 1:154.

32 BENJAMIN WHEELER$^{4}$ (Elizabeth$^{3}$ White, Resolved$^{2}$, William$^{1}$), b. Concord 29 Sept. 1693; d. New Marlborough 14 May 1759 in 66th yr. "son of Obidiah of Concord."

He m. HANNAH ----- who was living New Marlborough 15 May 1760.

Benjamin was the first settler of New Marlborough in the winter of 1739/40, having lived in Lancaster after his marriage and moved to Bolton between 1725 and 1732. He executed his last deed of Bolton land on 20 Nov. 1741, witnessed by Zenas Wheeler and Hannah Wheeler. In 1747 and on 19 Feb. 1759, he deeded land in New Marlborough the latter witnessed by Nehemiah Howe and Zenas Wheeler, presumably his son-in-law and son.

He left no probate records, but on 15 May 1760 his land was divided among his heirs: Hannah Wheeler, widow; Zenas Wheeler; Joshua Fosket and wife Hannah; Nehemiah Howe and wife Beulah; David Smith and wife Consolation; all of New Marlborough.

Children (WHEELER), first four b. Lancaster, fifth b. Bolton:

i HANNAH$^{5}$, b. 22 Dec. 1717; living New Marlborough 3 Jan. 1786; m. bef. 1750 JOSHUA FOSKET, b. Charlestown 5 April 1717 to Robert and Mercy (Goodwin) Fosket. Joshua bought land in New Marlborough 19 Feb. 1759 from Benjamin Wheeler. He was living in New Marlborough 13 March 1786 when he acknowledged a deed. The 1790 census for New Marlborough lists a Joshua Fosket with one female in his household. There is nothing on the Foskets in Hampshire or Berkshire Co. probate records or in Hampshire Co. land records.

Three (FOSKET) ch., first b. Bolton, rest b. New Marlborough: Jesse b. 1750, Susanna b. 1754 and John b. 1765.

ii JESSE (son), b. 15 May 1720; d. Bolton 16 Dec. 1744 in 23rd yr.

iii BULAH, b. 1 March 1724; d. ca. 1799; m. Bolton 4 March 1746/7 NEHEMIAH HOWE, b. Marlborough 13 Jan. 1720/1; d. Poultney VT in April 1777; son of Peter and Grace (Bush) Howe. Nehemiah was a miller; he moved from Marlborough to New Marlborough about 1749, and to Poultney VT in 1775. He served at Ticonderoga and Bennington in the Revolution.

Nine (HOWE) ch., first b. Marlborough: Abner b. 1747; eight b. New Marlborough: Olive b. 1750, Phoebe b. 1752, Beulah b. 1754, Peter b. 1756, Candis b. 1758, Phoebe b. 1761, John b. 1763 and Joel b. 1765.

iv ZENAS, b. 29 Dec. 1725; d. New Marlborough 6 Oct. 1785; m. bef. 1750 AZUBAH ----- ; d. New Marlborough 1 Oct. 1790 "wife of Zenas." The will of Zenas Wheeler of New Marlborough dated 26 Dec. 1783 and presented 1 Nov. 1785, names wife Azuba, eldest son Zenas, other son Benjamin, oldest daughter Hannah Wheeler, daughter Lois wife to John Hyde, daughter Azuba wife to John Hyde 2nd, daughter Eunice, and youngest daughter Dinah.

Nine (WHEELER) ch., last eight b. New Marlborough: Levi, Hannah b. 1750, Lois b. 1752, Eunice b. 1754, Zenas b. 1756, Luis b. 1759, Azubah b. 1761, Benjamin b. 1764 and Dinah b. 1766.

v CONSOLATION, b. Bolton 28 April 1732; d. New Marlborough bef. 4 April 1808; m. bef. 1753 DAVID SMITH, d. New Marlborough bef. 2 Feb. 1779. Bond was posted on administrators of the estate of David Smith late of New Marlborough, deceased, 2 Feb. 1779. His estate was distributed 3 May 1779 among his sons: Samuel, Benjamin, David, Richard, Obadiah, Laben and Gilbert, with widow Consolation receiving her rights. Administration on the estate of Consolation Smith late of New Marlborough was requested 4 April 1808.

Seven (SMITH) ch. b. New Marlborough: Samuel b. 1753, Benjamin b. 1755, David b. 1757, Richard b. 1761, Obadiah b. 1765, Laban b. 1768 and Gilbert b. 1771.

References: VR BOLTON, MARLBOROUGH. CONCORD VR p. 41. LANCASTER VR pp. 57-8, 274, 276, 278. New Marlborough VR (typescript at NEHG Soc.) pp. 23, 58.

Worcester Co. LR 21:393; 24:259(Benjamin Wheeler). Berkshire Co. LR 4:183(Benjamin Wheeler to Fosket); 20:198 (Hannah Fosket). Berkshire Co. PR #958(David Smith); #2552(Consolation Smith); #1290(Zenas Wheeler); #3347 (Hannah[6] Wheeler). Hampden Co. LR 12:739-42(Hepzibah and Samuel Wheeler); 10:626(Hepzibah Wheeler); 4:31(Hannah Wheeler et al). HOWE (JOHN) GEN pp. 34, 73, 148-50. WHEELER FAM 1:355-6; 2:1092. POULTNEY VT BY JOSLIN pp. 279-80. WORCESTER SOC COLL 5:158. MA HIST BY BARBER p. 83.

33 JOSHUA WHEELER[4] (Elizabeth[3] White, Resolved[2], William[1]), b. Concord 9 April 1696; d. Bolton 11 April 1778.

He m. about 1720 ANNA ----- , b. ca. 1702; d. Bolton 26 Oct. 1761 in 60th yr. "wife of Joshua."

Joshua was admitted to the Lancaster Church 4 Nov. 1716 and Anna was admitted 13 July 1729. They were in Bolton by 1747 when Joshua Sr. deeded land to son Joshua Jr. also of Bolton. The bond on Joshua Wheeler of Bolton, administrator of the estate of Joshua[4] Wheeler, late of Bolton deceased, was dated 8 June 1778.

Children (WHEELER), b. Lancaster:

i ANNA[5], b. 27 June 1721; living 21 April 1747 when she witnessed her father's deed to her brother.

ii JOSHUA, b. 13 Dec. 1723, bp. 19 Feb. 1722/3 (*sic*); living Bolton 2 Oct. 1794 when he and his wife Elizabeth acknowledged a deed; m. ELIZABETH BARNEY, b. Sudbury 15 May 1726; living Bolton 2 Oct. 1794; daughter of Thomas and Mary (-----) Barney. In the estate of Thomas Barney late of Sudbury on 8 March 1753, Joshua and his wife Elizabeth are listed among the heirs; on that day they received their portion "from brother Thomas Barney." Joshua and Elizabeth were in Hopkinton 1753-67 (deed and births of their children) and in Bolton by 1778.

Nine (WHEELER) ch., first two b. Sudbury, last seven b. Hopkinton: Elizabeth b. 1748/9, Mary b. 1751, Sarah b. 1754, Mary b. 1756, Philadelphia b. 1758, Matilda b. 1760, Joshua b. 1762, Anna b. 1764 and Thankful b. 1767.

iii ELIZABETH, b. 1 Nov. 1725, bp. 20 June 1725 (*sic*); d. Bolton 11 March 1745.

iv THANKFUL, b. 16 July 1728; d. Bolton bef. 11 July 1804. She was a weaver living in Bolton 20 July 1778 when she acknowledged a deed of land to her brother. On 11 July 1804 Timothy and Matilda Bruce (her niece and niece's husband) requested that an administrator be appointed for her estate.

References: VR BOLTON. CONCORD VR p. 41. LANCASTER VR pp. 65, 271, 272, 277, 279. Worcester Co. PR #63437(Joshua Wheeler Sr.); #63564(Thankful Wheeler). Worcester Co. LR 24:260(Joshua[4] Wheeler); 121:150; 125:461(Joshua[5] Wheeler); 80:542(Thankful Wheeler). Middlesex Co. PR 37:292-3(Thomas Barney). WHEELER FAM 1:356; 2:611.

34 JOSIAH[4] WHITE (Josiah[3], Resolved[2], William[1]), bp. Salem Village (now Danvers) 20 May 1705 "adult"; d. prob. Sutton bet. 26 Aug. 1761 and 13 Aug. 1764.

He m. Sutton 28 April 1737 MARY TAYLOR, prob. b. Reading 25 June 1708 to Thomas and Mary (-----) Taylor, although no proof of Mary Taylor's parentage was found in probates of Essex, Middlesex and Worcester Counties or in Middlesex deeds. In Josiah White's will he gives to his son Caleb a chest of his grandfather Taylor.

Josiah was of Salem in Aug. 1720 and "of Sutton, formerly of Salem" 19 Nov. 1725. The will of Josiah White of Sutton "far advanced in age," dated 26 Aug. 1761 and filed 13 Aug. 1764, names his son Caleb and daughter Mary White; they were to care for their brother Josiah, an idiot. The executor was Josiah White Jr., a nephew.

Children (WHITE), b. Sutton:

i JOSIAH[5], b. 8 July 1738; d.y.

ii MARY, b. 8 July 1741; d. after 2 Feb. 1808 when she gave bond on her husband's estate; m. Sutton 24 Nov. 1761 THOMAS PARKER, b. there 27 April 1733; d. there bef. 2 Feb. 1808; son of Samuel and Hannah (-----) Parker.

Seven (PARKER) ch. b. Sutton: Polly b. 1761, Betty b. 1763, John b. 1767, twins Lucy and Parley b. 1770, Roby b. 1773 and Fally b. 1775.

iii JOSIAH, b. 1 April 1745; living 1787 "idiot" when Thomas Parker asked that a guardian be appointed.

iv CALEB, b. 31 July 1747; living 2 Jan. 1787 when he deeded land; m. Sutton 26 Feb. 1767 REBECCA MARSH, living 2 Jan. 1787 when she signed the above deed. Caleb's father left him a considerable estate and the care of his idiot elder brother. In 1781 the selectmen of Sutton asked that a guardian be appointed for Caleb who appeared to be non-compos. He left the state in 1787.

Two (WHITE) ch. b. Sutton: Sally b. 1768 and Chloe b. 1771.*

References: MD 8:165-7. VR READING, SUTTON. MA MARR 1:100. Essex Co. LR 37:162; 49:269(Josiah White). Worcester Co. PR #45241(Thomas Parker); #64218 (Caleb White gdn.). Worcester Co. LR 101:266(Caleb White). BOSTON TRANSCRIPT 26 July 1922 #9636. STANSTEAD CO QUEBEC HIST pp. 221-2. SUTTON BY BENEDICT pp. 254, 747.

35 JOSEPH[4] WHITE (Josiah[3], Resolved[2], William[1]), d. Sutton bet. 12 July 1750 and 20 Dec. 1750.

He m. (1) Boxford 31 Aug. 1711 BEATRIX HOLTON, who was living 12 Jan. 1725/6 "near Sutton"; he m. (2) Salem 23 Nov. 1738 SARAH GARDNER, living 20 Dec. 1750.

Joseph was in Salem 29 July 1720 and in Sutton 21 Oct. 1723. He was a joiner of Sutton on 12 July 1750 when he acknowledged a deed to Josiah White Jr. On 20 Dec. 1750 Sarah White, widow, and eldest son Jonathan consented to sons Joseph and Josiah Jr. as administrators of the estate of Joseph White. In the order to divide the estate, dated 27 July 1753, Josiah White of Sutton was to pay brothers Jonathan, Joseph and John, and sisters Mary, Abigail wife of Jonathan Church, and Sarah wife of Ebenezer Brown.

Children (WHITE) by first wife:

i JONATHAN[5], d. Pomfret CT 20 April 1795; m. there 4 or 19 May 1743 SARAH BACON, b. there 27 March 1718; living 20 March 1795; daughter of Daniel and Sarah (Pooly) Bacon. On 20 March 1795 Jonathan, wife Sarah, and their "son and daughter" Daniel and Sarah White Jr., all of Pomfret CT deeded land received from Mr. Daniel Bacon of Pomfret, dec.

Two (WHITE) ch. b. Pomfret CT: Daniel b. 1746 and Sarah b. 1749.

ii JOSEPH, d. Woodstock CT 19 Feb. 1794 in 81st yr.; m. Pomfret CT 9 Nov. 1745 MARTHA SAWYER, b. there 9 May 1719 (original rec.); d. Woodstock 12 Oct. 1804 in 86th yr. "the widow Martha"; daughter of James and Mary (-----) Sawyer.

Five (WHITE) ch., first b. Pomfret, rest b. Sutton: Cornelius b. 1746, Peregrine b. 1747,

---

*Two other (WHITE) children, Caleb b. 1777 and Dexter b. 1781, were supposedly born to them in Sutton. [See STANSTEAD CO QUEBEC HIST.] We have not found certain proof that these two were sons of Caleb and Rebecca; nevertheless the Mayflower Society does accept descent through Caleb[6].

Joel b. 1751, Mary b. 1757 and Anna b. 1759.

iii JOSIAH, JR., d. Barre bet. 16 May 1803 and 16 July 1804; m. (1) Sutton 2 Jan. 1745/6 HANNAH GARDNER; m. (2) Sutton 28 Nov. 1751 LUCY WHIPPLE, b. there 25 Feb. 1723/4; d. bef. 16 May 1803, not mentioned in her husband's will; daughter of John and Mary (-----) Whipple. The will of Josiah White of Barre, yeoman, dated 16 May 1803 and filed 16 July 1804, names sons Ebenezer, Josiah, Abel, Elias, and Job, daughters Hannah wife of John Moore, Beatrix widow of Joseph Lawrence, Lucy, Hannah, Rachel wife of Ezra Houtson (Hudson), and son Noah.

Eleven (WHITE) ch., first ten b. Sutton, first two by first wife: Hannah b. 1746, Beatrix b. 1748/9, Ebenezer b. 1752, Abel b. 1754, Jephthah b. 1755, Josiah b. 1758, Elias b. 1759, Noah b. 1761, Lucy b. 1764, Job b. 1766 and Rachel.

iv JOHN, certified as non compos mentis 27 Aug. 1750 and in need of a guardian. The last account of his guardian dated May 1756 does not mention his death.

v ABIGAIL, d. Granville 7 Oct. 1794 ae. 76 "wife of Jonathan"; m. Sutton 15 Jan. 1740/1 JONATHAN CHURCH, b. Plainfield CT 17 July 1714; d. Granville "of old age" 1809 ae. 95; son of Samuel and Mary (Edwards) Church.

Five (CHURCH) ch. b. Granville: Josiah b. 1742, Abijah b. 1745, Hannah b. 1749, Batheuel b. 1752 and Jonathan b. 1755.

vi SARAH, living 17 March 1773; m. Pomfret CT 28 Dec. 1748 EBENEZER BACON, b. 8 Aug. 1715; d. Pomfret bef. 5 July 1768; son of Isaac Bacon. On 10 June 1746 Ebenezer Bacon of Pomfret sold his part of the estate of his father Isaac, late of Pomfret, dec. On 5 July 1768 Sarah Bacon of Pomfret was bonded as administratrix on the estate of Ebenezer Bacon of Pomfret.* The last record of Sarah is a deed of 17 March 1773, wherein Hannah, her husband Elihu Sabin, and Sarah Bacon, spinster, sold their portion of

---

*Although the settlement of the estate of Joseph White, Sarah's father, twice refers to her husband as Ebenezer Brown, the authors are convinced that she married Ebenezer Bacon. First, the name Bacon is rare in Worcester County and can easily be misread for the more common name of Brown in the hand of the period. Further, Jonathan White co-signed Sarah's bond as administratrix of the estate of Ebenezer Bacon, late of Pomfret, 5 July 1768; and was made guardian to Bacon children: Abigail, Dorothy, Rhoda and Mary in 1771; Lucy and Sarah in 1772.

the estate left by their father Ebenezer Bacon, late of Pomfret, dec., except their mother's thirds.

Eight (BACON) ch. b. Pomfret CT: Hannah b. 1749, Sarah b. 1751, Abigail b. 1754, Ebenezer b. 1756, Lucy b. 1757, Dorothy b. 1760, Rodah b. 1762 and Molly b. 1766.

vii MARY, living 27 July 1753, settlement of her father's estate.

References: MD 8:165-8. VR BOXFORD, GRANVILLE, SALEM, SUTTON. CSL Barbour Index:Pomfret, Plainfield, Stonington (Church-Edwards m.). E. Granville Ch. Rec., (Typescript at Berkshire Athenaeum, Pittsfield) p. 108. Worcester Co. PR #64372(Josiah White); #64354 and A615:491(Joseph White); #64331(John White gdn.). Pomfret CT PR #242, #243, #237, #255, #258(Ebenezer Bacon et al). Worcester Co. LR 29:145(Joseph White). Essex Co. LR 38:79(Joseph White). Pomfret CT LR 6:84(Sabin and Bacon); 8:40(Jonathan White et al); 8:48(Jonathan White); 3:138 (Ebenezer Bacon). NEHGR 67:374-5; 120:174-87. TAG 34:135. WOODSTOCK CT BY BOWEN 2:283, 305. WINDHAM CO CT BY LARNED 1:529. SUTTON BY BENEDICT p. 747. WHITE FAM REC pp. 49, 273 (confuses Joseph$^5$ with Joseph son of Daniel).

36 SAMUEL$^4$ WHITE (Josiah$^3$, Resolved$^2$, William$^1$), b. Salem 4 Sept. 1696; d. Danvers 5 Dec. 1773.

He m. DINAH KINNEY, b. Salem 9 Dec. 1698; living 3 Jan. 1774; daughter of Henry and Priscilla (Lewis) Kinney. The will of Henry Kenney of Sutton, dated 1 Feb. 1727/8 and proved 10 Aug. 1732, names daughter Dinah, wife of Samuel White of Salem.

Samuel was a wheelwright and turner; he was in Salem until Feb. 1734/5, and of Danvers in Sept. 1753. The will of Samuel White of Danvers, dated 21 Aug. 1771 and proved 3 Jan. 1774, names wife Dinah, daughters Jerusha Peabody, Eunice How, Anna Nichols and Mary Nichols, and son Samuel White, executor. The consent of his wife to the provisions of the will is on file.

Samuel never lived in Shrewsbury. The Samuel and Sybil "bp. Shrewsbury" in 1739 to Samuel and Dinah appear to be children of Samuel and Dinah (Ward) White who were married in Marlboro and later went to Killingly CT.

Children (WHITE) bp. Salem:

i JERUSHA$^5$, bp. 13 Sept. 1719; d. Middleton 27 Sept. 1809 ae. 92 "widow of Zerubbabel"; m. Middleton 20 Oct. 1743 ZEROBABEL PEABODY, b. Boxford 26 Feb. 1707; d. Middleton 28 Dec. 1781; son of Joseph and Mary (Symonds) Peabody, not a descendant of Pilgrim John Alden. He m. (1) 21 Feb. 1733 Lydia Fuller by whom he had three ch. The will of Zorobabel Peabody of Middleton, yeoman, dated 28 Dec. 1772 and proved 5 March 1781, names wife Jerusha, daughters Bethiah and Lydia (by his first wife), daughter Elizabeth and sons Andrew and Joseph.

Three (PEABODY) ch. b. Middleton to Zerobabel and Jerusha: Andrew b. 1745, Joseph b. 1747 and Elizabeth b. 1749.

ii EUNICE, bp. 14 May 1721; d. Middleton 2 Dec. 1803 ae. 84y 29d "widow of Mark Howe"; m. 20 April 1741 ISRAEL KINNEY, b. Boxford 24 Aug. 1712; d. Middleton bef. 20 April 1747; son of Daniel and Mary (Richards) Kinney. The bond on Eunice as administratrix of the estate of her husband Israel Kinney, late of Middleton deceased, is dated 20 April 1747. On the same day, Eunice was named guardian of Israel Kinney Jr., son of Israel, then under 14 years; on 8 Dec. 1760 Israel Jr., over 14, chose his uncle Zerubabel Peabody as guardian.

Eunice m. (2) Middleton 4 June 1752 MARK HOWE, b. Boxford 18 April 1701; d. bet. 21 April 1768 and 2 Nov. 1778; son of John and Sarah (Cave) Howe. He had earlier m. (1) in 1725 Lydia Wilkins; (2) Dorothy ----- ; and (3) in 1740 Mary Stevens. "Eunice Kenney alias Howe" rendered an account on the estate of her late husband, Israel Kenney, 6 Nov. 1752; a later account was signed by Eunice Howe and Mark Howe. The will of Mark How of Middleton, yeoman, dated 21 April 1768 and proved 2 Nov. 1778, names wife Eunice, son Asa, daughters Lydia How and Mary Stiles (both by his first marriage), and daughters Eunice Howe and Sarah How.

One (KINNEY) ch. b. to Israel and Eunice: Israel b. 1748.

Three (HOW) ch. b. Middleton to Mark and Eunice: Eunice b. 1753, Sarah b. 1755 and Asa b. 1756.

iii ANN, bp. 21 July 1723; d. Merrimack NH in 1807; m. Danvers 26 May 1760 SAMUEL NICHOLS, b. Topsfield 25 Feb. 1714/5; d. Merrimack in 1793; son of John and Mary (Golthright) Nichols. He m. (1) in 1742 Abigail Eliot, by whom he had seven ch. including Amos who m. Ann's sister Mary (see v below). Samuel and Ann moved to Merrimack from Middleton about 1777, but did not transfer their church membership until 1785.

Two (NICHOLS) ch. b. Middleton to Samuel and Ann: Samuel b. 1761 and Asa b. 1762.

iv SAMUEL, bp. 7 Dec. 1729; d. Danvers bet. 4 Jan. 1799 and 5 May 1800; m. Salem 10 May 1751 MARTHA PRITCHET, bp. Topsfield 29 April 1733; d. bef. 4 Jan. 1799; daughter of John and Martha (Gould) Pritchet. Samuel was a wheelwright. The will of Samuel White, yeoman of Danvers, dated 4 Jan. 1799 and proved 5 May 1800, names sons John, Joseph, Samuel and daughters Mehitable Preston, Lydia Knight and Anna White (unm.).

Six (WHITE) ch. b. Danvers: Mehitable b. 1752, John b. 1753, Joseph b. 1762, Samuel b. 1764, Lydia b. 1765 and Anna b. 1775.

v MARY, bp. 16 May 1736; d. Merrimack NH in 1796 "widow Mary Nichols"; m. Middleton 5 July 1770 AMOS NICHOLS, b. there 19 Sept. 1747; d. Merrimack in 1783; son of Samuel and Abigail (Eliot) Nichols (see iii above). They apparently moved to Merrimack before Nov. 1774 where they had a son recorded.

One (NICHOLS) ch. b. Merrimack NH: Peregrine b. 1774.

References: MD 8:165-70. VR BOXFORD, DANVERS, GRAFTON, MIDDLETON, SALEM, TOPSFIELD. Essex Co. PR 350:79(Samuel White); 354:39(Zorobabel Peabody); 331:55 and #15324(Israel Kinney); #15325(gdn. of Israel Kinney Jr.); 353:263(Mark How); 367:391(Samuel White). First Cong. Ch. of Merrimack NH (original records at clerk's home) 1:43, 276, 277. TAG 34:102. NEHGR 2:363. PEABODY GEN pp. 23, 30, 50. HOWE GENS pp. 169, 170. ESSEX INST HIST COLL 3:30, 31; 62:384. KINNE GEN pp. 136, 137, 149. TINGLEY ANCY pp. 141, 185, 187. WHITE (THOMAS) DESC p. 9.

37 JOHN[4] WHITE (Daniel[3], Peregrine[2], William[1]), b. Marshfield 26 April 1675; d. there 9 Sept. 1753 in 79th yr.

He m. Marshfield 18 Feb. 1700 SUSANNA SHERMAN, b. there; d. there 22 Dec. 1766 in 88th yr. "wife of John White"; daughter of Samuel and Sarah (Doggett) Sherman.

The will of John White of Marshfield, yeoman, aged and infirm, dated 26 Oct. 1747 and proved 5 Nov. 1753, mentions his "beloved wife"; daughter Hannah White; daughter Sarah Phillips; grandchildren, children of son John deceased: John, Susanna, Hannah, James and Andrew White; and sons Abijah and Jesse to be executors.

The will of John's daughter Hannah White of Marshfield, spinster, dated 14 July 1775 and proved 6 May 1776, names brother Abijah White; sister Sarah Phillips; sister Anna White wife of Abijah; Sylvanus; Abijah Jr.; William and Sybeline White; Anna White daughter of Abijah; Priscilla White; Sarah White daughter of Abijah; Susannah

White daughter of Abijah; Christiana wife of William Lewis; daughters of Abijah White: Anna, Priscilla, Sarah and Susanna White.

Children (WHITE) b. Marshfield:

i HANNAH[5], b. 28 March 1702; d. Marshfield 29 July 1775, unm. She was the first recorded school dame of Marshfield; see her will above.

ii JOHN, b. 17 Aug. 1704; d. Marshfield bef. 4 Aug. 1746; m. there 16 Jan. 1729/30 JOANNA SPRAGUE, b. there 10 Sept. 1711; d. bef. 29 May 1756; daughter of Nathan and Margaret (Randall) Sprague. The will of Nathan Sprague of Marshfield, dated 29 May 1756 and proved 25 April 1758, names wife Margaret and five granchildren, children of his daughter "Jonne" White, dec., late wife of John White, dec: John, James, Andrew, Susanna and Hannah. An administrator was appointed on the estate of John White Jr. late of Marshfield dec., on 4 Aug. 1746; guardians were appointed on 12 Aug. 1746 for his ch: John, Susanna, James, Hannah, Andrew and Nathan White.

Six (WHITE) ch., first rec. in Marshfield: John b. 1732, Susanna, Hannah, James, Andrew and Nathan.

iii ABIJAH, b. 8 Oct. 1706; d. Boston 29 Oct. 1775 in 70th yr. and bur. King's Chapel; m. Marshfield 1 Feb. 1738 ANNA LITTLE, b. there 30 Jan. 1715/6; d. there 11 March 1791 in 76th yr. "widow of Abijah White Esq."; daughter of John and Constant (Fobes) Little, and a descendant of Pilgrims John Alden and Richard Warren. The will of John Little of Marshfield, dated 14 Jan. 1764 and proved 6 March 1761, names wife Constant (Fobes) Little and daughter Anna White; the will of Constant Little, dated 18 Nov. 1767 and probated 6 Aug. 1772, names son-in-law Abijah White and his wife Anna. Abijah was a loyalist refugee. There is no probate of the estate of Abijah, but in a land record "Silvanus White, William White, Sarah White and Susannah White, singlewomen,...Ezra Edson and Anna his wife in her right...divide among ourselves and to mother Anna White, widow, relict of Abijah White Esq. deceased, land of which our father Abijah White died seized"; they all signed 26 May 1784.

Ten (WHITE) ch. b. Marshfield: Anna b. 1739, Priscilla b. 1740, Sylvanus b. 1742, Abijah b. 1745, Deborah b. 1746, Abijah b. 1747, Sarah b. 1749, William b. 1752, John b. 1753 and Susanna b. 1756.

iv SARAH, b. 31 May 1710; d. Marshfield 15 Feb. 1788 in 78th yr. "widow of Isaac Phillips"; m. there 25 Jan. 1727/8 ISAAC PHILLIPS, b. Marshfield 5 March 1701/2 or 1702/3; d. there 18 Sept. 1787 in 86th yr.; son of Benjamin and Sarah (Thomas) Phillips. Isaac was a mariner. There is no probate record in Plymouth County for either Isaac or Sarah. On 7 Jan. 1782 Isaac Phillips of Marshfield sold to his son Isaac of Boston all his real estate including buildings "where I now dwell," and his pew in the meeting house.
Seven (PHILLIPS) ch. b. Marshfield: Isaac b. 1728, David b. 1731, Sarah b. 1735, Anna b. 1736/7, James b. 1739, Rebecca b. 1742 and Solomon b. 1750.

v REBECCA, b. in Dec. 1713; d. in 1716.

vi SYLVANUS, b. 24 July 1718; d. 19 Dec. 1742. On 7 Feb. 1742 John White of Marshfield was appointed administrator of the estate of Sylvanus, coaster, late of Marshfield; the appraisal reads "all shown to us by Mr. John White, father to deceased." No record of marriage or children has been found.

vii JESSE, b. 7 Dec. 1720; living in May 1765; m. Boston 28 Dec. 1743 CATHERINA CHARLOTTE WILHELMINA SYBELLINA WARNER, b. in Germany; living 1 Aug. 1774 when she gave Sybilline White of Marshfield her power of attorney. In March 1754 witnesses appeared in Plymouth to attest the signature of Jesse White, mariner, to a deed, he "now out of the Province." On 29 July 1757 part of Jesse's property was appraised to satisfy a debt and his wife exercised his power of attorney. Jesse was living in Marshfield 6 May 1765, when he gave his wife Catherine power of attorney. No probate record was found for Catherina in Plymouth, Middlesex or Suffolk Counties, but the will of Sybilline White names his mother Catherina and his sister Christiana in 1770.
Three (WHITE) ch. b. Marshfield: two sons named Sybelene b. 1744 and 1748, and Christiana b. 1750.

References: MD 19:165. VR SCITUATE. MARSHFIELD VR pp. 30, 43, 406. BOSTON VR 28:342. Plymouth Co. PR 13:149; #22576(John White); 14:501(Nathan Sprague); 24:135(Hannah White); 10:276(John[5] White); 9:32(Sylvanus White); 28:151(Sybilline White). Plymouth Co. LR 42:198; 44:168(Jesse White); 56:71(Isaac White); 62:243(Abijah White). Hampden Co. LR 2:799; 14:40(Jesse White); 14:43 (Catherina White). TAG 28:10. SHERMAN DESC pp. 7, 23, 24.

MARSHFIELD BY RICHARDS pp. 42-4. SCITUATE BY DEANE p. 23. DOGGETT FAM p. 355.

38 JOSEPH$^4$ WHITE (Daniel$^3$, Peregrine$^2$, William$^1$), b. Marshfield 1 March 1677/8; d. Lebanon CT bef. 27 March 1764.

He m. Scituate 21 Dec. 1710 ELIZABETH DWELLY, b. there 25 Aug. 1687; d. Lebanon 30 May 1751 ae. 64; daughter of Richard and Amy (or Eame) (Glass) Dwelly. The estate of Richard Dwelly on 23 Sept. 1709 names widow Amy and one child Elizabeth.

Joseph White lived in Marshfield while his children were born. On 15 June 1748 Joseph White of Marshfield, gentleman, sold to Abijah White "all my dwelling house, barns and land formerly my father Daniel White's"; his wife Elizabeth released her dower. Thus it appears that Joseph and Elizabeth did not leave Marshfield until 1748, although their daughter Ruth m. at Lebanon CT in 1736, twelve years earlier. There are no deeds in Lebanon for Joseph White.

The will of Capt. Joseph White of Lebanon, dated 6 Nov. 1753 and proved 27 March 1764, names daughter Ruth Thomas late of Lebanon, dec., son-in-law Amos Thomas, and their children: Ruth, Bethia, Abijah, Lucy, Amos and Molly (none of age); daughter Elizabeth Tilden, son-in-law Joseph Tilden, and their child Elizabeth Tilden. Sons-in-law Thomas and Tilden were executors.

Children (WHITE) b. Marshfield:

i DEBORAH$^5$, b. 7th of an unknown month 1712; bp. Scituate 23 Aug. 1713; n.f.r.

ii [RUT]H, b. 12th ---ber 1715, bp. 15 July 1716; d. Lebanon CT 12 Sept. 1753 ae. 37 "wife of Amos Thomas"; m. there in May 1736 AMOS THOMAS, b. Marshfield 22 Oct. 1703; d. Lebanon 17 Dec. 1787 ae. 84; son of Israel and Bethiah (Sherman) Thomas. The will of Ruth's father names her living children (see above). On 3 July 1734 Amos Thomas of Marshfield bought 250 acres of land in Lebanon. Amos m. (2) Colchester CT 19 March 1761 the widow Lydia (-----) Kellogg. The will of Amos Thomas of Lebanon CT, dated 17 Sept. 1787 and proved 21 Jan. 1788, names wife Lydia, eldest son Abijah, son Amos, and granddaughter Molly Anne Veals.

Nine (THOMAS) ch. b. Lebanon CT to Amos and Ruth: Ruth b. 1737, Bethia b. 1738, Anne b. 1740, Abijah b. 1741/2, Lucy b. 1743, Deborah b. 1745, Amos b. 1747, Joseph White b. 1750 and Molly b. 1753.

iii ELIZABETH, b. 10 Jan. 1720; d. Lebanon CT 10 March 1773 ae. 54; her gravestone, beside Joseph's, calls her "wife of Samuel" (*sic*); m. Lebanon CT 14 June 1750 JOSEPH TILDEN, b. Marshfield 15 Sept. 1721; d. Lebanon 13 March 1733 in 52nd yr.; son of Ebenezer and Mary (Vinal) Tilden, and a descendant of Pilgrim Richard Warren. Joseph m. (1) Lebanon 11 Nov. 1744 Elizabeth Brewster. Division of the estate of Joseph Tilden of Lebanon dated 13 April 1733 names "eldest and only son Ebenezer, eldest daughter Elizabeth Tilden, other daughter Chloe Tilden."

Three (TILDEN) ch. b. Lebanon to Joseph and Elizabeth: Elizabeth b. 1752, Chloe b. 1754 and Ebenezer b. 1757.

References: MD 20:61; 31:122. VR SCITUATE. MARSHFIELD VR pp. 25, 31, 32, 34, 42, 43, 84, 353. CSL Barbour Index:Lebanon. CSL Hale Cem Recs:Lebanon. Plymouth Co. PR 3:25(Richard Dwelly). Plymouth Co. LR 39:161 (Joseph White). CT PR #4121(Joseph White); #3763(Joseph Tilden). Windham CT PR 12:210(Amos Thomas). Lebanon CT LR 5:64(Amos Thomas). HANOVER BY DWELLEY p. 154. SHERMAN DESC p. 35. SHIPBUILDING ON NORTH RIVER p. 159. CT MARR 3:103. WHITE FAM REC pp. 49, 273.

39 CORNELIUS[4] WHITE (Daniel[3], Peregrine[2], William[1]), b. Marshfield 28 March 1682; d. there 21 Jan. 1755 ae. 76.

He m. Scituate 22 May 1706 HANNAH RANDALL, b. there 7 March 1677/8; d. Marshfield 24 Feb. 1768 in 90th yr. "wife of Cornelius White"; daughter of Joseph and Hannah (Macomber) Randall. The will of Joseph Randall of Scituate, dated 17 Nov. 1720 and proved 17 March 1720/1, names wife Hannah and daughter Hannah White.

The will of Cornelius White, shipbuilder of Marshfield, dated 16 April 1754 and probated 23 March 1756, names wife Hannah, his brother John White, his sons Lemuel, Cornelius, Paul, Daniel, Gideon who received a house in Plymouth, Benjamin a house in Hanover, daughter Joanna Phillips wife of Nathaniel, grandson Cornelius White under 21. The will of Hannah White of Marshfield, relict of Cornelius, late of Marshfield deceased, spinster, dated 10 Sept. 1767 and proved 2 March 1768, names sons Lemuel, Cornelius, Paul, Daniel, Gideon and Benjamin; daughter Joanna Phillips, wife of Nathaniel; granddaughter Lucy, daughter of Lemuel White and wife of Ezekiel Young; granddaughter Alice White, daughter of my son Cornelius; granddaughter Hannah White, daughter of my son Paul; granddaughter Joanna Turner, wife of Thomas Jr.; granddaughter Abigail White, daughter of my son Daniel; granddaughter Hannah White, daughter of my son Gideon; and Hannah White, daughter of my son Benjamin.

Children (WHITE) b. Marshfield:

i LEMUEL[5], b. 24 March 1706[/07]; m. Marshfield 3 Feb. 1731 ANNA SCOTT "of Dorchester." Lemuel and Anna were both living in Marshfield in 1771 and as late as 21 May 1783 when they acknowledged the sale of house, land and meadows etc. to (their son-in-law) Ezekiel Young. Lemuel was a Loyalist refugee.

Four (WHITE) ch. b. Marshfield: Nathaniel b. 1732, Lusanah b. 1735, Joanna b. 1737 and Giddeon b. 1741.

ii CORNELIUS, b. 9 March 1708; d. Marshfield 9 Jan. 1796 in 88th yr.; m. Kingston 22 Feb. 1738 SARAH FORD, b. Marshfield 23 Sept. 1721; d. there 17 April 1777 in 55th yr. "wife of Capt. Cornelius White"; daughter of Peleg and Alice (Warren) Ford, and a descendant of Pilgrims Edward Doty and Richard Warren. The will of Peleg Ford of Marshfield, dated 17 Nov. 1762 and proved 14 Jan. 1769, names his daughter Sarah White. The claim that Cornelius' wife was Sarah Hewitt of Bridgewater has been refuted. There are no probate records for Sarah White or Cornelius in Plymouth County.

Eleven (WHITE) ch. b. Marshfield: Charles b. 1740, Alice b. 1742, Sarah b. 1744, Ruth b. 1746, Lucy b. 1748, Cornelius b. 1750, Cornelius b. 1752, Olive b. 1754, Cornelius b. 1756, Warren b. 1758 and Peleg b. 1760.

iii PAUL, b. 1 Nov. 1711; d. 27 Aug. 1775 ae. 63y 9m 26d "died from home"; bur. Marshfield; m. Hanover 24 Feb. 1736/7 ELIZABETH CURTIS, bp. Scituate 28 May 1721; d. Marshfield 15 Jan. 1802 ae. 85y 11m 28d "widow of Capt. Paul"; daughter of John and Experience (Palmer) Curtis. The will of John Curtis of Hanover, dated 12 Sept. 1737 and proved 3 Dec. 1750, names wife Experience and daughter Elizabeth White. The will of Paul White of Marshfield gentleman, aged, dated 6 Sept. 1768 and proved 2 Sept. 1776, names wife Elizabeth; three sons Paul, Christopher and Peregrine; daughters Experience Clapp and Hannah White.

Six (WHITE) ch. b. Marshfield: Joseph b. 1737, Paul b. 1739, Experience b. 1741, Christopher b. 1743, Hannah b. 1745 and Perigrine b. 1748. [The John White who m. Sybil Buckminster was not one of Paul's children.]

iv JOANNA, b. 5 Dec. 1713; d. Marshfield 3 Feb. 1798 in 85th yr. "widow of Capt. Nathaniel Phillips"; m. Duxbury 16 Jan. 1734/5 NATHANIEL PHILLIPS, b. Marshfield 22 July 1713; d. there 15 May 1795 in 82nd yr.; son of John and Patience (Stevens) Phillips. The will of Nathaniel Phillips of Marshfield, gentleman, dated 1 March 1782 and proved 1 June 1795, names wife Joanna and her father Cornelius White, late of Marshfield dec., son Nathaniel, daughter Joanna Turner, and son Daniel Phillips. The will of Joanna Phillips of Marshfield, widow of Nathaniel, dated 8 March 1796 and proved 4 June 1798, names the same three children.

Five (PHILLIPS) ch. b. Marshfield: John b. 1739, Nathaniel b. 1742, Johanna b. 1744, Patience b. 1747 and Daniel b. 1752.

v DANIEL, b. 4 May 1716; d. Marshfield 27 Dec. 1785 in 71st yr. "Captain"; m. ABIGAIL TURNER b. Scituate 30 May 1725; d. Marshfield 15 March 1796 in 70th yr. "widow of Capt. Daniel White"; daughter of Capt. Samuel and Abigail (Leavitt) Turner. The will of Samuel Turner of Scituate, gentleman, dated 21 May 1757 and probated 22 Nov. 1759, names daughter Abigail White. The will of Daniel White of Marshfield, gentleman, dated 6 Sept. 1785 and probated 21 Jan. 1786, names wife Abigail, daughter of Capt. Samuel Turner of Scituate; son Daniel; daughters Abigail Soule, Lydia White, Cate Lewis, Urania White; son Samuel; and daughter Temperance White. Son-in-law James Lewis was an executor. Daniel was an innholder of Marshfield and a Loyalist refugee.

Eight (WHITE) ch. prob. b. Marshfield: Daniel, Abigail, Lydia, Keturah (Katy), Uraniah, Betsey, Samuel and Temperance.

vi GIDEON, b. 19 July 1717; d. Plymouth 6 March 1779 ae. 62; m. there 23 Feb. 1743/4 JOANNA HOWLAND, b. there 7 May 1716; d. there 23 Sept. 1810 in 95th yr. "wife of Capt. Gideon White"; daughter of Thomas and Joanna (Cole) Howland, and a descendant of Pilgrim John Howland. [See *The John Howland Family* for more extensive data regarding the children of Gideon$^5$ White and Joanna$^4$ Howland.] The will of Gideon White of Plymouth, yeoman, dated 1 May 1766 and proved 7 June 1779, names wife Joanna; sons Cornelius and Gideon; daughters Joanna, Hannah, Mary and Elizabeth White. The estate was not settled until after wife Joanna's death. The will of Joanna White of Plymouth, widow advanced in life, dated 11 March 1806 proved 4 May 1811, names daughters Joanna

Winslow, Hannah White and Elizabeth Earl; son Gideon; daughter Mary to be provided for by the executors.

Nine (WHITE) ch. prob. b. Plymouth: Cornelius, two Elizabeths, Hannah bp. 1747, Experience (daughter), Gideon, Polly, Thomas and Joanna.

vii BENJAMIN, b. 4 Feb. 1720; d. Hanover 10 Feb. 1786 ae. 65; m. Marshfield 3 April 1743 HANNAH DECROW, b. there 15 Feb. 1720; d. Hanover 22 March 1814 ae. 93 "widow Hannah White"; daughter of Robert and Susanna (Tilden) Decrow. Division of the estate of Robert Decroe late of Marshfield on 18 April 1761 named wife Susannah and daughter Hannah White. The will of Benjamin White of Hanover, yeoman, dated 28 Dec. 1785 and proved 8 March 1786, names wife Hannah; children of "my daughter Hannah Crooker"; three sons Robert, Benjamin and Cornelius White.

Five (WHITE) ch. bp. Hanover: daughter Peninniah bp. 1754, Benjamin bp. 1754, Hannah bp. 1754, Cornelius bp. 1755 and Robert bp. 1757.

References: MD 8:199; 14:160; 20:61-7; 28:27-33. VR DUXBURY, KINGSTON, SCITUATE. DORCHESTER VR 36:209. HANOVER VR p. 13. MARSHFIELD VR pp. 31, 32, 34, 41, 42, 59, 73, 74, 79, 81, 91, 97, 98, 140, 172, 349, 352, 371, 372, 407. Plymouth Co. PR 4:270(Joseph Randall); 20:51(Hannah White); 24:195 and #22603(Paul White); 11:518 (John Curtis); 35:268 and #15886(Nathaniel Phillips); 36:374 and #15870(Joanna Phillips); 15:432(Samuel Turner); 43:446(Joanna White); 16:138(Robert Decroe); 29:469(Benjamin White); 20:181(Peleg Ford); 25:304 and #22553(Gideon White). Plymouth Co. LR 57:63; 62:74; 76:276(Lemuel White); 58:160(Cornelius White et al). SHIPBUILDING ON NORTH RIVER p. 353. (PLYMOUTH) ANC LANDMARKS 2:283, 360. HANOVER BY DWELLEY p. 440. SCITUATE BY DEANE pp. 323, 329. (PLYMOUTH) BURIAL HILL pp. 31, 32, 34, 51, 117, 195, 202, 207. TAG 48:154. HANOVER FIRST CH pp. 89, 133. MARSHFIELD BY RICHARDS p. 58. HOWLAND GEN p. 334.

40 BENJAMIN[4] WHITE (Daniel[3], Peregrine[2], William[1]), b. Marshfield 12 Oct. 1684; d. there 12 May 1724 ae. 39.

He m. Marshfield 2 Dec. 1714 FAITH OAKMAN, b. there 15 May 1697; d. there 26 Dec. 1758 ae. 61y 6m "wife of Thomas Foster"; daughter of Tobias and Elizabeth (Doty) Oakman, and a descendant of Pilgrim Edward Doty. She m. (2) Thomas Foster. The will of Tobias Oakman of Marshfield, dated 21 March 1745 and proved 26 July 1750, names his daughter Faith Foster. [See *The Edward Doty Family*.]

Benjamin was a boatman of Marshfield. Faith White was granted administration on the estate of Benjamin White, late of Marshfield, dec., 7 July 1724. The account of Faith Foster, administratrix on Benjamin's estate was rendered 17 June 1741 "for support of Benjamin's children and lying-in with my son Benjamin born after said Benjamin deceased" and support for Jedidah and Lydia.

Children (WHITE) b. Marshfield:

i ABIGAIL[5], b. 5 Nov. 1715; d. Marshfield 19 July 1736 "wife of John Stetson"; m. there 29 Dec. 1732 JOHN STETSON, perhaps the one b. Scituate in March 1694 to Samuel and Lydia (Pickles) Stetson; d. there 13 or 24 Jan. 1787 ae. 92. John Stetson was of Marshfield in Sept. 1730 and Dec. 1736 and "of Scituate otherwise called John Stutson of Marshfield" in March 1743. There are no probate records for John in Barnstable, Bristol or Plymouth Counties and nothing in *Acts and Resolves of the Province of Massachusetts Bay*.*

One (STETSON) child b. Marshfield: John b. 1734.

ii TABITHA, b. 30 Oct. 1717; d. Marshfield 7 July 1742, unm.

iii LYDIA, b. 1 Aug. 1719; m. Marshfield 12 Oct. 1748 THOMAS HOLMES, b. there 15 Oct. 1720; d. Scituate 23 Dec. 1792 in 73rd yr.; son of John and Sarah (Thomas) Holmes. Nothing was found in Plymouth Co. land or probate records for Lydia, Thomas or John.

Six (HOLMES) ch. b. Marshfield: Benjamin b. 1749, Sarah b. 1751, Faith b. 1753, daughter Christiane b. 1755, Thomas b. 1758 and Lydia b. 1760.

iv JEDIDAH, b. 6 Nov. 1721; d. Duxbury 26 March 1794 in 73rd yr. "widow of Joseph Brewster"; m. Marshfield 26 Nov. 1740 JOSEPH BREWSTER, b. Duxbury 3 July 1718; d. there either 3 Sept. 1791 in 71st yr. or "3-5" 1791 ae. 73; son of Nathaniel and Mary (Dwelly) Brewster, and a descendant of Pilgrim William Brewster. Nothing was found in Plymouth Co. land or probate records.

Six (BREWSTER) ch. 1st, 5th, 6th bp. Duxbury, 2nd, 3rd, 4th said to be bp. Attleboro: Zadok bp. 1742, Mary, Joseph, Ruth, Nathaniel bp. 1755 and son Truelove bp. 1760.

---

*A statement in *The Descendants of Cornet Robert Stetson of Scituate, Mass*. (p. 48) is confusing. The John Stetson who married Abigail Crocker was "of Pembroke" and his wife Abigail was still living and they were having children at the time John Stetson of Marshfield registered his intentions of marriage at Scituate with Ruth Penniman.

v BENJAMIN, b. 23 Jan. 1724/5; d. Marshfield 8 Sept. 1783 in 59th yr.; m. there 29 Dec. 1748 MERCY THOMAS, b. there 27 June 1725; d. there 27 May 1808 in 83rd yr. "widow of Benjamin White"; daughter of Gideon and Abigail (Baker) Thomas, and a descendant of Pilgrim William Bradford. The will of Gideon Thomas of Marshfield, dated 10 May 1764 and proved 14 Jan. 1766, mentions daughter Mercy White wife of Benjamin, and grandson Gideon Thomas White. Benjamin gave patriotic service during the Revolution. There is no estate for him or his wife Mercy in Plymouth Co. probate records.

Four (WHITE) ch. b. Marshfield: Benjamin b. 1749, Tobias b. 1753, Gideon Thomas b. 1755 and Luther b. 1758.

References: MD 10:28; 22:36. VR DUXBURY, SCITUATE. MARSHFIELD VR pp. 32, 36, 40, 42, 44, 54, 79, 80, 86, 87, 94, 97, 99, 140, 159-161, 167, 402, 413. Plymouth Co. PR 12:90(Tobias Oakman); 4:423; 8:387; #22511 (Benjamin White); 19:415(Gideon Thomas). Plymouth Co. LR 10:490(Benjamin White). MARSHFIELD BY RICHARDS pp. 43-6. NEHGR 26:399. GILES MEM p. 192. BREWSTER GEN 1:85, 140. (PLYMOUTH) ANC LANDMARKS 2:42. Plymouth Co. Rec. C. C. Pleas 4:245; 6:63; 8:498.

41 ELEAZER[4] WHITE (Daniel[3], Peregrine[2], William[1]), b. Marshfield 8 Nov. 1686; d. there bef. 14 April 1737.

He m. Marshfield 29 Sept. 1712 MARY DOGGETT, b. there 26 April 1687; daughter of Samuel and Mary (Rogers) Doggett. The will of Samuel Doggett of Marshfield, dated 13 Jan. 1724 and proved 4 Oct. 1725, mentions his daughter Mary White.

On 14 April 1737, John White of Marshfield was appointed guardian of Elkanah White, son of Eleazer late of Marshfield deceased, aged bet. 14 and 21. There are no Plymouth probate records for Eleazer or any of his children, except this one guardianship, and no Plymouth land records for Eleazer.

Children (WHITE) b. Marshfield:

i NEHEMIAH[5], b. 13 or 14 Jan. 1712[/3]; m. Scituate 25 April 1737 RACHEL CURTIS, b. there 6 June 1717; daughter of William and Rachel (Stodder) Curtis. No further data were found on either Nehemiah or Rachel White in the probate records of Barnstable, Norfolk, Plymouth, Suffolk or Worcester Cos. and nothing in land records of

Plymouth or Worcester Cos. But was she the Rachel White, widow, admitted to the First Church at Scituate 4 June 1758?

Nehemiah is definitely not the father of Nicholas and Philip, nor is he the Nehemiah from Braintree who d. Ashford CT 3 Oct. 1754.

ii PEREGRINE, b. 18 Sept. or 17 Oct. 1715; n.f.r.

iii ELEAZER, b. 8 March 1716/7 or 25 Sept. 1717; did he m. Philander Chase in Newport RI 8 April 1741?

iv ELKANAH, b. 10 Dec. 1719; living 14 April 1737 when a gdn. was appointed.

v MARY, b. 23 March 1720/1; undoubtedly the Mary who was warned out of William Hyland's house in Scituate 1 Jan. 1765. No marriage record was found for Mary.

One (WHITE) child b. Marshfield: daughter Orphan b. 1743.

vi BENAJAH, b. 19 Sept. 1724; Benajah White of Marshfield was warned out of Pembroke 8 Jan. 1745, and out of Scituate 21 Feb. 1750; n.f.r.

vii PENELOPE, b. 13 June 1727; d. Plympton 4 May 1818 ae. 91y 10m 10d "widow of Thomas Harlow"; m. there 29 July 1778 THOMAS HARLOW, prob. the one b. Plymouth 26 July 1712 to Thomas and Jedidah (Churchill) Harlow. He m. (1) Plympton in 1736 Patience Tilson, (2) in 1762 Anne Fuller; he had six ch. by his first wife, and one by the second. Penelope White, singlewoman from Pembroke, was warned out of Plympton 6 April 1767. No records of the family appear in Plymouth Co. land or probate records, unless he is the one described above. Thomas and Penelope apparently had no children.

viii THOMAS, b. 29 June 1729; n.f.r.

ix REBECCA, b. 18 April 1731; m. Marshfield 1 Nov. 1759 JOHN HYLAND of Scituate. A John Hyland, transient person, was warned out of Marshfield 14 June 1779. No John Hyland was located in probate records of Barnstable, Bristol, Middlesex, Norfolk, Plymouth or Suffolk Counties.

References: MD 7:209; 11:142; 14:36; 15:115; 16:87; 20:61; 26:41. VR PLYMPTON, SCITUATE. RI VR 8:479. MARSHFIELD VR pp. 18, 32, 37, 39, 65, 89, 147. Plymouth Co. PR 5:97(Samuel Doggett); 7:395(gdn. Elkanah White). Plymouth Co. Rec. Sess. (Mss.) 2:12, 314. Plymouth Co. Gen. Sess. Ct. Rec. 1760-1782 (Mss.) 3:110, 197. Gen. Sess. of Peace 1730-1749 (Mss.) p. 225. Plymouth Co. C. C. Pleas 1760-1782 (Mss.) 3:521. WHITE (NICHOLAS) FAM pp. 37, 73. WHITE FAM REC pp. 165, 167. DOGGETT FAM pp. 346, 362. CSL Barbour Index:Ashford. TAG 49:138-42.

42 EBENEZER$^4$ WHITE (Daniel$^3$, Peregrine$^2$, William$^1$), b. Marshfield, 3[torn] Aug. 1691; d. Hebron CT 18 May 1733.

He m. Marshfield 9 March 1712/3 HANNAH DOGGETT, b. there 28 Dec. 1693; d. Hebron 4 May 1734 "widow of Ebenezer White"; daughter of John and Mehitable (Trewant) Doggett. The will of John Doggett of Marshfield, dated 21 Jan. 1716, names daughter Hannah White.

Ebenezer White and wife Hannah of Marshfield sold their house and land in Marshfield on 13 April 1723 and moved to Hebron CT.

The will of Ebenezer White of Hebron, dated 14 May 1733 and exhibited 3 July 1733, names wife Hannah, executrix; sons Obadiah, Ebenezer and Joseph; daughter Rebecca (under 21); and three youngest daughters Hannah, Cheanne and Mehetabell. On 13 March 1738/9 property remained to be distributed, a double portion to Obadiah, and the remainder to Ebenezer, Rebecca, Hannah, Chene and Mehitabell White. On 1-2 Jan. 1744/5 a guardianship was on file for Ebenezer White minor, and there was a distribution of the lands of Ebenezer White of Hebron CT deceased to: eldest son Obadiah White, 18 acres and a dwelling house; son Ebenezer, 25 acres; daughters Cheny, Rebecca and Hannah, 4 acres each.

Children (WHITE) first four b. Marshfield, last three b. Hebron CT:

i OBADIAH$^5$, b. 27 March 1716; d. Hebron CT 3 March 1801 ae. 88 (*sic*); m. Hebron CT 2 Jan. 1745/6 ELIZABETH ALLEN, b. Windham CT 21 Aug. 1728; d. 3 July 1810; daughter of Joseph and Mary (Utley) Allen. The will of Joseph Allen of Hebron "advanced in age," dated 10 April 1778 and proved 22 Aug. 1778, names daughter Elizabeth White, wife of Obadiah. The will of Obadiah White of Hebron, dated 18 March 1793 and proved 16 March 1801, names wife Elizabeth; sons Joseph, Obadiah and Daniel; daughters Elizabeth, Anna, Mary and Sarah; and sons Ebenezer, Peregrine and Benjamin.
Eleven (WHITE) ch. recorded Hebron CT, except first one and last two: Joseph b. 1747, Daniel b. 1749, Obadiah b. 1751, Obadiah b. 1753, Elizabeth b. 1756, Sarah b. 1758, Ann b. 1760, Perregrine b. 1762, Mary b. 1764, Ebenezer and Benjamin.

ii REBECCA, b. 17 Nov. 1718; d. Granville MA in 1769; m. Hebron CT 18 May 1737 JOHN ROOT, b. there 4 Oct. 1712; d. Granville 12 Jan. 1804 ae. 91; son of Jacob and Sarah (Goodale) Root. John m. (2) [Mary?] Simons. John and Rebecca were living in Glastonbury CT in 1750, 1753 and on 22 March 1757 when they sold land she had received from her father's estate. They were in Granville, Hampshire Co. when they sold land in Hebron 19 Jan. 1761. Nothing further was found in the probate records of Hampshire, Hampden or Berkshire Cos., or in the land records of Berkshire or Hampshire Cos.

Seven (ROOT) ch., first b. Hebron CT: Sibet (*sic*) b. 1738; three b. Glastonbury CT: Sybil b. 1740, Dorcas b. 1742 and Amos b. 1745; three b. Granville: Prudence b. 1748, John, and Israel b. 1759.

iii HANNAH, b. 13 March 1720/1; d. Middletown CT 3 May 1763 "wife of Asa Foster"; m. Lebanon CT 4 Feb. 1744/5 ASA FOSTER, b. Topsfield "15, 11, 1710"; son of Daniel and Mary (Dresser) Foster. On 25 May 1753 Hannah and her husband Asa, both of Lebanon, sold the 4 acres of land in Hebron which was set off to her from the estate of her father Ebenezer White late of Hebron, deceased.* Asa was in Lebanon on 25 Oct. 1756 when he sold "the 70 acre farm where I dwell," and on 25 April 1757 when he bought 60 acres in Middletown CT.

Nine (FOSTER) ch., first seven b. Lebanon, last two b. Middletown: Mary b. 1745, Samuel b. 1747, Daniel b. 1747/8, Asa b. 1750, Mary b. 1753, William b. 1755, Hannah b. 1757, Ephraim b. 1759 and Alpheus b. 1761.

iv CHENE (also spelled Chenneyanne, Cheanne, Cheney, etc.), b. 16 July 1722; living 25 May 1753; m. (1) Norwich CT 1 Nov. 1744 EPHRAIM FARNUM, b. Windham CT 20 March 1721; d. Norwich bef. 17 Jan. 1750/1; son of Henry and Phebe (Russell) Farnum. Chene m. (2) bef. May 1752 JOHN LOUDEN, b. ca. 1720; son of Thomas and Mary (Wheeler) Lowden. Chenney Anne Farnum was administratrix of the estate of Ephraim Farnum late of Norwich deceased, by 17 Jan. 1750/1; by May 1752 Chenyanna Lowden and John Lowden were administrators of the same estate. An account of John and his wife Chenyanna includes money paid to the widow for taking care of two small children. On 25 May 1753 John and Cheney Louden of Norwich sold the 4 acres of land in Hebron CT which was set off from the estate of "her father Ebenezer White..." This is the last record of Chene found.

In July and Aug. 1759 John Lowden of Norwich,

---

*For proof that Hannah White who married Josiah Owen in Hebron CT in 1741/2, and died there in 1747, was not the daughter of Ebenezer and Hannah (Doggett) White, see TAG 48:150-3.

merchant, sold land, dwelling house, shop and barn in Norwich. In June 1784, a judgement was recovered against "John Lowden late of Norwich, now of Nova Scotia." This could refer either to Chene's husband or to his son John by a previous wife as mentioned below.

The *Yarmouth [N. S.] Herald* of 4 Sept. 1934 provides the approximate birth year and parents of John Lowden. It adds that he grew up in Pelham MA, moved to Leicester and then to Voluntown CT where in 1741 he married (1) Jean Campbell, by whom he had John and Mary, both living in 1773. John (the father) received a grant of one and one half shares (1000 acres) at Cornwallis, N.S., in 1764.

There is no record of children to John Louden and wife Chene in the Vital Records of Norwich CT or deeds of Lebanon CT; however a copy of the Cornwallis Nova Scotia Record book lists marriages and parents for Thomas, Jerusha and Fanny Louden, ch. of John and Cheneyanne, in 1773, 1781 and 1790 respectively, and of Ebenezer Farnam, son of "Epharum" Farnam and wife Cheneanna in 1782.

Two (FARNUM) ch., b. Norwich CT to Ephraim and Chene: Ephraim b. 1745 and Ebenezer b. 1747.

Three (LOUDEN) ch., b. CT or Nova Scotia to John and Chene: Thomas b. ca. 1754, Jerusha and Fanny.

v EBENEZER, b. 30 Jan. 1726/7; d. Willsboro NY ca. 1767; m. HANNAH ROOT, b. Hebron CT 22 Jan. 1735/6; d. Willsboro NY; daughter of William and Hannah (Pinnock) Root. The will of William Root of Hebron, dated 29 March 1764 and proved in 1769, names wife Hannah and daughter Hannah White. Ebenezer may have left Hebron about 1 May 1749 when he sold 31 acres of land to his brother Obadiah.

One (WHITE) ch.: William b. 1765.

vi JOSEPH, b. 11 March 1728; d. Hebron CT 14 Dec. 1736.

vii MEHITABLE, b. 24 Jan. 1730/1; d. Hebron CT 30 Jan. 1741/2

References: VR GRANVILLE, TOPSFIELD. MARSHFIELD VR pp. 17, 32, 37, 39, 40, 84. CSL Barbour Index: Glastonbury, Hebron, Middletown, Windham. NORWICH CT VR p. 240. CT MARR 5:42. Plymouth Co. PR 4:120(John Doggett). Norwich CT LR 13:533; 15:115; 25:370(John Lowden). Middletown CT LR 16:481; 17:424; 18:54, 55(Asa Foster). Lebanon CT LR 9:1(Asa Foster). Hebron CT LR 3:227, 260-1 (John Root); 4:96, 97(John Root from John Lowden); 4:217; 5:15(John Root); 3:54(Joseph Allen grantee). Plymouth Co.

LR 16:187(Ebenezer White). MANWARING 3:131, 209. Colchester CT PR 1:76, 87-88(Ebenezer White). CT PR #2669 (Obadiah White); #2624(William Root); #3762(Ephraim Farnum). Cornwallis N.S. Rec. Bk. (Mss. NEHG Soc.) pp. 28, 36, 38, 44. Bible Record (at CSL) pp. 275, 278(Ebenezer and Obadiah White). East Granville Ch. Rec. (Mss. at Berkshire Athenaeum, Pittsfield MA) pp. 219, 226, 228. ROOT RECS pp. 112, 133. FOSTER GEN 1:132, 154. YARMOUTH N.S. HERALD GEN 4 Sept. 1934 #380(Lowden). KINGS CO N.S. HIST pp. 736-7. CSL Hale Cem Recs. TAG 48:150-3. DOGGETT FAM pp. 354-5.

43 ESTHER[4] WHITE (Jonathan[3], Peregrine[2], William[1]), b. ca. 1685; d. Warwick RI 23 July 1738 ae. 53 "wife of Capt. John Drake."

She m. (1) Yarmouth 7 Nov. 1707 JOHN JOYCE, d. there 10 Jan. 1714/5; son of Hosea and Elizabeth (Chipman) Joyce, and a descendant of John Howland. [See *The John Howland Family*.] The will of John Joyce, husbandman of Yarmouth, dated 28 Dec. 1714 and proved 6 April 1715, names his unm. daughters Fear and Desire, his wife's sister Elizabeth White, his wife Esther, and his brothers.

Esther m. (2) Boston 25 June 1719 JOHN DRAKE, b. Weymouth 30 Sept. 1694; d. Warwick RI 21 June 1733 in 39th yr.; son of John and Sarah (King) Drake. The will of John Drake of East Greenwich RI, dated 16 June 1733 and proved 30 June 1733, names wife Esther Drake; Desier Arnold, wife of John; Fear Smith, wife of Christopher; daughter Elizabeth Drake under 18; and son Francis Drake under 21. In the inventory of his estate John is called a mariner.

The will of Esther Drake of East Greenwich RI, widow, dated 11 July 1738, mentions daughters Deziah (*sic*) Arnold, Fear Smith, Elizabeth Drake under 18, and son Francis Drake. She gave to her daughter Elizabeth Drake "my pine box marked H. W."

In a release on the estate of Jonathan[3] White dated 14 Nov. 1741 the following statement is made on behalf of Francis Drake: "My grandfather Jonathan White late of Yarmouth deceased, by will dated 14 July 1736, gave to my mother Esther Drake deceased £5 and personal estate."

Children (JOYCE) b. Yarmouth to John and Esther:

i JOHN[5], d. Yarmouth 27 Dec. 1710.

ii DESIRE, b. 17 Jan. 1709; d. East Greenwich RI 18 July 1771 "wife of John Arnold"; m. E. Greenwich or Warwick RI 1 March 1732/3 JOHN ARNOLD; d. East Greenwich 20 June 1801; son of Capt. William and Deliverance (Whipple) Arnold. John was an innholder and was called Major in the E. Greenwich land records. There is no mention of

John or Desire in the E. Greenwich probate records.

Seven (ARNOLD) ch., first three b. Warwick RI, last four b. East Greenwich RI: Phebe b. 1734, Barbara b. 1735, John b. 1737, William b. 1739, Elizabeth b. 1741, Ann b. 1744 and Sarah b. 1747.

iii FEAR, b. 15 Feb. 1712/3; d. Warwick RI 10 June 1748 in 36th yr. "wife of Capt. Christopher Smith"; m. East Greenwich RI 9 Jan. 1731/2 CHRISTOPHER SMITH, b. Warwick RI 14 Oct. 1703; d. there 10 Feb. 1752 in 50th yr.; son of Capt. Simon and Mary (Andrews) Smith. The will of Christopher Smith of Warwick, dated 25 July 1751 and probated 13 April 1752, names daughter Phebe Smith under 18, sons Benjamin, Job and Christopher Jr. under 21, and daughter Freelove Smith.

Five (SMITH) ch.: Phebe, Benjamin, Job, Christopher and Freelove.

Children (DRAKE) b. East Greenwich RI to John and Esther:

iv ELIZABETH, b. 1 March 1724/5; m. (1) East Greenwich RI 3 April 1743 WILLIAM COREY, d. Warwick RI bef. 6 Oct. 1746; son of John and Elizabeth (-----) Corey. William may have m. (1) East Greenwich RI 21 Jan. 1724 Sarah Matteson. On 6 Oct. 1746 the inventory of William Cory deceased of Warwick was reported at Warwick RI. Records of the estate include the bond of John Arnold, administrator, of East Greenwich (see ii above). On 5 Jan. 1746 Elizabeth Cory, relict and widow of the deceased swore to the inventory. William Corey was of East Greenwich when he married the first time and when he bought land in Warwick 23 April 1726. He was of North Kingstown RI when he married Elizabeth in 1743.

Elizabeth m. (2) East Greenwich 15 Feb. 1748 THOMAS COREY, d. bef. 13 Feb. 1761; son of John and Elizabeth (-----) Corey.

The will of John Corey, father of Elizabeth's two husbands, dated 18 March 1768 and proved in the same year, names granddaughter Easter (*sic*) Corey, daughter of Thomas Corey deceased. James Fones was appointed administrator on the estate of Thomas Corey on 13 Feb. 1761. The will of Mary Corey, singlewoman, proved 11 Nov. 1776, names her "nephew" Esther Slocum, wife of Ebenezer; nephew Daniel Corey, son of Thomas; nephews Gideon and John, sons of Thomas; and also names Elizabeth Corey, "wife of ----- deceased," presumably the widow of Mary's two brothers.

Six (COREY) ch. b. North Kingstown, first two by William, last four by Thomas: William, Francis, Esther, John, Daniel and Gideon. (Note: Three ch. b. East Greenwich RI 1755-1763 were b. to a different Thomas and Elizabeth Corey.)

v FRANCIS, b. 29 May 1727; d. East Greenwich RI 9 April 1748

References: MD 7:248; 9:122. VR WEYMOUTH. BOSTON VR 28:81. YARMOUTH VR pp. 17, 132, 133, 137. RI VR:East Greenwich pp. 3, 23, 43, 65, 95, 113, 114 (original records say Drake not Deake); Warwick pp. 4, 108, 202; N. Kingstown p. 68. East Greenwich RI PR 1:215 (Esther Drake); 1:341(John Drake). Warwick RI PR 2:171 (Christopher Smith); 2:37(William Corey). North Kingstown RI PR 9:371(John Corey); 9:127(Thomas Corey); 10:198 (Mary Corey). Barnstable Co. PR 3:344(John Joyce); 6:59 (Jonathan White). East Greenwich RI LR 7:140(John Arnold). Warwick RI LR 3:333(William Corey). Arnold Cem Rec Elmwood Library, Providence RI. Arnold's Gravestones (MSS. RIHS) Warwick:4:79-86. Benn's Cem Rec (microfilm RIHS) 4:123. TAG 43:5-8. WEYMOUTH BY CHAMBERLAIN 3:206. ARNOLD MEM pp. 92, 111. DRAKE FAM pp. 4, 297. RI GEN DICT p. 56.

44 JONATHAN[4] WHITE (Jonathan[3], Peregrine[2], William[1]), living Jan. 1739/40 when he signed a release on the estate of his father.

He m. Yarmouth ca. 1717 DORCAS (GODFREY) HAMBLEN (marriage entered bet. those dated 1716 and 1717); daughter of John and Martha (Joyce) Godfrey, but not a descendant of Pilgrim John Howland. Dorcas m. (1) Yarmouth 29 March 1715 Israel Hamblen, by whom she had a son Israel, whose birth is recorded with her White children. The will of John Godfrey of Yarmouth, dated 7 Aug. 1735 and sworn 23 Oct. 1735, names daughter Darkis White. There is no land record for Israel or Dorcas Hamblen in Barnstable Co.

Jonathan and Dorcas White and their children apparently left Yarmouth about 1740, since there is no further record in land, probate or vital records of the town or county. It is possible they went to the southern district of Dutchess Co. NY, where a 1746 tax list indicates a Jonathan White and a John White were living either together or in neighboring houses. Additionally, an Eleazer Hamlin of Barnstable MA and a John White were at Carmel NY in 1755-6; an Israel Hamlin was living in Frederickstown NY in 1790; and a John White died in Fishkill NY in 1797, leaving eleven children, including Joseph who had daughter Dorkis born in 1780.

Children (WHITE) b. Yarmouth:

i DORCAS[5], b. 8 Dec. 1717; m. Yarmouth 29 May 1740 JOSEPH THORP of Barnstable, poss. the one b. Chatham 16 April 1720 to Thomas and Mehitable (-----) Thorp. There is no land or probate record of Dorcas or Joseph in Barnstable Co.
ii JOHN, b. 15 Feb. 1719, n.f.r.
iii MARTHA, b. 1 Sept. 1722, n.f.r.
iv TEMPERANCE, b. 8 April 1725, n.f.r.
v SUSANNA, b. 25 July 1727, n.f.r.
vi THANKFUL, b. 18 Aug. 1729, n.f.r.
vii DESIRE, b. 1 Oct. 1732, n.f.r.
viii FEAR, b. 14 April 1735, n.f.r.

References: MD 4:185. YARMOUTH VR pp. 74, 140, 151, 179. WHITE FAM (YARMOUTH) pp. 1, 5. Desc. of Richard Godfrey of Taunton by Geo. A. Dary 1920 (MS. NEHG Soc.). Barnstable Co. PR 5:253(John Godfrey). 1790 CENSUS NY:83. NYGBR 34:131. Dutchess Co. NY PR #4367 (Sarah White). Fam. Rec. owned by Mrs. Nathan Davis of Holmes, Dutchess Co. 1746 Tax List, Dutchess Co.

45 EBENEZER[4] WHITE (Jonathan[3], Peregrine[2], William[1]), b. Yarmouth 9 Aug. 1698; d. Harwich 9 July 1772 in 74th yr.

He m. Harwich 13 July 1727 MERCY SMITH, d. there 10 Sept. 1769 ae. 69y 1m 4d; daughter of John Smith. The recorded copy of the will of John Smith of Harwich, dated 16 Aug. 1732 and probated 19 Dec. 1748, names daughter "Mary" White; in an account of the estate, "Marcy" White received her legacy 7 May 1751. There are no probate records in Barnstable Co. for Ebenezer or Mercy.

Children (WHITE) b. Yarmouth:

i ELIJAH[5], b. 6 April 1728; d. Frederickstown (now Carmel) NY 7 Feb. 1804; m. Carmel NY 7 June 1756 MERCY HOPKINS, b. Harwich 21 Feb. 1719/20; d. Frederickstown 26 March 1798; daughter of Nathaniel and Mercy (Mayo) Hopkins, and a descendant of Pilgrim Stephen Hopkins. The will of Nathaniel Hopkins of Harwich, yeoman, dated 25 March 1765 and proved 21 Oct. 1766, names wife Mercy and daughter Mercy White.

Five (WHITE) ch. b. Frederickstown NY: John M. b. 1757, Marcy S. b. 1759, Elijah b. 1761, Ebenezer b. 1763 and Susanna b. 1765.

ii THANKFUL, b. 1 Jan. 1729/30; d. Harwich 19 Aug. 1806 in 77th yr. "widow of Ebenezer Paine"; m. Yarmouth 2 Sept. 1756 EBENEZER PAINE, b. Eastham 26 Nov. 1722; d. Harwich 28 April 1795 in 74th yr.; son of Ebenezer and Hannah (Hopkins) Paine, and a descendant of Pilgrims Stephen Hopkins and William Brewster. Ebenezer m. (1) Yarmouth 21 Feb. 1750/1 Mary Allen. Ebenezer was a cordwainer and farmer. On 3 May 1792 Ebenezer and wife Thankful of Harwich sold rights in land from her father Ebenezer White of Yarmouth. There are no probate records in Barnstable Co. for Thankful or Ebenezer.

Ebenezer deeded his lands, dwelling house, etc. to sons Isaac, Ebenezer Jr. and Seth on 11 July 1794, reserving to his daughters Mary (Mercy?) and Ruth the privilege of living in the house.

Eight (PAINE) ch. b. Harwich: Isaac b. 1759, Mercy, Betsey b. 1765, Hannah b. 1765, Ruth, Patience b. 1772, Ebenezer b. 1774 and Seth b. 1777.

iii THOMAS, b. 9 Feb. 1731/2; m. Yarmouth 1 July 1765 MERCY (GRAY) SEARS; daughter of Samuel and Ruth (Allen) Gray of Tisbury. Mercy Gray "of Chisbe" m. int. (1) Yarmouth in 1754 Thomas Sears, by whom she had three children. The will of Samuel Gray of Tisbury, dated 4 Oct. 1768 and proved 21 Dec. 1768, names wife Ruth, brother-in-law Joseph Allen, son Isiah (*sic*) Gray, daughter Mercy White; and grandchildren Sarah Sears and Allen Sears children of my sd. daughter.

The last certain record of Thomas White is the bp. of a child 14 June 1778 in West Yarmouth. There is no mention of Thomas or Mercy White in the probate or land records of Barnstable or Plymouth Cos. He is probably Thomas White of Caughnawaga, Montgomery Co., NY in the 1790 census.

Six (WHITE) ch. b. or bp. Yarmouth: Sylvia (Silva) bp. 1766, Ruth bp. 1768, Persalah (Priscilla) bp. 1770, Marcy bp. 1772, Thomas bp. 1775 and Isaiah Gray bp. 1778.

iv EBENEZER, b. 1733; d. 1733.

v MARCY, b. 1735; d. 1735.

vi DANIEL, b. 6 Oct. 1738; prob. d. Yarmouth 23 Dec. 1801; m. int. Yarmouth 8 April 1775 JENNY (or Jane) SMITH, d. in Sept. 1830 "widow of Daniel White." She may be the daughter Jane Smith mentioned in the will of William Smith of Harwich, yeoman, dated 12 March 1773.

On 6 Feb. 1795 Daniel and wife Jane, both of Yarmouth, deeded land there. But he had died by 10 April 1813 when "widow Jane White," Solomon Rogers and wife Tamson, Joseph Rider and wife Thankful, Daniel White and Marcy White, all of Yarmouth, sold land in Yarmouth. There are no records of Daniel or Jane in Barnstable Co.

Five (WHITE) ch. b. Yarmouth: Tamson b. 1778, Daniel Smith b. 1782, Patience b. 1786, Marcy b. 1789 and Thankful b. 1792.

References: MD 1:175; 14:30; 16:28. VR TISBURY. YARMOUTH VR pp. 62, 74, 162, 168, 169, 191, 199, 227-8, 256, 318, 396, 488, 541. Barnstable Co. PR 8:348, 467(John Smith); 13:246(Nathaniel Hopkins). Barnstable Co. LR Yarmouth:2:321(Ebenezer Paine); 2:528; 3:217(Daniel White); Harwich:3:371, 374(Ebenezer Paine). NEHGR 22:190; 102:54; 105:203, 308, 311; 106:102. WHITE FAM (YARMOUTH) pp. 1, 5, 6, 7. PAINE FAM REC 2:4:81-2; 2:8:186-8. Dukes Co. PR 1663-1850 (MSS. by Banks at NEHG Soc.) p. 155 (Samuel Gray). MARTHA'S VINEYARD BY BANKS 3:182-3. SEARS DESC pp. 172, 268. TAG 51:29-31. 1790 CENSUS NY:103.

46 JOSEPH$^4$ WHITE (Jonathan$^3$, Peregrine$^2$, William$^1$), b. ca. 1702; d. Yarmouth 4 June 1782 in 80th yr.

He m. Yarmouth 21 June 1737 LYDIA BAKER, b. there 28 Feb. 1705/6; d. there 4 May 1780 in 75th yr.; daughter of Nathaniel and Elizabeth (Baker) Baker. The will of Nathaniel Baker of Yarmouth, dated 5 Sept. 1750 and proved 20 Sept. 1757, names wife Elizabeth and daughter Lydia White.

The will of Joseph White of Yarmouth, dated 7 March 1775 and proved 20 Aug. 1782, names wife Lydia, daughter Anna Crowell, granddaughter Huldah Crowell, and son Joseph White.

Children (WHITE) b. Yarmouth:

i (H)ANNA$^5$ (or Anne), b. 21 Feb. 1737/8; d. Yarmouth 21 Nov. 1789 in 52nd yr. "Annas, wife of John Crowell"; m. Yarmouth 10 Feb. 1760 JOHN CROWELL, b. there 27 Jan. 1734/5; d. there 2 June 1820 ae. 86; son of Ephraim and Rose (Gorham) Crowell, and a descendant of Pilgrim John Howland. No probate or land records were found for John or Hannah in Barnstable Co.

Two (CROWELL) ch. b. Yarmouth: Henry b. 1761 and Jenne b. 1763.

ii HULDAH, b. 18 Nov. 1739; d. bef. 7 March 1775, not mentioned in her father's will; m. Yarmouth 16 Dec. 1773 AARON CROWELL, b. there 4 April 1743; living in Dennis 18 Dec. 1816; son of Aaron and Mercy (Howes) Crowell; he m. (2) 29 Feb. 1776 Rebecca Crowell (Rebecca in int., Ruth in m. rec.). On 18 Dec. 1816 Aaron Crowell of Dennis, yeoman, sold land to Aaron Jr. of Dennis, shipwright, the deed being signed by Aaron and Rebecca Crowell.

One (CROWELL) ch. rec. Yarmouth and Dennis, to Aaron and Huldah: Huldah b. 1775.

iii JOSEPH, b. 20 March 1742/3; d. Yarmouth 3 Nov. 1812 in 71st yr.; his gravestone says "He is the fourth from the first man born in New England"; m. Yarmouth 29 Nov. 1764 REBECCA BRAY, b. there 10 March 1742/3; d. there 14 or 16 Nov. 1827 in 86th yr. "widow of Deacon Joseph White"; daughter of Thomas and Mary (Crowell) Bray. The will of Joseph White, yeoman of Yarmouth, dated 28 Aug. 1800 and proved 12 Jan. 1813, names wife Rebecca, son Isaac, sons Peregrine and Joseph, daughters Lydia Black wife of Alexander, Polly Hall wife of Peter, children of daughter Azubah Hallet, deceased, and grandchild Harriet Hallett.

Seven (WHITE) ch. b. Yarmouth: Lydia b. 1765, Joseph b. 1768, Azubah b. 1770, twins Rebecca and Isaac b. 1775, Molly b. 1777 and Peregrine b. 1785.

References: MD 6:91; 7:161; 9:122, 142, 253; 12:44. YARMOUTH VR pp. 21, 53, 68, 79, 150, 198, 203, 209-10, 245, 281, 282, 315, 319, 323, 429, 552, 560, 822, 823, 833. Barnstable Co. PR 9:348(Nathaniel Baker); 36:41 (Aaron Crowell); 37:45(Joseph White); 14:134(Joseph White). Barnstable Co. LR Dennis:1:239(Aaron Crowell). Baker Fam (MSS). WHITE FAM (YARMOUTH) pp. 3, 5, 6. CROWELL (JOHN) FAM pp. 3, 4. BRAY FAM p. 1.

47 MARY[4] WHITE (Jonathan[3], Peregrine[2], William[1]), b. prob. Yarmouth and prob. bef. 1703.

She m. Yarmouth 14 Aug. 1729 JAMES RUSSELL. He is just possibly the James Russell "of Yarmouth" whose m. int. are recorded at Gloucester 21 April 1739 to Deborah (Elwell) Carlisle, widow of Joseph.

No further information was found on this family in the Barnstable VR or Barnstable Co. probate records; nor was anything helpful found in the probate records of Berkshire, Bristol, Franklin, Hampshire, Middlesex, Norfolk or Suffolk Cos. (James Russell of Holliston is not the one who m. Mary White.)

Child (DELL) b. Yarmouth:

i JONATHAN[5], b. 8 Nov. 1719 "to Mary White"; living 14 July 1736, named in the will of his grandfather Jonathan White.

Children (RUSSELL) b. Yarmouth:

ii JAMES, b. 13 May 1730, n.f.r.
iii JOB, b. 24 June 1732; d. Yarmouth 27 April 1733.
iv BARNABAS, b. 29 Aug. 1734; poss. m. New Braintree 23 Nov. 1758 JUDITH SPENNY, and bought land in July 1770 "of Warwick," and sold it in Nov. 1770 "of Guilford, Cumberland Co. NY." This became Guilford, Windham Co. VT, where a widow Russell and other Russells are listed in the 1790 census. The 1772 Guilford census lists a Barnabas in Guilford with a wife and two ch.
v MARY, b. 22 April 1737, n.f.r.

References: YARMOUTH VR pp. 61, 145. VR GLOUCESTER, NEW BRAINTREE. Hampden Co. LR 10:64; 10:191 (Barnabas Russell). GUILFORD VT HIST p. 119. 1790 CENSUS VT:49.

48 GEORGE YOUNG$^4$ (Sarah$^3$ White, Peregrine$^2$, William$^1$), b. Scituate 30 Nov. 1689; d. Boston in May 1771 ae. about 80 yrs.

He may have m. (1) Scituate 16 Aug. 1716 MARGARET FRANK.

He m. Scituate 5 or 25 April 1722 MARY STOCKBRIDGE, b. there 31 March 1701; living 10 Dec. 1766; daughter of Thomas and Sarah (Reed) Stockbridge. The settlement of the estate of Thomas Stockbridge, late of Scituate, dated 9 April 1725 mentions his widow Sarah and daughter Mary Young, wife of George. The will of widow Sarah Stockbridge of Hanover dated 25 May 1758 names daughter Mary Young.

George Young was living at Scituate on 7 March 1761 when he, wife Mary, and others divided land that descended to them from Mary's mother. On 10 Dec. 1766 the following persons who had come from Scituate in October were warned out of Marshfield: George Young, his wife Mary, their daughters Deborah Young, Priscilla Young, Lillis Young and Lucy Young, and Wales Young son of Lucy Young.

George Young was a currier and a weaver. The *Boston Newsletter* of 2 May 1771 says, "Died at North End, Mr. Young, weaver, aged above 80 years"; the issue of 9 May 1771 adds, "The death of Mr. George Young, in our last... he was grandson to Peregrine White."

There are no probate records for George or Mary Young in Suffolk or Plymouth Cos.

Children (YOUNG) b. Scituate to George and Mary:

i ISAAC$^5$, b. 15 March 1722/3; bp. 18 Aug. 1723; n.f.r.

ii JAMES, b. 22 May 1724; d. bef. 28 Nov. 1760; m. int. Scituate 13 Jan. 1753 MEHITABLE HATCH, poss. the one b. Hanover 12 Aug. 1730, daughter of Isaac and Sarah (Stevens) Hatch. Mehitable Yongue widow of Scituate was appointed administratrix on the estate of James Yongue, late of Scituate, mariner, 28 Nov. 1760; she rendered an account 30 July 1761. According to SCITUATE BY DEANE they had daughter Mehetabel; and a death notice in NEHGR claims Elisha, of Groton, was their son. No additional evidence was found for either child, but the Mayflower Society accepts lines through Elisha.

Two possible (YOUNG) ch.: Elisha and Mehetabel.

iii MARY, b. 10 Jan. 1725; d. Abington 10 Nov. 1810 ae. 86 "Mary Young Reed, widow of Samuel"; m. Abington 26 May 1763 SAMUEL REED, d. there bef. 5 Aug. 1776. He possibly m. Abington in 1730 Martha Noyes, and he did m. there in 1737 Elizabeth Hayward. On 5 Aug. 1776 Mary Reed, widow, of Abington was appointed one of the administrators of the estate of Samuel Reed late of Abington; on the same day Mary was appointed guardian to Sarah Reed aged 11, and Deborah Reed aged 8, daughters of Samuel. On 17 April 1777 the residual estate was divided among Sarah Reed, Deborah Reed, and the children of Elizabeth Askins, late widow of Jeremiah deceased and daughter of Samuel Reed. (Elizabeth was born to Samuel Reed and his wife Elizabeth.)

Two (REED) ch. b. Abington to Samuel and Mary: Sarah b. 1765, and Deborah b. 1768.

iv DEBORAH, b. 6 Oct. 1727; living unm. 10 Dec. 1766.

v REUBEN, b. 17 June 1729. The Mayflower Society accepts lineages on the basis that this is the Reuben who m. Scituate 2 July 1780 ABIGAIL BATES, bp. Scituate with six siblings 26 May 1776; d. Scituate 17 April 1794 "wife of Reuben Young"; daughter of Reuben and Mary (Hayden) Bates. No probate records were found for Reuben in Barnstable, Norfolk, Plymouth or Suffolk Cos., nor anything helpful in Plymouth land records.

Reuben and Abigail Young had seven children b. Scituate: Mehitable b. 1781, Reuben Bates b. 1782, Mary Thomas b. 1784, James b. 1786, Jane Bates b. 1788, Abigail Bates b. 1791, and Caleb Bates b. 1793.

vi JOB, b. 25 March 1731; d. Hanover bef. 5 March 1782; m. there 6 June 1762 ELIZABETH STOCKBRIDGE, b. there 22 April 1739; d. there 1 June 1813 "wife of Benjamin Stetson"; daughter of David and Deborah (Cushing) Stockbridge. Elizabeth m. (2) Hanover in 1784 Benjamin Stetson. The will of her father David Stockbridge of Hanover, dated 22 Aug. 1786 and proved 3 Feb. 1789, names his daughter Bettie Stetson. Job was a trader of Hanover. Job Young of Hanover and wife Betty in 1768 sold to "their father David Stockbridge ... land and our dwelling house." On 5 March 1782 David Stockbridge of Hanover was appointed administrator on the estate of Job Young late of Hanover.

Seven (YOUNG) ch. bp. Hanover First Cong. Ch.: Betty b. 1763, Job b. 1765, John b. 1766, Jane b. 1768, Charles b. 1769, Deborah Cushing b. 1771 and Bethia b. 1773.

vii PRISCILLA, b. 23 Feb. 1732; living unm. 10 Dec. 1766.

viii LUSANNAH, b. 22 Dec. 1734; n.f.r.

ix LILLIS, b. 5 Nov. 1736; d. Scituate 7 Aug. 1812 ae. 75 widow; m. Scituate 12 Nov. 1776 ELISHA SILVESTER, bp. there 24 April 1720; d. bet. 17 July 1805 and 17 Dec. 1807; son of Zebulon and Mary (Turner) Silvester. Elisha m. int. (1) Scituate in 1746 Hannah Hunt; he m. (2) Scituate in 1751 Grace Ruggles. The will of Elisha Silvester of Scituate, yeoman, advanced in age, dated 17 July 1805 and proved 17 Dec. 1807, names wife Lillis, five children by his earlier marriages, and "granddaughter Mary Stockbridge Cushing daughter of my late daughter Lillis Cushing." The will of Lillis Silvester of Scituate, widow, dated 10 June 1810 and proved 7 Sept. 1812, names her granddaughter Mary Stockbridge Cushing.

One (SILVESTER) ch. b. Scituate: Lillis b. 1778.

x SYLVANUS, b. 2 April 1739; n.f.r.

xi LUCY, b. 31 March 1740; living 10 Dec. 1766; nothing further found in Plymouth Co. probate records.

One (YOUNG) ch. b. Scituate: Wales b. 1765 "to Lucy Young."

xii JENNY, b. 15 March 1742; n.f.r.

References: MD 10:71, 230. VR ABINGTON, SCITUATE. BOSTON VR 28:158. HANOVER VR pp. 13, 127. Plymouth Co. PR 5:123(Thomas Stockbridge); 15:64(Mary Stockbridge); 16:189; 17:2(James Young); 22:77; 23:99; 24:388 (Samuel Reed); 27:82(Job Young); 30:507(David Stockbridge); 42:209(Elisha Silvester); 44:325 and #19998(Lillis Silvester). Plymouth Co. LR 46:256(George Young); 52:205; 54:20 (Job Young). Plymouth Ct. of Sess. 1760-1782 3:193(George Young and family). BOSTON NEWSLETTER 2 May 1771 and 9 May

1771(George Young). NEHGR 24:198; 84:269; 86:291-2. TAG 38:187. SCITUATE BY DEANE pp. 254, 394. ABINGTON BY HOBART pp. 374-6. HANOVER FIRST CH pp. 93, 98, 136-139, 207.

49 THOMAS YOUNG[4] (Sarah[3] White, Peregrine[2], William[1]), b. Scituate 18 May 1700; d. there bef. 12 April 1776.

He m. (1) Scituate 12 April 1737 MARY HOUSE, prob. the one b. there 27 Oct. 1711; daughter of Samuel and Sarah (Pinson) House.

Thomas m. (2) Scituate 19 Feb. 1756 JAEL WHITING (or Whiton and other variations), perhaps the one b. Hingham 3 July 1722; daughter of Solomon and Jael (Dunbar) Whiton.

He m. (3) Scituate 11 Dec. 1760 the widow HANNAH (-----) BARKER, d. Scituate bet. 22 Feb. 1777 and 7 Dec. 1778.

Thomas Young of Scituate was a housewright in 1744 when he and others divided land in Connecticut.

On 12 April 1776 Hannah Young declined administration on her deceased husband's estate in favor of Ezekiel Young.

The will of Hannah Young of Scituate, widow of Thomas Young late of Scituate deceased, dated 22 Feb. 1777 and presented 7 Dec. 1778, names her cousins Mary Brown and Robert Brown, daughter-in-law (stepdau.) Sarah Young and son-in-law (stepson) Thomas Young. The estate of Thomas Young of Ashford CT mentions distribution 22 March 1820 of the estate of Thomas Young late of Scituate between Sally Young of Scituate and the legatees of Thomas Young late of Ashford deceased.

Children (YOUNG) b. Scituate to second wife:

i SARAH[5], b. 2 Dec. 1757 and bp. 31 July 1757 (*sic*); d. Scituate 3 Dec. 1831 ae. 75. On 3 Dec. 1819 a group of "relations and friends of Sally Young of Scituate" prayed for a guardian to be appointed for her, since she was entitled to considerable real estate in Connecticut; on 30 May 1821 through an agent she sold her Connecticut land.

ii THOMAS, b. 20 Sept. 1758; d. Ashford CT 21 Oct. 1818; m. (1) Scituate 3 Oct. 1779 MABEL STODDER, d. Ashford 31 Oct. 1795 "wife of Thomas Young." She was poss. the one b. Hingham 3 June 1755 to Samuel and Ruth (Litchfield) Stodder. There is no Plymouth Co. probate record of a Samuel or Ruth Stodder who could be Mabel's parents to confirm this speculation. Thomas m. (2) Ashford 2 March 1796 MARY (SLATE) FLINT, b. Mansfield CT 15 Aug. 1758; living 6 June 1818; daughter of

Ezekiel and Mehitabel (Hall) Slate. Mary was divorced from Luke Flint, her first husband.

Thomas Young was of Ashford 22 Oct. 1785 when he sold land there.

The will of Thomas Young of Ashford CT, dated 6 June 1818 and proved 26 Oct. 1818, names wife Mary; her son-in-law Erastus Back; sons Thomas and David; daughter Mabel Howard; sons John, Mark and Noah; housekeeper Mary Hoskin, and Justis, Job and Harriet her children.

Twelve (YOUNG) ch. recorded Ashford CT, seven by first wife: Thomas b. 1780, David b. 1782, Hannah b. 1785, Mabel b. 1787, John b. 1790, Mark b. 1792 and Noah b. 1794; one by second wife: Job b. 1797; and four recorded to "Thomas Young and Mary Haskins": Justis* b. 1811, Harriet* b. 1813, Job* b. 1816 and James* b. 1818.

References: VR COHASSET, SCITUATE. CSL Barbour Index: Ashford, Mansfield. Plymouth Co. PR #23590 (Thomas Young); 25:134(Hannah Young). CT PR #4590(Thomas Young). Ashford CT LR 12:14, 36; D:139(Thomas Young). NEHGR 111:133. SCITUATE BY DEANE p. 394. HINGHAM HIST 3:195, 291.

50 JOSEPH YOUNG[4] (Sarah[3] White, Peregrine[2], William[1]), b. Scituate 10 Oct. 1701; d. Scituate bef. 24 Oct. 1763.

He m. Scituate 5 Sept. 1729 LYDIA BARRELL, b. there 15 Dec. 1709; d. there 30 May 1734 "wife of Joseph Young"; daughter of William Jr. and Elizabeth (Bailey) Barrell, and a descendant of Pilgrim William Brewster.

On 24 Oct. 1763 administration of the estate of Joseph Yongue (*sic*) late of Scituate deceased, yeoman, was granted to Ezekiel Youngue of Scituate.

Children (YOUNG) b. Scituate:

i RUTH[5], b. 24 Nov. 1729; d. prob. before April 1754; m. Scituate 11 Aug. 1748 DAVID DAMON, d. there bef. 3 Dec. 1760. He prob. m. int. (2) Scituate 1754 widow Mary (-----) Clap, by whom he had three children; the second was named Ruth prob. for his first wife. On 3 Dec. 1760 an administrator was appointed on the estate of David Damon late of Scituate, mariner deceased, and on 12 Aug. 1762 widow Mary Damon was appointed guardian to her two children by David Damon, Luther and Ruth.

Although the CLAPP MEM states that a child

---

*May have used either Young or Haskins as last name.

David was born to David and Ruth in 1752, no proof has been found that they had any children.

ii EZEKIEL, b. 22 June 1731; d. Scituate 10 Feb. 1814 ae. 82 "husband of Lusanna"; m. in 1755 LUSANNA WHITE, b. Marshfield 26 Oct. 1735; d. Scituate 28-30 June 1825 ae. 90 "wife of Ezekiel Young"; daughter of Lemuel and Anna (Scott) White (see #39 i). On 5 Sept. 1814 dower was set off to Lusanna Young, widow of Ezekiel, and a division of his estate was ordered among his children: Joseph, Gideon, Christopher, Ebenezer Scot, Stephen Fulington, Lydia Gannett and Joanna White Prouty. On 6 Dec. 1826 an order to divide the estate of Lusanna Young names the same children, calling Lydia Gannett deceased.

Eight (YOUNG) ch. b. Scituate: Joseph b. 1755, Lydia b. 1758, Gideon b. 1761, Christopher b. 1764, Stephen b. 1769, Ebenezer Scott b. 1772, Joanna White b. 1776 and William b. 1779.

iii SARAH, b. 10 June 1733; n.f.r.

References: MD 20:62, 66. VR SCITUATE. MARSHFIELD VR p. 97. Plymouth Co. PR #23571; 17:116(Joseph Yongue); 17:26; 18:95, 103(David Damon); 45:473(Ezekiel Young); 60:407(Lusanna Young). Plymouth Co. LR 51:22(Mary Damon). SCITUATE BY DEANE pp. 217, 384. CLAPP MEM p. 142.

51 JOSHUA YOUNG$^4$ (Sarah$^3$ White, Peregrine$^2$, William$^1$), b. Scituate 27 Sept. 1704; d. there bef. 29 Oct. 1757.

He m. (1) Scituate 22 Aug. 1732 ELIZABETH CUDWORTH, living 10 Nov. 1748 when she released her dower rights. (Their son named his second daughter after her.)

He m. (2) Boston 11 Dec. 1751 LYDIA BARNARD, bur. Scituate 28 Sept. 1793 ae. 87.

Joshua Young of Scituate was a saddler when he sold land of "my father Thomas late of Scituate" on 11 May 1733. There is no probate record in Plymouth Co. for Joshua; but on 29 Oct. 1757 a bond was posted on Thomas Young of Scituate as guardian to Joshua Young, minor son of Joshua Young late of Scituate deceased.

Children (YOUNG) by first wife:

i HANNAH$^5$, bp. Scituate 23 Sept. 1733 "daughter of Joshua"; d. unm. Scituate 23 Dec. 1821 ae. 90. On 5 July 1752 Hannah, "daughter of Joshua," was admitted to communion at the 1st Church of Scituate.

ii JOSHUA, b. ca. 1742; m. bef. Dec. 1772 CELIA LITTLE, b. Marshfield 20 Dec. 1754; d. Scituate 29 Aug. 1802 in 49th yr. "wife of Capt. Joshua

Young"; daughter of Ephraim and Alice (Baker) Little, and a descendant of Pilgrims William Bradford, Edward Doty and Richard Warren. On 15 Aug. 1809 creditors of the estate of Ephraim Little late of Marshfield deceased included "children of Selah [Celia] Young." (The following appears to refer to son Joshua[6] rather than to Joshua[5]: Joshua Young m. int. Hanover and Scituate in Feb. 1804 Mary Lenthal Eells of Hanover; sale of property was ordered of the insolvent estate of Joshua Young Jr. late of Scituate deceased 8 Dec. 1813; Mary Lenthall Young of Scituate married Marshfield 8 Nov. 1812 Jedidiah Ewel.)

Twelve (YOUNG) ch. b. Scituate: Elcia (Alice) Baker b. 1772, Elezebeth Cudworth b. 1775, Celia b. 1777, Betsey b. 1780, Joshua b. 1782, Patience b. 1785, Ephraim b. 1787, Peabody b. 1789, poss. an unnamed child b. 1791, Zynthia b. 1793, Emily b. 1795 and Peabody b. 1798.

References: MD 11:139, 141. BOSTON VR 38:347. VR SCITUATE. MARSHFIELD VR p. 57. HANOVER VR p. 257. MA OBITS (bur. of Lydia Young). Plymouth Co. PR #23573(gdn. Joshua Young); 43:75(Ephraim Little); 45:167 (Joshua Young). Plymouth Co. LR 28:22; 39:272(Joshua Young). SCITUATE BY DEANE p. 394.

52 WILLIAM[4] WHITE ( Sylvanus[3], Peregrine[2], William[1]), b. ca. 1683; d. Dartmouth bef. 3 Oct. 1780.

He m. bef. 1718 ELIZABETH CADMAN, living Dartmouth 6 Jan. 1768; daughter of George and Hannah (Hathaway) Cadman, and a descendant of Pilgrims Francis Cooke and Richard Warren. The will of George Cadman of Dartmouth, dated 24 Nov. 1718 and proved 6 Jan. 1718/9, names daughter Elizabeth White wife of William. William White was a blacksmith.

The will of William Whight gentleman of Dartmouth very aged, dated 6 Jan. 1768 and probated 3 Oct. 1780, names son William; ten grandchildren, Israel, Peleg, William, Sylvanus, Obed, Ruth, Sarah, Hannah, Mary and Unice, children of deceased son George; daughters Sarah Brown and Hannah Taber; sons Roger, Christopher and Thomas; children of daughter Elizabeth Slowcum deceased; sons Oliver and Abner; granddaughter Phebe Smith; daughter Susanna White; wife Elizabeth.

Children (WHITE) were:

i WILLIAM[5], d. Dartmouth bet. 17 Feb. 1777 and 3 Oct. 1780; m. Little Compton RI 2 Oct. 1729 ABIGAIL THURSTON, b. there 7 May 1700; daughter of

Jonathan and Sarah (-----) Thurston. The will of "Jonathan Thurston of Little Compton, now living in Dartmouth," dated 22 Aug. 1735 and proved 15 April 1740, mentions daughter Abigail White. The will of "William White son of William White of Dartmouth...blacksmith" dated 17 Feb. 1777 and probated with his father's will on 3 Oct. 1780, mentions the farm "my grandfather George Cadman gave me after the decease of my father and mother" and names son Jonathan White, eldest daughter Hannah Kirby, second daughter Elizabeth Peckham, and youngest daughter Abigail White.

Five (WHITE) ch., first two b. Dartmouth: Sarah b. 1730, Hannah b. 1731, Jonathan, Elizabeth and Abigail.

ii GEORGE, d. Dartmouth bet. 28 Dec. 1762 and 29 March 1764; m. Little Compton RI 18 Feb. 1730 DEBORAH SHAW, d. Dartmouth bet. 15 Jan. and 24 Nov. 1766; prob. the daughter b. Little Compton RI 15 July 1711 to Israel and ----- (Tallman) Shaw, but no land or probate records in Little Compton or Tiverton prove this. The will of George White of Dartmouth, dated 28 Dec. 1762 and proved 29 March 1764, names wife Deborah; sons Israel, Peleg, William, Silvenus, and Obed; daughters Ruth Wilcox, and Hannah Wing; and three unm. daughters Sarah, Mary, and Eunice. The will of Deborah White of Dartmouth, widow of George of Dartmouth deceased, dated 15 Jan. and proved 24 Nov. 1766, names the same children, except that Mary is called Mary "Sowle."

Eleven (WHITE) ch. b. Dartmouth: Israel b. 1730, Peleg b. 1732, Salvenus b. 1734, Ruth b. 1736, Sarah b. 1740, William b. 1741/2, Hannah b. 1744, Mary b. 1746, Eunice b. 1748, Silvanus b. 1750 and Obed b. 1755.

iii SARAH, d. Tiverton RI in Oct. 1795 ae. 86 "wife of John Brown"; m. Portsmouth RI 23 May 1726 JOHN BROWN, b. Little Compton RI in 1705; d. Tiverton RI in April 1773 ae. 68; son of Tobias and Alice (Burrington) Brown. The will of John Brown of Tiverton, gentleman, dated 24 Feb. and proved 5 May 1773, names wife Sarah; sons William and Thomas; daughters Elizabeth Howland, Abigail Gray, Mary Gray, Ruth Devol and Sarah Almy; father Tobias Brown; brother Nicholas Brown; grandchildren: Holder, son of Joseph and Sarah Almy, Meribah Shaw widow of Gideon deceased, Elizabeth Brown daughter of son John Brown deceased; grandsons Daniel, Elisha and John Brown.

Nine (BROWN) ch. b. Little Compton RI: William b. 1727, Elizabeth b. 1728, Abigail b. 1730, Mary b. 1733, John b. 1734, Ruth b. 1737, George b. 1739, Thomas b. 1741 and Sarah b. 1743.

iv HANNAH, d. Dover Plains, Dutchess Co. NY 9 June 1792 ae. 81; m. Dartmouth 27 Dec. 1730 WILLIAM TABER, b. there 18 Feb. 1704/5; d. there bef. 4 April 1758; son of Phillip and Margaret (Wood) Taber, and a fifth generation descendant of Pilgrims Francis Cooke and Richard Warren. William m. (1) Dartmouth in 1727 Merebah Soule, a descendant of George Soule of the *Mayflower*. An administrator was appointed on the estate of William Taber late of Dartmouth deceased on 4 April 1758.

Five (TABER) ch. b. Dartmouth to William and Hannah: Merebah b. 1731, Thomas b. 1732/3, Philip b. 1734, Hannah b. 1735/6 and Job b. 1737.

v ROGER, d. Hopkinton RI bef. 17 June 1802; m. Little Compton RI 4 May 1736 REBECCA GRINNELL, b. there 16 Dec. 1710; living 1 May 1749; daughter of Richard and Patience (Amory) Grinnell. Rebecca White and husband Roger signed a receipt 1 May 1749 for a legacy "given me by my mother Patience Grinnell." Roger White was one of the founders of Hopkinton RI in 1757. The inventory of the estate of Roger White of Hopkinton RI was dated 17 June 1802, Daniel White administrator. Proof of the parentage of Roger's three children is the inclusion in the marriage records of the first two that they were "of Roger"; and a deed wherein the third sold land in Hopkinton formerly of "my father Roger White."

Three (WHITE) ch.: Job, Hannah and Daniel.

vi CHRISTOPHER, d. Tiverton RI bet. 18 Dec. 1793 and 5 Oct. 1795; he m. (1) Little Compton RI 4 March 1738/9 ELIZABETH THURSTON, b. there 24 or 29 Sept. 1719; living 2 Aug. 1782; daughter of Edward and Sarah (Carr) Thurston. The will of Edward Thurston of Little Compton RI, dated 20 March 1738 and proved 15 Jan. 1739, names wife Sarah and daughter Elizabeth White. The last record of Elizabeth was her release of dower on 2 Aug. 1782.

Christopher m. (2) widow SARAH (-----) EARL, d. bef. 5 March 1810. There were no children of this marriage; Sarah m. before 12 Aug. 1804 John Perry, as indicated in a codicil to her will, which was presented 5 March 1810.

Christopher White "late of Little Compton RI, now residing in Tiverton," deeded property to his son "Perry G. White" 11 Nov. 1794.

The will of Christopher White of Little Compton, blacksmith, feeble, dated 18 Dec. 1793 and presented at Tiverton 5 Oct. 1795, names wife Sarah; sons Noah, Perigrin, and Thomas; daughters Sarah Hilyard, Mary Baley, Elizabeth Brown, and Ruth Mayhew.

Twelve (WHITE) ch. b. Little Compton RI: Sarah b. 1740, Thurston b. 1741, William b. 1742, Mary b. 1744, Noah b. 1745, Peregrine b. 1748, Susanna b. 1751, Elizabeth b. 1753, Lucy b. 1755, Pardon, Thomas and Ruth.

vii SUSANNA, living 3 Oct. 1780 when she was granted administration of her father's estate. No marriage record has been found for Susanna, but Phoebe White "daughter of Susannah White of Dartmouth" was married in 1756 to Gershom Smith, and "granddaughter Phebe Smith" is named in the will of Susanna's father in 1768. Nothing further was found in probate records of Bristol Co.

One (WHITE) child: Phebe.

viii ELIZABETH, d. bef. 13 Feb. 1748/9 according to the will of her grandmother Cadman; m. Little Compton RI 24 April 1737 BENJAMIN SLOCUM, b. Newport RI 11th month, 30th day, 1714; d. Adams MA 15th, 4th month, 1792; son of Giles and Mary (Paine) Slocum. Benjamin m. (2) Mercy (Smith) Scott by whom he had three children. Benjamin lived at Exeter and Smithfield RI, and finally moved to Adams bet. 1773 and 1779.

The will of Benjamin Slocum of Adams, yeoman, dated 20th of the 4th month 1782 and presented 7 June 1791 (*sic*), names sons Benjamin and Peleg; daughters Hannah Smith, Mary Sayles and Achsah Shearman; grandsons John Slocum, William Slocum and Benjamin Coopper; granddaughters Sarah Coopper, Hipzibah Coopper and Abra Slocum; and wife Marcy Slocum.

Five (SLOCUM) ch. b. Exeter RI to Benjamin and Elizabeth: Hannah b. 1737, Mary b. 1738, Peleg b. 1740, Elizabeth b. 1742 and Sarah b. 1743/4.

ix OLIVER, d. Hopkinton RI bef. 19 April 1791; m. No. Kingstown RI 21 Jan. or Feb. 1747 in all probability MARY SHERMAN. What remains of the original record reads "Olliver White of Newport and Mary (torn)armon of North Kingstown married 21 day (torn)uary 1747." [The name Sherman is frequently spelled Sharmon or Shearmon in RI records of the period.] Mary was b. No. Kingstown RI 10 Aug. 1725 to Stephen and Sarah (-----) Sherman. The will of Stephen Sherman of No. Kingstown, dated 29 Feb. 1772 and proved 3 Sept. 177[2], names his (third) wife [Gi]ffe and daughter (torn)y White.

An Oliver White "of Newport" was admitted freeman in 1746, and probably is the one who came to No. Kingstown to marry in 1747. Oliver died before 19 April 1791, when his son Oliver signed a receipt to Walter White, administrator of the estate of their father Oliver.

Proof of Oliver's progeny lies in a division of real estate on 21 Nov. 1791 naming his eight children: Walter, Oliver, Godfrey, Clark Wilbur and Sarah his wife, Oliver Davis and Penelope his wife, Susannah White, Christopher, and Joshua Collins and his wife Mary.

Eight (WHITE) ch., first two b. Hopkinton RI: Godfrey b. 1761, Susanna b. 1766, Walter, Mary, Sarah, Oliver, Christopher and Penelope.

x ABNER, b. Dartmouth 24 April 1725; d. Mabbetsville, Dutchess Co. NY bet. 30 June and 14 Nov. 1794; m. Little Compton RI 14 April 1746 RUTH BROWNELL, b. there 29 Dec. 1727; d. Mabbetsville 28 March 1806 ae. 78y 8m 22d; daughter of Charles and Mary (Wilbor) Brownell. The will of Charles Brownell of Little Compton RI, dated 21 March 1768 and proved in March 1774, names wife Mary and daughter Ruth White. Abner moved to Dutchess Co. about 1752. His will, dated 30 June 1794 and proved 14 Nov. 1794, names wife Ruth; sons Charles, William, James and Thomas; daughter Mary Harris; grandsons Thomas and Jeremiah Doty; and daughter Ruth Merritt.

Six (WHITE) ch., first b. Little Compton RI, next three b. Mabbetsville NY: Mary b. 1748, Charles b. 1753, William A. b. 1756, Thomas b. 1770, James and Ruth.

xi THOMAS, living in 1768, named in his father's will. He was prob. not the one who m. Elizabeth Jenney in Dartmouth in 1751, but he might be the Thomas White who m. Newport RI 23 or 25 Oct. 1755 Sarah Norton, and had there Elizabeth b. 1756, John b. 1757, and Thomas b. 1760.

References: MD 22:2-11. NYGBR 84:218(Abner White). TAG 17:195; 20:118, 182-3. NEHGR 71:363; 72:18; 91:185; 117:136. VR DARTMOUTH. RI VR:Exeter p. 59; Hopkinton p. 53; Little Compton pp. 66, 86, 94, 95, 122, 176; North Kingston p. 51; Newport pp. 76, 115, 123; Portsmouth p. 11. Hopkinton RI PR Counc. Rec. 4:235(Mary White); 4:1 (Roger White); 3:18(Oliver White). Bristol Co. PR 9:390 (Edward Thurston); 26:286 and original papers(William White); 18:318(George White); 19:438(Deborah White); 16:6 (William Taber). Tiverton RI PR 4:172(John Brown); 6:309 (Sarah Perry); 5:268(Christopher White). Little Compton

RI PR 1:55, 71(Patience Grinnell); 9:206(Edward Thurston); North Kingstown RI PR 10:116(Stephen Sherman). Hopkinton RI LR 6:192(Daniel White); 5:25, 27(Oliver White). Berkshire Co. PR #1523(Benjamin Slocum). Little Compton RI LR 2:425(Christopher White). Tiverton RI LR 5:285(Christopher White). Recs. of Col. of RI, J. R. Bartlett (1857) 5:163(Oliver White). NEB-MW GEN REC 4:231(Abner White). THURSTON pp. 520, 524. RI GEN DICT p. 174. LITTLE COMPTON FAMS pp. 552, 701. FALMOUTH N.S. HIST p. 386. TABER GEN pp. 64-5, 119. TABER DESC pp. 15, 64. HOPKINTON BY GRISWOLD p. 17. GRINNELL ANCY p. 10. SLOCUM GEN pp. 89, 114.

# ABBREVIATIONS

| | | | |
|---|---|---|---|
| ae. | aged | MS(S). | manuscript(s) |
| b. | born | n.d. | no date |
| bef. | before | n.f.r. | no further record found |
| bet. | between | | |
| bp. | baptized | n.p. | no place |
| bur. | buried | N.S. | new style |
| ca. | about | O.S. | old style |
| Cem. | cemetery | p./pp. | page/pages |
| ch. | children | pos./poss. | possibly |
| Ch. | church | PR | probate record |
| Co. | county | prob. | probably |
| Col. | colony | pub. | published |
| Comm. | committee | rec. | record(s) |
| d. | died | rem. | removed |
| dau(s). | daughter(s) | repr. | reprinted |
| dec. | deceased | res. | resided |
| d.s.p. | died without issue | sic | copy correct |
| d.y. | died young | Soc. | society |
| ed. | edition | TR | town record(s) |
| G.S. | gravestone | unm. | unmarried |
| gdn. | guardian | unpub. | unpublished |
| granddau. | granddaughter | VR | vital record(s) |
| LR | land record | yr(s). | year(s) |
| m. | married | -y -m -d | years, months, days |
| m. int. | marriage intentions | vol(s). | volume(s) |

Unless otherwise stated, all places are in Massachusetts.

# KEY TO ABBREVIATED TITLES

The following is an alphabetical list of abbreviated titles used in the references of the three family genealogies in this volume. When the abbreviated title is in capital letters, the reference is in print -- a book or periodical. When the abbreviated title is not in capital letters, it represents unpublished material -- handwritten or typed. With respect to printed vital records, the abbreviated titles VR MANSFIELD, DUXBURY etc. indicate alphabetized vital records; the abbreviated titles MARSHFIELD VR, TRURO VR etc., followed by page numbers, indicate vital records published non-alphabetically.

Other abbreviations used in the references and in the genealogies themselves, as well as in this Key to Abbreviated Titles, appear on the page opposite this.

**ABINGTON BY HOBART**
Hobart, Benjamin
*History of Abington, Mass.*
Boston, 1866.

**ADDISON CO VT HIST**
Smith, H.P.
*History of Addison Co. VT.* Syracuse NY, 1886.

**ALDEN MEM**
Alden, Ebenezer
*Memorial of the Descendants of the Hon. John Alden.* Randolph MA, 1867.

**ALLEN (PHINEHAS) DESC**
Allen, George H.
*Phinehas Allen's Descendants of Lincoln, Mass. 1745 and A Complete Genealogy of the Descendants of Benjamin Allen of Ashby, Mass. 1777.* Boston, 1898.

**ARBER**
Arber, Edward
*The Story of the Pilgrim Fathers....* Boston and New York, 1897; repr. New York, 1969.

**ARNOLD MEM**
Arnold, E.S.
*Arnold Memorial.* Rutland VT, 1935.

**Aspinwall Papers**
Aspinwall, Algernon A.
Manuscripts at New England Historic Genealogical Society, Boston.

**Attleboro 1st Ch**
Wilmarth, Elizabeth J.
Baptisms, Marriages and Deaths of 1st Church 1740-1856. Mimeographed. Attleboro, 1928.

**Attleboro 2nd Church**
Carter, Marion W. P.
Membership and Vital Records of 2nd Church. Mimeographed. Washington DC, 1924.

**Baker Fam**
Clark, Bertha W.
Baker family. Typescript at R.I. Historical Society, Providence, and NEHG Society, Boston. 1951.

**BALLARD FAM**
De Forest, Louis E.
*Ballard and Allied Families.* New York, 1924.

**BALLARD GEN**
Farlow, Charles F.
*Ballard Genealogy. William Ballard (1603-1639) of Lynn Mass. and William Ballard (1617-1689) of Andover, Mass. and Their Descendants.* Boston, 1911.

**BANKS ENGLISH ANCESTRY**
Banks, Charles E.
*The English Ancestry and Homes of the Pilgrim Fathers....* New York, 1929; repr. Baltimore, MD, 1962, 1968.

**BARNSTABLE FAMS**
Swift, C. F.
*Genealogical Notes of Barnstable Families, being a reprint of the Amos Otis Papers.* Barnstable MA, 1888-90.

**BASSETT FAM (1926)**
Bassette, Buell B.
*One Bassett Family in America....* Springfield MA, 1926.

**BISBEE FAM**
Lapham, William B.
*Family records of some of the descendants of Thomas Besbedge (Bisbee) of Scituate, Mass. 1634.* Augusta ME, 1876.

**BISBEE GEN**
Bisbee, Frank J.
*Genealogy of the Bisbee Family, Descendants of Thomas Besbeech (Bisbee) of Scituate, Duxbury & Sudbury, Mass.* Hampton Falls NH, 1956.

**BLAIR FAM**
Leavitt, Emily W.
*The Blair Family of New England.* Boston, 1900.

**BOLTON CT VR**
*Vital Records of Bolton to 1854 and Vernon to 1852.* Conn. Hist. Soc. Hartford CT, 1909.

**(BOSTON) GRANARY BUR GD**
Codman, Ogden
Gravestone Inscriptions and Records of Tomb Burials in the Granary Burying Ground. Salem MA, 1918.

**(BOSTON) KINGS CHAPEL**
Bridgeman, Thomas
*Memorials of the Dead in Boston, Containing exact transcripts of inscriptions ...in King's Chapel Burying Ground....* Boston, 1853.

**BOSTON NEWS LETTER**
*The Boston Newsletter.*
Established as a newspaper 1704, name changed after 1763 several times. Available on microfilm in historical and educational libraries.

**BOSTON NEWS OBITS**
*Index of Obituaries in Boston Newspapers 1704-1800.* 3 vols. Boston, 1968.

**BOSTON TRANSCRIPT**
Genealogical column of the Boston Transcript, available on microcards from Godfrey Mem. Lib., Middletown CT. Published 1906-1941.

**BOSTON VR**
*Reports of the Record Commissioners.* Vols. 9 and 24, births, marriages and deaths 1630-1699 and births 1700-1800. Boston, 1883 and 1894. Vols. 28 and 30, marriages 1700-1751 and 1751-1809. Boston, 1898 and 1902.

**BOSWORTH GEN**
Clarke, Mary B.
*Bosworth Genealogy; a History of the Descendants of Edward Bosworth who Arrived in America in 1634.* Six parts. San Francisco CA, 1926-40.

**BOWDOIN COLLEGE CAT**
*General Catalogue of Bowdoin College and the Medical School of Maine, 1794-1912.* Brunswick ME, 1912.

**BOWDOIN COLLEGE HIST**
Cleveland, Nehemiah
*History of Bowdoin College with Sketches of its graduates from 1806-1879, inclusive.* Boston, 1882.

**BRADFORD'S HIST (1898)**
Bradford, William
*History "of Plimoth Plantation." From the Original Manuscript.* Boston, 1898.

**BRADFORD'S HIST (1908)**
Bradford, William
*History of Plymouth Plantation 1606-1646.* Edited by W. T. Davis. New York, 1908.

**BRADFORD'S HIST (1952)**
Bradford, William
*Of Plymouth Plantation,1620-1647.* Edited by Samuel E. Morison, Modern Lib. NY, 1952.

**BRAINERD -BRAINARD**
Brainard, Lucy Abigail
*The Genealogy of the Brainerd-Brainard Family in America, 1649-1908.* 3 vols. Hartford CT, 1908.

**BRAINTREE RECS**
Bates, Samuel A.
*Records of the Town of Braintree 1640-1793.* Randolph MA, 1886.

**BRATTLEBORO ANNALS**
Cabot, Mary R.
*Annals of Brattleboro VT 1681-1895.* Brattleboro VT, 1921/22.

**BRAY FAM**
*Bray Family of Yarmouth.* Library of Cape Cod History and Genealogy #86. Yarmouthport MA, 1912.

**BREWSTER GEN**
Jones, Emma C. Brewster
*The Brewster Genealogy 1566-1907; Record of the Descendants of William Brewster of the Mayflower....* 2 vols. New York, 1908.

**BRIDGEWATER BY MITCHELL**
Mitchell, Nahum
*History of the Early Settlement of Bridgewater... including an extensive Family Register.* Boston, 1840; repr. Bridgewater, 1897; Baltimore MD, 1970.

**BRUNSWICK-TOPSHAM-HARPSWELL HIST**
Wheeler, G.A. and Wheeler, H.W.
*History of Brunswick, Topsham and Harpswell, Maine.* Boston, 1878.

**CARPENTER (REHOBOTH) GEN**
Carpenter, Amos B.
*A Genealogical History of the Rehoboth Branch of the Carpenter Family in America....* Amherst MA, 1898.

**CHARLESTOWN BY WYMAN**
Wyman, Thomas B.
*The Genealogies and Estates of Charlestown....* 2 vols. Boston, 1879.

**CHESTERFIELD HIST**
*The History and Genealogy of the Families of Chesterfield, Mass. 1762-1962.* Pub. by Bicentennial Gen. Comm. of Chesterfield, 1962.

**CLAPP MEM**
Clapp, Ebenezer
*The Clapp Memorial. Record of the Clapp Family containing sketches of the original six emigrants....* Boston, 1876.

**COBB FAM**
Cobb, Philip L.
*A History of the Cobb family.* 3 vols. Cleveland OH, 1907-1923.

**COLONIAL CLERGY**
Weiss, Frederick L.
*Colonial Clergy and Colonial Churches of New England.* Lancaster MA, 1936.

**CONANT FAM**
Conant, Frederick O.
*A History and Genealogy of the Conant Family... 1520-1887.* Portland ME, 1887.

**CONCORD VR**
*Concord, Massachusetts. Births, Marriages and Deaths 1635-1850.* Boston, 1895.

**COOLEY GEN**
Cooley, Mortimer E.
*The Cooley Genealogy, Descendants of Ensign Benjamin Cooley, an Early Settler of Springfield and Longmeadow Mass....* Rutland VT, 1941.

**CORNWALL BY STARR**
Starr, Edward C.
*A History of Cornwall Conn., a Typical New England Town.* New Haven, 1926.

**CRAPO GEN**
Crapo, Henry H.
*Certain Comeoverers.* 2 vols. New Bedford MA, 1912.

**CROWELL (JOHN) FAM**
*The Crowell Family of Yarmouth. Descendants of John.* Library of Cape Cod History and Genealogy #72. Yarmouthport MA, 1913.

**CSL Barbour Index**
Bound volumes of alphabetized vital records to about 1850, from all CT towns, as copied by Lucius B. Barbour. Also a statewide alphabetical card index of these records, interfiled with similar entries from private sources. At CT State Library.

**CSL Census Index**
Alphabetical card index of persons in Federal censuses for CT, 1790 to 1850. WPA project. At CT State Library.

**CSL Ch Rec**
Bound volumes of alphabetized vital records from over 600 CT churches and a single alphabetical card index for them all. At CT State Library.

**CSL Hale Cem Recs**
Hale collection of cemetery records copied by the WPA from CT cemeteries about 1932. Bound volumes for each town, and a single alphabetical card index. At CT State Library.

**CT MARR**
Bailey, Frederick W.
*Early Connecticut Marriages as found on ancient church records prior to 1800.* 7 vols. New Haven CT, 1896-1906; repr. with additions, 1 vol. Baltimore MD, 1968.

**CUSHMAN GEN**
Cushman, Henry W.
*A Historical and Biographical Genealogy of the Cushmans: The Descendants of Robert Cushman. the Puritan, 1617-1855.* Boston, 1855.

**DAKIN DESC**
Dakin, Albert H.
*Descendants of Thomas Dakin of Concord, Mass.* Rutland VT, 1948.

**DAR LINEAGE**
*Lineage Book, National Society of the Daughters of the American Revolution.* Vol.1-- 1895--. Harrisburg PA.

**DAR PATRIOT INDEX**
*DAR Patriot Index.* Pub. by National Society of the Daughters of the American Revolution. Washington DC , 1966.

**DEERFIELD BY SHELDON**
Sheldon, George
*History of Deerfield, Mass.* Greenfield MA, 1896.

**DeMARANVILLE GEN**
Randall, George L.
*Descendants of Louis DeMaranville.* New Bedford MA, 1921.

**DEXTER**
Dexter, Henry M. and Dexter, Morton
*The England and Holland of the Pilgrims.* Boston, 1905.

**DOGGETT FAM**
Doggett, Samuel B.
*A History of the Doggett Family.* Boston, 1894.

**DORCHESTER VR**
*Report of the Record Comissioners.* Vol. 21, to 1825. Boston, 1891; vol. 36, 1826-49. Boston, 1905.

**DORCHESTER VR INDEX**
Gladden, Sanford C.
*An Index to the Vital Records of Dorchester, Mass.* Boulder, CO, 1970.

**DOTY GEN**
Doty, Ethan A.
*The Doty-Doten Family in America. Descendants of Edward Doty, an Emigrant by the Mayflower,1620.* 2 vols. Brooklyn, 1897.

**DRAKE FAM**
Drake, Louis S.
*The Drake Family in England and America, 1360-1895, and the Descendants of Thomas Drake of Weymouth, Mass. 1635-1691.* Boston, 1896.

**DUXBURY RECS**
Etheridge, George, copyist.
*Copy of the Old Records of the Town of Duxbury, Mass. from 1642 to 1770.* Plymouth, 1893.

**DUXBURY BY WINSOR**
Winsor, Justin
*History of the town of Duxbury, Mass. with Genealogical Registers.* Boston, 1849; repr. Boston, 1970.

**DWIGHT FAM**
Dwight, Benjamin W.
*The History of the Descendants of John Dwight of Dedham, Mass.* 2 vols. New York, 1874.

**EATON NEWS**
Molyneux, Nellie Z. R.
*History, Genealogical and Biographical of the Eaton Families.* Syracuse NY, 1911.

**EATONIAN NEWS**
Published semi-annually by Eaton Families Association. #1 Jan. 1933.

**EDDY FAM**
Eddy, Charles
*Genealogy of the Eddy Family.* Brooklyn, 1881.

**EDDY GEN**
Eddy, Ruth S.D.
*The Eddy Family in America, a Genealogy.* Boston, 1930; repr. Ann Arbor MI, 1965.

**EDSON GEN**
Edson, Jarvis B.
*Edsons in England and America and Genealogy of the Edsons.* New York, 1903.

**ESSEX INST HIST COLL**
*Historical Collections of the Essex Institute.* Vol. 1-- Apr. 1859--. Published Salem MA for the Essex Institute.

**FAIRBANKS GEN**
Fairbanks, Lorenzo S.
*Genealogy of the Fairbanks Family in America, 1633-1897.* Boston, 1897.

**FALMOUTH N.S. HIST**
Duncanson, J. V.
*Falmouth, a New England Township in Nova Scotia.* Windsor, Ont., 1965.

**FAM OF PILGRIMS**
Shaw, Hubert K.
*Families of the Pilgrims.* Boston, 1956.

**FAUNCE DESC**
Faunce, James F
*The Faunce Family History and Genealogy. Ancestry and Descendants of John Faunce of Purleigh, Essex, England and Plymouth, Mass.* 1967.

**FOLGER**
Folger, Herbert
*A record of the Names of the Passengers of the good ship Mayflower in December, 1620...with the names of some of the husbands of their married daughters, granddaughters, and great-granddaughters.* Berkeley CA, 1920; new edition, NJ, n.d. Revised by Lewis Neff AL,1959.

**FOSTER GEN**
Pierce, Frederick C.
*Foster Genealogy; being the record of the posterity of Reginald Foster of Ipswich in New England. Also the record of all other American Fosters.* Chicago IL, 1899.

**FOWLER HIST**
Fowler, Christine C.
*History of the Fowlers.* Batavia NY, 1950.

**Freetown VR**
Freetown, Mass. Vital Records, Births, Marriage Intentions, and Deaths 1686-1793. Typescript in Fall River Public Library and NEHG Society, Boston. n.d.

**FULLER GEN 1**
Fuller, William H.
*Genealogy of some Descendants of Edward Fuller of the Mayflower.* Palmer MA, 1908.

**FULLER GEN 2**
Fuller, William H.
*Genealogy of some Descendants of Dr. Samuel Fuller of the Mayflower....* Palmer MA, 1910.

**FULLER GEN 3**
Fuller, William H.
*Genealogy of some of the Descendants of Captain Matthew Fuller, John Fuller of Newton, John Fuller of Lynn, John Fuller of Ipswich, Robert Fuller of Dorchester and Dedham.* Palmer MA, 1914.

**GEN ADVERTISER**
Greenlaw, Lucy H., ed.
*The Genealogical Advertiser, a Quarterly Magazine of Family History.* vols. 1-4, 1898-1901; repr. Baltimore MD, 1974.

**GILBERT (THOMAS) DESC**
Brainard, Homer W.; Gilbert, Harold S.; and Torrey, Clarence A.
*Descendants of Thomas Gilbert, 1582-1659, of Mt. Wollaston (Braintree), Windsor and Wethersfield.* New Haven CT, 1953.

**GILES MEM**
Vinton, John A.
*The Giles Memorial. Genealogical Memoirs of the Families Bearing the Names of Giles, Gould, Holmes (and others).* Boston, 1864.

**GOSS FAM**
Goss, Paul
*Criticism and Brief on the Goss Family.* n.p., n.d.

**GRANBERRY FAM**
Jacobus, Donald L.
*Granberry Family and Allied Families....* Hartford CT, 1945.

**GREAT BARRINGTON BY TAYLOR**
Taylor, Charles J.
*History of Great Barrington [MA].* Great Barrington MA, 1882.

**GREENLEAF FAM(1896)**
Greenleaf, James E.
*Genealogy of the Greenleaf Family.* Boston, 1896.

**GRINNELL ANCY**
Emery, William M.
*Ancestry of the Grinnell Family.* Boston, 1931.

**GROSVENOR ANCY**
Kent, Daniel
*The English Home and Ancestry of John Grosvenor of Roxbury Mass.* Boston, 1918.

**GUILFORD VT HIST**
*Official history of Guilford 1678-1961.* Guildford VT, 1961.

**HALIFAX VR**
Bowman, George E.
*Vital records of the Town of Halifax, Mass. to the end of the year 1849.* Boston,1905.

**HAMILTON FAM**
Hamilton, Charles W. Jr.
*Hamilton Family of America.* 1933.

**HAMILTON, HOUSE OF**
Hamilton, George
*A History of the House of Hamilton.* Edinburgh, 1933.

**HAMLIN FAM**
Andrews, H. Franklin
*History of the Hamlin Family; with Genealogies of early settlers of the Name in America, 1639-1894.* Part 1. Exira IA, 1894.

**HANOVER FIRST CH**
Briggs, L. Vernon
*History and Records of the First Congregational Church, Hanover, MS. 1727-1865.* Boston, 1895.

**HANOVER BY DWELLY**
Dwelley, Jedediah and Simmons, John F.
*History of the Town of Hanover, Massachusetts with Family Genealogies.* Hanover MA, 1910.

**HANOVER VR**
*Records of Births, Marriages and Deaths and of Intentions of Marriage of the Town of Hanover, Mass. 1727-1857.* Rockland MA, 1898.

**HARRIS FAM (1909)**
Harris, Dwight J. and Harris, N. D., editors.
*Harris Family from AD 1630 in two lines.* 1909.

**HARTFORD TIMES**
Genealogical columns in the Hartford [CT] Times. Newspaper files available on microfilm in a number of libraries.

**HARVARD BY NOURSE**
Nourse, H. S.
*History of the town of Harvard, Mass., 1732-1893.* Harvard, 1894.

**HARVARD GRADS**
Sibley, John L.
*Biographical sketches of graduates of Harvard University in Cambridge, Mass.* Cambridge vol. 1-- 1873--.

**HARWICH BY PAINE**
Paine, John
*A History of Harwich Mass., 1620-1800, including the early history of that part which is now Brewster.* Rutland VT, 1937.

**HATHAWAY GEN (1970)**
Versailles, Elizabeth S.
*Hathaways of America.* Northhampton MA, 1970.

**HAYWARD (JAMES) GEN**
Adams, William F.
*James Hayward, born April 4, 1750, Killed...April 19, 1775, with Genealogical Notes relating to the Haywards.* Springfield MA, 1911.

**HILDRETH ANCY**
Davis, Walter G.
*Ancestry of Sarah Hildreth.* Portland ME, 1958.

**HINGHAM HIST**
*History of the Town of Hingham, Mass.* 3 vols. in 4. Pub. by the town. Hingham MA, 1893.

**HOPKINTON BY GRISWOLD**
Griswold, S.S.
*Historical Sketch of the Town of Hopkinton, Rhode Island from 1757 to 1876....*
Hope Valley RI, 1877.

**HORSFORD FAM**
Hosford, Henry H.
*Horsford-Hosford Families....* Cleveland OH, 1936.

**HOWE GENS**
Howe, Daniel W.
*Howe Genealogies. Genealogies of Abraham of Roxbury, James of Ipswich, Abraham of Marlborough and Edward of Lynn, Mass., also the appendix.* Vol 2. Boston, 1929.

**HOWE (JOHN) GEN**
Howe, Daniel W.
*Howe Genealogies. The genealogy of John Howe of Sudbury and Marlborough, Mass.* Vol 1. Boston, 1929.

**HOWLAND GEN**
Howland, Franklyn
*A Brief Genealogical and Biographical History of Arthur, Henry, and John Howland, and their descendants.* New Bedford MA, 1885.

**JENKINS DESC**
Jenkins, Samuel B.
*Descendants of John Jenkins.* Library of Cape Cod History and Genealogy #2. Yarmouthport MA, 1929.

**KEENE NH VR**
Whitcomb, Frank H.
*Vital Statistics of the Town of Keene NH....* Keene NH, 1905.

**KING PHILIP'S WAR**
Bodge, George M.
*Soldiers in King Philip's War.* 3rd ed., 1906; repr. Baltimore MD, 1967.

**KINGS CO N.S. HIST**
Eaton, Arthur W. H.
*History of Kings County, Nova Scotia.* Salem, 1910.

**KINNE GEN**
Robertson, Florance K.
*Genealogy of Henry and Ann Kinne....*
Los Angeles CA, 1947.

**LANCASTER VR**
Nourse, Henry S.
*Births, Marriages, and Deaths Register, Church Records and Epitaphs.* Lancaster, 1890.

**LANESBORO BY PALMER**
Palmer, C. J.
*History of the Town of Lanesborough [Mass.] 1741-1905.* 1905.

**LEACH GEN**
Leach, F. Phelps
*Lawrence Leach of Salem Massachusetts and some of his Descendants.* East Highgate VT, 1924-26.

**LEWISIANA**
*Lewisiana; or, The Lewis Letter.* vols.1-17 in 8. Pub. by the Lewis League, Lisle NY, 1887-1907.

**LEYDEN DOCUMENTS**
Plooij, Dr. D. and Harris, Dr. J. Rendel
*Leyden Documents Relating to the Pilgrim Fathers.*
Leiden, Holland, 1920.

**LITCHFIELD ME HIST**
*History of Litchfield Maine and an Account of its Centennial Celebration, 1895.* Augusta ME, 1897.

**LITTLE COMPTON FAMS**
Wilbour, Benjamin F.
*Little Compton Families published by the Little Compton Historical Society from records compiled by Benjamin F. Wilbour.* Providence RI, 1967.

**LIVERMORE FAM**
Thwing, Walter E.
*The Livermore Family of America.* Boston, 1902.

**LONGMEADOW CENT**
*Proceedings at the Centennial Celebration of the Incorporation of the Town of Longmeadow [Mass.]....* with a Town Genealogy. Longmeadow, 1884.

**LUMBERT-LOMBARD**
Otis, Amos
*The Lumbert-Lombard Family.* Library of Cape Cod History and Genealogy #54. Yarmouthport MA, 1912.

**MA BAY ACTS & RESOLVES**
*Acts and Resolves of the Province of Massachusetts Bay.* 21 vols. Boston, 1869-1922.

**MA BAY RECS**
Shurtleff, Nathaniel B.
*Records of the Governor and Company of the Massachusetts Bay in New England.* 5 vols. in 6. 1853-4; repr. NY, 1968.

**MA HIST BY BARBER**
Barber, John W.
*Historical collections...of every town in Mass.....* Worcester MA, 1841.

**MA MARR**
Bailey, Frederic W.
*Early Massachusetts Marriages Prior to 1800.* 3 vols. in 1. 1897-1900; repr. Baltimore MD, 1968.

**MA OBITS**
*Index of obituaries on the Massachusetts Centinel and the Columbian Centinel, 1784-1840.....* 5 vols. Boston, 1961.

**MA PIONEERS**
Pope, Charles H.
*The pioneers of Massachusetts....* Boston, 1900; repr. Baltimore MD, 1965.

**MANWARING**
Manwaring, Charles W.
*A Digest of the Early Connecticut Probate Records.* 3 vols. Hartford CT, 1902-6.

**MARSHFIELD BY RICHARDS**
Richards, Lysander S.
*History of Marshfield, Mass., with Genealogy.* 2 vols. Plymouth, 1901-5.

**MARSHFIELD VR**
Sherman, Robert M. and Sherman, Ruth W.
*Vital Records of Marshfield, Massachusetts to the year 1850.* Warwick RI, 1969.

**MARTHA'S VINEYARD BY BANKS**
Banks, Charles E.
*History of Martha's Vineyard, with Genealogy.* 3 vols. Boston, 1911-25; repr. Edgartown MA, 1966.

**MATTHEWS FAM**
*The Matthews Family of Yarmouth.* Library of Cape Cod History and Genealogy #81. Yarmouthport, MA, 1912.

**MD**
Bowman, George E., editor.
*The Mayflower Descendant: a quarterly magazine of Pilgrim history and genealogy.* 34 vols. 1899-1940.

**ME-NH GEN DICT**
Noyes, Sybil; Libby, C.T.; Davis, Walter G.
*Genealogical Dictionary of Maine and New Hampshire.* 1928-1935; repr. Baltimore MD, 5 parts in 1, 1972.

**MEDFIELD BY TILDEN**
Tilden, William S.
*History of Medfield [Mass.]* Boston, 1887.

**MERRILL MEM**
Merrill, Samuel
*A Merrill Memorial; an account of the descendants of Nathaniel Merrill, an early settler of Newbury, Mass.* 2 vols. Cambridge MA, 1917-1928.

**MIDDLEBORO BY WESTON**
Weston, Thomas
*History of the town of Middleboro [Mass.]* Boston, 1906.

**MIDDLEBORO DEATHS**
Wood, Alfred
*Record of Deaths, Middleboro, Massachusetts.* Boston, 1947.

**MIDDLEFIELD BY CHURCH-SMITH**
Church, Edward and Smith, Philip M.
*A history of the town of Middlefield, Massachusetts with genealogies.* Menasha WI, 1924.

**MOORE ANCY**
DeForest, L.E.
*Moore and Allied Families: the ancestry of William Henry Moore.* New York, 1938.

**MORSE GEN**
Morse, J. Howard and Leavitt, Miss Emily W.
*Morse Genealogy, being a revision of the Memorial of the Morses published by Abner Morse in 1850.* 2 vols. New York, 1903-1905.

**MORSE MEM**
Lord, Henry D.
*Memorial of the family of Morse.* Cambridgeport MA, 1896.

**MQ**
*The Mayflower Quarterly.* Vol 1-- 1935-- . Published Plymouth MA for the General Society of Mayflower Descendants.

**MSSR**
*Massachusetts Soldiers and Sailors of the Revolutionary War.* 17 vols. Boston, 1896-1908.

**MURDOCK GEN**
Murdock, Joseph B.
*Murdock Genealogy. Robert Murdock of Roxbury, Mass., and some of his descendants....*
2 parts. Boston, 1925.

**NASH FAM**
Nash, Sylvester
*The Nash Family; or records of the descendants of Thomas Nash of New Haven, Conn., 1640.*
Hartford CT, 1853.

**NEB-MW GEN REC**
*The Nebraska and Midwest Genealogical Record.* Vols. 1-22. Lincoln NE, 1923-44.

**NEHGR**
*New England Historical and Genealogical Register.* Vol. 1-- Jan. 1847--. Published at Boston by the New England Historic Genealogical Society.

**New Bedford Mercury Obits**
*New Bedford Mercury deaths 1807-1845.* Typescript, New Bedford MA Pub. Lib. and RI Hist. Soc. Lib., Providence RI.

**NGSQ**
*National Genealogical Society Quarterly.* Vol. 1-- 1912--. Published at Washington DC by the Society.

**NICKERSON GEN**
Hawes, James W.
*Children of William Nickerson.* Library of Cape Cod History and Genealogy #91. Yarmouthport MA, 1912.

**NJ ARCH**
*Archives of the state of New Jersey.*
47 vols. Trenton NJ, 1880-1949.

**NJ GEN MAG**
*Genealogical Magazine of New Jersey.* Vol. 1-- 1925--. Published by the Genealogical Society of New Jersey, Newark NJ.

**NORTH BRIDGEWATER BY CARY**
Cary, Moses
*Genealogy of the families who have settled in the North Parish of Bridgewater....* 1824; repr. 1903.

**NORTH BROOKFIELD BY TEMPLE**
Temple, Josiah H.
*History of North Brookfield... Brookfield records, 1686-1783 ... with a genealogical register.*
Boston, 1887.

**NORTH DESC**
North, Dexter
*John North of Farmington Conn., and his descendants, with a short account of other early North families.* Concord NH, 1924.

**NORTH YARMOUTH BY ROWE**
Rowe, William H.
*Ancient North Yarmouth and Yarmouth, Maine 1636. A history of Yarmouth.* Yarmouth ME, 1937.

**NORTON HIST**
Clark, George F.
*History of the town of Norton, Bristol County, Mass. from 1669 to 1859.* Boston, 1859.

**NORWICH CT VR**
*Vital Records of Norwich, Conn., 1659-1848.*
2 vols. Hartford CT, 1913.

**NOVA SCOTIA CENSUSES**
*Report of Board of trutees of Public Archives of Nova Scotia.* Halifax N.S., 1935.

**NYGBR**
*The New York Genealogical and Biographical Record.* Vol. 1-- 1870--. Published by the Society.

**OLD TIMES**
*Old Times; a magazine devoted ...to the early history of North Yarmouth, Maine, including... the towns of Harpswell, Freeport, Pownal, Cumberland and Yarmouth....* 8 vols. Yarmouth ME, 1877-1884.

**OTIS FAM**
Otis, William A.
*A genealogical and historical memoir of the Otis family in America.* Chicago IL, 1924.

**OXFORD ME BY KING**
King, M. F.
*Annals of Oxford, Maine from 1829 to 1850, prefaced by a brief account of Shepardsfield Plantation, now Hebron and Oxford, with genealogical notes.* Portland ME, 1903.

**PAINE FAM REC**
Paine, H. D.
*Paine Family Records. A journal of genealogical and biographical information respecting the American families of Payne, Paine, Payn, etc.* 2 vols. in 1. New York, 1880-1883.

**PASTOR OF PILGRIMS**
Burgess, Walter H.
*The Pastor of the Pilgrims, a biography of John Robinson.* New York, 1920.

**PEABODY GEN**
Peabody, Selim H.
*Peabody (Paybody, Pabody, Pabodie) Genealogy.* Boston, 1909.

**PEIRCE FAM (1870)**
Peirce, Ebenezer W.
*The Peirce family of the Old Colony; or the lineal descendants of Abraham Peirce who came to America as early as 1623.* Boston, 1870.

**PEIRCE'S CONTRIB**
Peirce, Ebenezer W.
*Contributions, biographical, genealogical and historical on the following families: Barnaby, Bartlett, Booth, Brownell, Caswell, Gardiner, Godfrey, Harlow, Howland, Pearse and others.* Boston, 1874.

**PETTINGELL GEN**
Pettingell, John M.
*A Pettingell Genealogy.* Boston, 1906.

**PHELPS FAM**
Phelps, Oliver S. and Servin, Andrew T.
*The Phelps Family of America and their English ancestors.* 2 vols. Pittsfield MA, 1899.

**PIERCE FAMS (1936)**
Pierce, H. C.
*Seven Pierce Families.* Washington DC, 1936.

**(PLYMOUTH) ANC LANDMARKS**
Davis, William T.
*Ancient Landmarks of Plymouth.* 2nd edition; 1899; repr. of Part Two under title *Genealogical Register of Plymouth Families.*
Baltimore MD, 1975.

**(PLYMOUTH) BURIAL HILL**
Kingman, Bradford
*Epitaphs from Burial Hill, Plymouth Massachusetts, from 1657 to 1892. With biographical and historical notes.* Brookline MA, 1892.

**PLYMOUTH CH RECS**
*Plymouth Church Records, 1620-1859.* 2 vols. New York, 1920-23; repr. Baltimore MD, 1975.

**PLYMOUTH COLONY RECS**
Shurtleff, Nathaniel B. and Pulsifer, David
*Records of the colony of New Plymouth in New England.* 12 vols. Boston, 1855-61; repr. 12 vols. in 6, New York, 1968.

**Plymouth Col. LR**
Also known as Old Colony Deeds. 6 vols. MSS. at Plymouth Co. Register of Deeds. Vol 1 appeared in print as Vol. 12 of *Plymouth Colony Recs* (see above); Vol. 2 and Vol. 3, as far as p. 27 have been printed in MD.

**PLYMOUTH SCRAPBOOK**
Pope, Charles H.
*The Plymouth Scrapbook.* Boston, 1918.

**PN&Q**
Bowman, George E.
*Pilgrim Notes and Queries.* 5 vols. Boston, 1913-1917.

**POPE FAM**
Pope, Charles H.
*A history of the Dorchester Pope family 1634-1888.* Boston, 1888.

**POULTNEY VT BY JOSLIN**
Joslin, Joseph
*History of Poultney Vermont, to 1875. With family and biographical sketches.* Poultney VT, 1875.

**PRESTON CH**
*First Congregational Church of Preston CT 1698-1898....* Preston CT, 1900.

**PROUTY GEN**
Pope, Charles H.
*Prouty (Proute) Genealogy.* Boston, 1910.

**PUTNAM CO NY BY PELLETREAU**
Pelletreau, William S.
*History of Putnam Co., N.Y. with biographical sketches of its prominent men.* Philadelphia PA, 1886.

**PUTNAM FAM**
Putnam, Ebenezer
*A History of the Putnam Family in England and America.* 2 vols. Salem MA, 1891-1908.

**RANDOLPH FIRST CH**
*150th Anniversary of First Congregational Church, Randolph, Mass.* Boston, 1881.

**RAYMOND FAMS**
Raymond, Samuel
*Genealogies of the Raymond Families of New England 1630-1 to 1886, with a historical sketch of some of the Raymonds of early times....* New York, 1886.

**REHOBOTH BY BLISS**
Bliss, Leonard Jr.
*History of Rehoboth, Bristol County, Mass....* Boston, 1836.

**REHOBOTH VR**
Arnold, James N.
*Vital Record of Rehoboth, 1642-1896. Marriages, intentions, births, deaths ....*
Providence RI, 1897.

**RI GEN DICT**
Austin, John O.
*The Genealogical Dictionary of Rhode Island, comprising three generations of settlers who came before 1690.* Albany NY, 1887; repr. Cleveland OH, 1967 and Baltimore MD, 1969.

**RI VR**
Arnold, James N.
*Vital Record Of Rhode Island, 1636-1850.* 21 vols. Providence RI, 1891-1912.

**RICE GEN**
Ward, Andrew H.
*A Genealogical History of the Rice Family; descendants of Deacon Edmund Rice, who settled at Sudbury, Mass. in 1638 or 9.* Boston, 1858.

**RICH GEN**
Rich, C. T.
*Genealogy of Rich Family.* 1887.

**ROCKAWAY NJ RECS**
Crayon, Joseph P.
*Rockaway Records* Rockaway NJ, 1902.

**ROOT RECS**
Root, James P.
*Root Genealogical Records, 1600-1870, comprising the general history of the Root and Roots families in America.* New York, 1870.

**SAVAGE**
Savage, James
*A Genealogical Dictionary of the first settlers of New England, showing three generations of those who came before May 1692....* 4 vols. Boston 1860-62; repr. Baltimore MD, 1965.

**SCITUATE BY DEANE**
Deane, Samuel
*History of Scituate, Mass., from its Settlement to 1831.* Boston, 1831; repr. No. Scituate, 1899.

**SEARS DESC**
May, Samuel P.
*The Descendants of Richard Sares (Sears) of Yarmouth, Mass., 1638-1888.* With an appendix.... Albany NY, 1890.

**1790 CENSUS**
*Heads of Families at the First Census, 1790.* 12 vols. Washington DC, 1907-09; repr. Baltimore MD, 1852-66; Spartanburg SC, 1963-66.

**SHARON CT VR**
Van Alstyne, Lawrence
*A Record of Births, Marriages and Deaths in the Town of Sharon Conn. from 1721-1879.* Sharon, 1897.

**SHERMAN DESC**
Holman, Winifred L.
*Descendants of William Sherman of Marshfield.* Concord NH, 1936.

**SHIPBUILDING ON NORTH RIVER**
Briggs, L. Vernon
*History of Shipbuilding on North River, Plymouth Co, Mass.* Boston, 1889.

**SLOCUM GEN**
Slocum, Charles E.
*A short history of the Slocums, Slocumbs, and Slocombs of America, Genealogical and Biographical, from 1637 to 1881.* 2 vols. Syracuse NY, 1882 & 1908.

**SMALL DESC**
Underhill, Lora A. W.
*Descendants of Edward Small of New England and the allied families, with tracings of English Ancestry.* 3 vols. Cambridge MA, 1910.

**SMITH (JESSE) DESC**
Smith, L. Bertrand
*Jesse Smith, his Ancestors and Descendants.* New York, 1909.

**SMITH (THOMAS) MEM**
Smith, Susan A.
*A Memorial of Rev. Thomas Smith (second minister of Pembroke, Mass.) and his descendants.... 1707 - 1895.* Plymouth, 1895.

**SOUTHWORTH GEN**
Webber, Samuel G.
*A Genealogy of the Southworths (Southards), descendants of Constant Southworth, with a sketch of the family in England.* Boston MA, 1905.

**SPOONER DESC**
Spooner, Thomas
*Records of William Spooner of Plymouth, Mass., and his descendants.* Vol. 1. Cincinnati OH, 1883.

**STANSTEAD CO QUEBEC HIST**
Hubbard, B. F.
*History of Stanstead Co., Quebec, with sketches of more than five hundred families.* Montreal, 1874.

**STEARNS GEN**
Van Wagenen, Mrs. Avis S.
*Genealogy and memoirs of Isaac Stearns and his descendants.* Syracuse NY, 1901.

**STETSON DESC**
Stetson, Oscar F.
*Descendants of Cornet Robert Stetson of Scituate, Mass.* Vol. 1. Providence RI, 1933.

**STODDARD**
Stoddard, Francis R.
*The Truth about the Pilgrims.* New York, 1952; repr. Baltimore MD, 1974.

**STONINGTON CT FIRST CH**
Wheeler, R. A.
*History of the First Congregational Church Stonington Conn. 1674-1874 with statistics of the church.* Norwich CT, 1875.

**SUDBURY G S**
Greenlaw, Lucy H.
*Inscriptions from the old cemetery at Sudbury, Mass.* Boston, 1906.

**SUFFIELD CT CONG CH REC**
*Records of Congregational Church, 1710-1836.* Hartford CT, 1941.

**SUTTON BY BENEDICT**
Benedict William A. and Tracy, Hiram A.
*History of Sutton Mass., from 1704-1876 with genealogies.* Worcester MA, 1878.

**TABER DESC**
Randall, George L.
*Taber Genealogy. Descendants of Thomas, son of Philip Taber.* New Bedford MA, 1924.

**TABER GEN (1952)**
Wright, Ann A. and Wright, Albert H.
*Descendants of Josephand Philip, sons of Philip Taber.* Mimeo. Ithaca NY, 1952.

**TAG**
*The American Genealogist.* Vol. 1-- 1922--. Pub. at Des Moines IA in 1975.

**THOMSON (JOHN) DESC**
Thompson, Charles H.
*A Genealogy of descendants of John Thomson of Plymouth, Mass., also sketches of families of Allen, Cooke, and Hutchinson.* Lansing MI, 1890.

**THURSTON**
Thurston, Brown
*Thurston Genealogies 1635-1880.* Portland ME, 1880 & 1892.

**TILSON GEN**
Tilson, Mercer V.
*The Tilson genealogy from Edmond Tilson at Plymouth, N.E. 1638-1911....* Plymouth MA, 1911.

**TINGLEY ANCY**
Tingley, Raymond M.
*Some ancestral lines, being record of the ancestors of Guilford Solon Tingley. Some ancestral lines and ancestry of Guildford S. Tingley. Rutland VT, 1935.*

**Tinkham MSS.**
Tinkham, Horace W.
Tinkham Genealogy, descendants of Ephraim, 1614-1893. MSS. at NEHG Soc., Boston MA.

**VR**
Vital records for about 200 towns in Massachusetts have been printed. No page numbers are given in citing the alphabetized editions listed below to which reference is made in this volume.

ABINGTON 1912, ACTON 1923, BERLIN 1935, BEVERLY 1906-7, BILLERICA 1908, BOLTON 1910, BOXFORD 1905, BRIDGEWATER 1916, BROCKTON 1911, BROOKFIELD 1909, CAMBRIDGE 1915, CARVER 1911, CHESTER 1911, CHELMSFORD 1914, COHASSET 1916, CONWAY 1943, DANVERS 1909-10, DARTMOUTH 1929-30, DRACUT 1907, DUXBURY 1911, EAST BRIDGEWATER 1917, FOXBOROUGH 1911, GRAFTON 1906, GRANVILLE 1914, GLOUCESTER 1917-24, HANSON 1911, HARVARD 1917, HARDWICK 1917, HAVERHILL 1910-11, HEATH 1915, IPSWICH 1910, KINGSTON 1911, LEE 1903, LEICESTER 1903, LEOMINSTER 1911, MANSFIELD 1933, MARLBOROUGH 1908, MEDFIELD 1903, MEDFORD 1907, MENDON 1920, MIDDLETON 1904, NEW BRAINTREE 1904, NEWBURY 1911, NEW SALEM 1927, NEWTON 1905, NORTHBOROUGH 1921, NORTON 1906, OAKHAM 1905, PELHAM 1902, PEMBROKE 1911, PLYMPTON 1923, READING 1912, RICHMOND 1913, ROCHESTER 1914, ROXBURY 1928, SALEM 1916-25, SALISBURY 1915, SCITUATE 1909, SHERBORN 1911, SHREWSBURY 1904, SPENCER 1909, STOW 1911, SUDBURY 1903, SUTTON 1907, TAUNTON 1929, TISBURY 1912, TOPSFIELD 1903, WALPOLE 1902, WARREN 1910, WAYLAND 1910, WESTBOROUGH 1903, WEST BRIDGEWATER 1911, WESTON 1901, WEYMOUTH 1910, WORCESTER 1894, WORTHINGTON 1911.

**VT VR**
Vital records are kept by town clerks, and are all supposed to be collected in a statewide card file with the Secretary of State at Montpelier VT, but the file is not complete. When information is from the state file, it is cited VT VR, with the name of the town. When taken from the town records, it is cited [town] VT VR, with volume and page.

**WADHAMS GEN**
Stevens, Harriet W. W.
*Wadham Genealogy, preceded by a sketch of the Wadham Family in England.* New York, 1913.

**WAITSFIELD VT BY JONES**
Jones, M. B.
*History of Waitsfield, Vt.* Boston, 1909.

**WARNER (ANDREW) DESC**
Warner, Lucien C. and Nichols, Mrs. Josephine G.
*The descendants of Andrew Warner.* New Haven CT, 1919.

**WATERMAN GEN**
Jacobus, Donald L.
*Descendants of Robert Waterman of Marshfield, Mass.* Vols. 1 & 2. New Haven CT, 1939-42.
*Descendants of Richard Waterman of Providence, R.I.* Vol. 3. New Haven CT, 1954.

**WATERTOWN BY BOND**
Bond, Henry
*Genealogies of the families and descendants of the early settlers of Watertown [Mass.] including Waltham and Weston.* 2 vols. Boston, 1860.

**WESTON GEN**
Weston, Thomas Jr.
*The descendants of Edmund Weston of Duxbury Mass. for five generations.* Repr. from NEHGR 41:285-96 (1887). Boston, 1887.

**WEYMOUTH BY CHAMBERLAIN**
Chamberlain, G. W.
*History of Weymouth with genealogies....* Boston, 1923.

**WHEELER FAM**
Wheeler, Albert G. Jr.
*The genealogical and encyclopedic history of the Wheeler family in America.* 2 vols. Boston, 1914.

**WHEELER (OBADIAH) GEN**
Wheeler, Henry M.
*Genealogy of some of the descendants of Obadiah Wheeler of Concord and Thomas Thaxter of Hingham.* Worcester MA, 1898.

**WHITE FAM REC**
White, Thomas and White, Samuel
*Ancestral Chronological record of the William White Family 1607-8 to 1895.* Concord NH(?), 1895; repr. 1966.

**WHITE FAM (YARMOUTH)**
Davis, William P.
*The White family of Yarmouth [Mass.]* Library of Cape Cod History and Genealogy #88. Yarmouthport MA, 1912.

**WHITE (NICHOLAS) FAM**
Lothrop, Thomas J.
*The Nicholas White Family, 1643-1900.* Taunton MA, 1902.

**WHITE (THOMAS) DESC**
Ford, Ella W.
*Descendants of Thomas White, Sudbury, Mass., 1638.* Cleveland OH, 1952.

**WHITMAN DESC**
Farnam, Charles H.
*History of the descendants of John Whitman of Weymouth, Mass.* New Haven CT, 1889.

**WILDER GEN**
Wilder, Edwin M.
*Book of the Wilders.* Richmond VA, 1962.

**WILLARD MEM**
Willard, Joseph
*Willard Memoir or life and times of Major Simon Willard with ... his descendants ... in the United States.* Boston, 1858.

**WILLISON**
Willison, George F.
*Saints and Strangers....* New York, 1945.

**WINDHAM CO CT BY LARNED**
Larned, Ellen D.
*History of Windham County, Connecticut.* 2 vols. Worcester MA, 1874-80.

**WINSLOW MEM**
Holton, David P. and Holton, Mrs. Frances K.
*Winslow Memorial. Family records of the Winslows and their descendants in America with the English ancestry ....* 2 vols. NY, 1877-88.

**WOOD FAM INDEX**
Wood, J. S., Sr.
*Wood Family Index - a given name Index.* An Index of Wood Families in America. USA, 1966.

**WOOD (LEVI) DESC**
Pease, Verne S.
*Descendants of Levi Wood, 1755-1833, first of Middleboro, Mass....* Richland Center, WI, 1913.

**WOODSTOCK CT BY BOWEN**
Bowen, Clarence W.
*History of Woodstock, Conn.* 8 vols. Norwood MA, 1935--

**WOODSTOCK VT BY DANA**
Dana, H. S.
*History of Woodstock, Vermont.* Boston & New York, 1889.

**WOOLWICH ME RECS**
Lilly, G. H.
*Woolwich Maine Records*

**WORCESTER SOC COLL**
*Collections of the Worcester Society of Antiquity.* 16 vols. Worcester MA, 1881-99.

**YARMOUTH G S**
Bowman, George E.
*Gravestone records in the ancient cemetery and the Woodside cemetery, Yarmouth, Mass.* Boston, 1906; repr. in YARMOUTH VR, 1975.

**YARMOUTH N.S. HERALD GEN**
Genealogical columns in the Yarmouth, Nova Scotia Herald, Nov. 1896 to May 1902. Copies at NEHG Soc., Boston MA, and Mayflower Soc. Plymouth MA.

**YARMOUTH N. S. HIST**
Campbell, Rev. J. R.
*A History of the County of Yarmouth, Nova Scotia.* St. John, N.B. 1876; repr. Belleville, Ont., 1972.

**YARMOUTH VR**
Sherman, Robert M. and Sherman, Ruth W.
*Vital records of Yarmouth, Massachusetts to the year 1850.* Warwick RI, 1975.

# INDEX OF PLACES

This index of places references places within the United States and Canada associated in a relevant way with the subjects of this book. European place references and places associated with military activity have been disregarded. When a place is referenced on several consecutive pages,this fact is indexed thus 23-28; showing that on each of the pages 23,24,25,26,27,and 28 a reference was found.

**MASSACHUSETTS**

## INDEX OF NAMES

With a few exceptions, each name in the text or footnotes is indexed. The omissions are: heads of Mayflower families in cross references, authors or names mentioned in titles of references, and the names of heads of military units under whom the subject of the discussion served. Perhaps other incidental names could have been omitted, but it was decided to err on the side of thoroughness.

Married women are indexed both under maiden surname, e.g., Rachel EATON, and under married surname, Rachel(EATON) RAMSDELL, with the maiden name (or name before marriage) in parentheses. Widows who remarried receive the additional appropriate listings, but only the maiden surname is displayed.

When variant spellings of a surname appear the heading is, e.g., DOTY/DOTEY/DOTEN, or HAYWARD/HEYWOOD/HAWARD/HOWARD. Similar problems occur with given names. Sometimes the index entry is Mercy/Marcy, but in other places Mercy of the index may refer to both Mercy and Marcy on the page cited.

A hyphenated page reference, e.g., 16-18, means that a discussion of the person named begins on page 16 and ends on page 18. No systematic provision has been made for giving separate index entries to different persons with the same name discussed on the same page. Thus the index entry Ashley CURTIS 87 covers the three generations of Ashley Curtises treated on page 87. Similarly, Samuel RAMSDELL 28-29 refers to both Samuel Ramsdell[4] and his son Samuel Ramsdell[5] appearing on those pages.